RICHARD III

The RSC Shakespeare

Edited by Jonathan Bate and Eric Rasmussen

Chief Associate Editor: Héloïse Sénéchal

Associate Editors: Trey Jansen, Eleanor Lowe, Lucy Munro, Dee Anna Phares, Jan Sewell

Richard III

Textual editing: Eric Rasmussen

Introduction and Shakespeare's Career in the Theater: Jonathan Bate

Commentary: Charlotte Scott and Héloïse Sénéchal

Scene-by-Scene Analysis: Esme Miskimmin

In Performance: Karin Brown (RSC stagings), and Jan Sewell (overview)

Actor, Director, and Designer (interviews by Jonathan Bate and Kevin Wright): Simon Russell Beale, Bill Alexander, and Tom Piper

Reflections: Richard Eyre

The RSC Shakespeare

William Shakespeare

RICHARD III

Edited by Jonathan Bate and Eric Rasmussen

Introduction by Jonathan Bate

The Modern Library
New York

CONTENTS

INTRODUCTION

THE CYCLE OF HISTORY

Shakespeare's first group of historical plays comes to a harmonious conclusion with the defeat of wicked King Richard at the battle of Bosworth Field in 1485. The victorious Henry, Earl of Richmond, belongs to the House of Lancaster. He marries the Princess Elizabeth, of the House of York, thus unifying the nobility and bringing to an end the Wars of the Roses. In the final scene of *Richard the Third*, the Lord Stanley, Earl of Derby, places the crown on Richmond's head and he becomes King Henry VII, inaugurator of the Tudor dynasty. The play closes with a speech in which Henry looks back on the civil strife that has been the subject not just of this play but also of the *Henry the Sixth* sequence. It also looks forward to the golden age over which his wife's namesake, Queen Elizabeth, liked to believe that she reigned:

> England hath long been mad, and scarred herself;
> The brother blindly shed the brother's blood,
> The father rashly slaughtered his own son,
> The son, compelled, been butcher to the sire:
> All this divided York and Lancaster,
> Divided in their dire division.
> O, now let Richmond and Elizabeth,
> The true succeeders of each royal house,
> By God's fair ordinance conjoin together.
> And let thy heirs—God, if thy will be so—
> Enrich the time to come with smooth-faced peace,
> With smiling plenty and fair prosperous days!

On hearing these lines, Shakespeare's audience would themselves have looked both forward and back: back to a bloody period in the nation's history, with relief at how it was providentially ended by the

Tudor dispensation; forward to an uncertain future, in the knowledge that the queen was now too old to sustain the line.

Historians still debate the question of how villainous Richard III really was, and in particular whether he personally ordered the slaying of the princes in the Tower. What is not in doubt is that it was convenient for the Tudors to paint him as a villain, in order to make his opponent, the future Henry VII, into a hero and a saint. Sir Thomas More played a major part in the process with his *History of King Richard III*, written at the court of Richmond's son, Henry VIII. Shakespeare finished the work in the public theater of Henry VIII's younger daughter, immortalizing Richard as the scheming Crookback. The English are notorious for getting their theology from Milton and their history from Shakespeare, rather than from more orthodox sources. The endurance of the image of a Richard who is "determinèd to prove a villain" is proof of the power of drama to be more memorable than written history. *Richard the Third* is one of those core Shakespearean plays that everybody has heard of, even if they have never read it. The success of two film versions—first Sir Laurence Olivier's and subsequently Sir Ian McKellen's dazzling update to the fascist 1930s—has assured its continuing life.

As in the *Henry the Sixth* plays, the language is frequently elevated and highly rhetorical. The combination of formal language and a sense of symmetry in the events—action leading to reaction, bloody violence to revenge, a slippery rise followed by a crashing fall as the wheel of fortune turns—places the play in the tradition of the Roman tragedian Seneca. The influence on Shakespeare was probably both direct—Seneca had been published in English translation in the 1580s—and indirect, via the multiauthored *Mirror for Magistrates*, a highly Senecan collection of "complaint" poems, telling of misfortunes and wickedness, written in the voices of the victims of history, including both King Richard's brother George, Duke of Clarence, and King Edward IV's mistress, Jane Shore.

The Senecan symmetry is taken to an extreme in the role of Queen Margaret, the widow of King Henry VI, who had been such a powerful force throughout the Wars of the Roses plays. In Act 1 Scene 3, she formally curses Rivers, Dorset, Hastings, Buckingham, and Richard himself. All her curses are fulfilled and as each charac-

1. Engraving after William Hogarth's 1745 portrait of the actor David Garrick as Richard facing the ghosts on the night before the battle of Bosworth Field. Executed in the artist's studio, but influenced by the elaborate stage design of the period, this painting inaugurated the tradition of representing great moments in Shakespeare in the style of "history painting" that had hitherto been reserved for elevated biblical and classical stories. The original portrait is in the Walker Art Gallery, Liverpool.

ter dies, Richard realizes that this is the case. Senecan tragedy traditionally began with a ghost returning from the underworld and demanding revenge for his or her murder. In an elegant variation, Shakespeare withholds the ghosts for the climax of the play, bringing them on to taunt King Richard in his tent on the eve of the battle that will be his downfall. The scene in which Richard confronts those ghosts would duly become one of the great set pieces of the English stage: this was the play, and the moment within the play, chosen in the eighteenth century by the actor David Garrick and the painter William Hogarth for the portrait that immortalized Garrick and showed that Shakespeare was a fit subject for art of high moral and historical seriousness.

RICHARD THE PLAYER

Whereas nearly everybody in the *Henry the Sixth* plays appears to be caught up in a maelstrom of historical events that they are not able to control, Richard attempts to take command of his own and his country's destiny. There is little doubt that the part was written for Richard Burbage, just as he was becoming Shakespeare's closest friend in the theater world. *Richard the Third* is the first of the small group of Shakespearean plays that are not ensemble pieces—as the *Henry the Sixth* plays so clearly were—but star vehicles, in which the leading player has three times as many lines as anybody else. This play was the making of both the writer and the star. It accounts for their nicknames in a well-attested theatrical anecdote that has them as rivals in the bed of a theater-crazed citizen's wife: Burbage is "Richard the Third" and Shakespeare "William the Conqueror."

The trick that they seem to have worked out together was to make the leading character into the apparent author of his own script. From the very opening soliloquy, Richard takes the audience into his confidence and shares with them the role he will adopt and the plot of the drama that he intends to act out, which might be entitled "an unlovely but clever man plans his ascent to the throne, not letting anybody—even an innocent child—get in his way." He is master of the wink and the aside; he rejoices in playing the role of Iniquity, the Vice in the old tradition of morality plays. The audience enjoys his performance exactly because they know it is a performance.

The master actor needs a "straight man." For Richard, this role is played by Buckingham, who assists him as he stage-manages his public image for his appearance before the Lord Mayor and citizens of London:

> *Enter Richard aloft, between two Bishops*
> **MAYOR** See, where his grace stands 'tween two clergymen.
> **BUCKINGHAM** Two props of virtue for a Christian prince,
>   To stay him from the fall of vanity:
>   And, see, a book of prayer in his hand,
>   True ornaments to know a holy man.—
>   Famous Plantagenet, most gracious prince,

Lend favourable ear to our requests,
And pardon us the interruption
Of thy devotion and right Christian zeal.

In the previous play in the sequence, Henry VI's prayer-book was a
sign that he did not want to be king. Richard's is a sign that he is pretending not to want to be king, thus leading the Londoners to beg
him to take on the office. "Will you enforce me to a world of cares?"
he says, feigning reluctance—and in the next breath he whispers,
"Call them again," ensuring that the offer is renewed so that this
time it can be accepted. In all this, he is, as always, the consummate
actor.

There are two key turning points for Richard. One is when he con-
trives to lose his right-hand man, Buckingham. The comedian
begins to flounder without his stooge. The other is when the lamenting women who serve as a kind of Greek chorus to the action come
together and confront him in the enormously long fourth scene of
the fourth act. Richard's bravura seduction of the Lady Anne had
revealed his skill with words, but now his verbal power is matched by
the combined forces of Queen Margaret and Queen Elizabeth. If one
innovation in the writing of *Richard the Third* was the conversion of
the ensemble chronicle play into a star vehicle for a single huge theatrical personality, the other was the feminization of this traditionally masculine form. In Shakespeare's earlier history plays, in those
of other authors, and indeed in the tragedies of Marlowe, women are
bit-part players. Here, however, the boy-actors who play Elizabeth,
Margaret, and Anne are given larger parts and more richly inflected
rhetoric than all of their adult colleagues save the leading three who
play Richard, Buckingham, and Clarence. Symbolically, given that
Richard explains his own lust for power as a consequence of his
inadequacy in the arts of love, it is fitting that he meets his match in
the form of women and boys.

It is Richard's theatrical self-consciousness that ultimately sets
his play above the three parts of *Henry the Sixth*. In *The First Part of
Henry the Sixth*, Talbot is a manly hero and Joan an intriguing semi-
comic villain; in *The Second Part*, there is splendid energy (Queen
Margaret running amok) and variety (Jack Cade and the voice of the

discontented commons); in *The Third Part*, we witness a scene of high drama when York is taunted with a paper crown before being stabbed to death. But it is not until Richard of Gloucester gets into his stride that we meet a figure with the compelling theatrical presence of a Falstaff or an Iago. At the climax of his first long soliloquy in Act 3 of *The Third Part of Henry the Sixth*—a speech that the theatrical tradition has often imported into *Richard the Third*—he announces that he will "play the orator," "add colors to the chameleon," and "change shapes with Proteus for advantages." Each image is of the art of the actor, with his persuasive tongue and power of self-transformation.

BEYOND MARLOWE

Richard adds that he will "set the murderous Machevil to school." In his black farce *The Jew of Malta*, Christopher Marlowe had brought on a representation of Machiavelli, the Renaissance archetype of the scheming politician, to speak the prologue. As soon as the Prologue leaves the stage, Barabas the Jew is revealed, speaking his opening soliloquy. The audience thus makes the equation that Barabas is a Machiavellian schemer. In *Richard the Third*, Shakespeare made a bold advance on this device. He dispensed with a prologue and began the action with Richard's riveting soliloquy, "Now is the winter of our discontent." Where Marlowe had cast Barabas in the role of the machiavel by means of a pointed structural device, Shakespeare's Richard casts himself. He announces that since his crookback prevents him from playing the role of a stage lover, he will self-consciously adopt that of a stage villain. For good measure, he goes on in the second scene to show that he can in fact play the lover—with such accomplishment that he successfully woos Lady Anne over the very corpse of her father-in-law when she knows that he has been responsible for the murder of her first husband. As promised, he plays the orator to supreme effect. By the third act, he is changing shapes with Proteus and, as we have seen, appearing between two bishops in the color of a holy man. By means of the orator's art of saying the opposite of what he means—"I cannot, nor I will not" accept the crown—he wins over the Mayor and the citizens of London.

The character of Richard III is Shakespeare's overstepping of the Marlovian antihero. Marlowe's Tamburlaine, Barabas, and Dr. Faustus fashion their identities by assuming roles—scourge of God, machiavel, conjuror. They do not stop to think that such roles are precisely that: flimsy theatrical impersonations. If they did stop, the whole Marlovian house of cards would come tumbling down. But Shakespeare began from a different place. He was an actor himself. This was the one trump card that was unavailable to Marlowe. Richard is quintessentially Shakespearean, supremely charismatic in the theater, because he knows that he is a role-player. He revels, and makes the audience revel, in playacting. He is the first full embodiment of a Shakespearean obsession that culminates in Macbeth's "poor player" and Prospero's "These our actors." It is Iago in *Othello* who says, "I am not what I am." But Richard could have said it too. And, as the critic Lionel Trilling remarked in a study of *Sincerity and Authenticity* (1972), so could almost every one of Shakespeare's most memorable characters: Hamlet has no sooner heard out the Ghost than he resolves to be what he is not, a madman. Rosalind in *As You Like It* is not a boy, Portia in *The Merchant of Venice* is not a doctor of law, Romeo's beloved Juliet is not a corpse, in *Measure for Measure* the Duke is not a friar and Mariana is not Isabella (nor is Helen Diana in *All's Well That Ends Well*), Edgar in *King Lear* is not Tom o' Bedlam, Hermione in *The Winter's Tale* is neither dead nor a statue.

Marlowe's characters invest everything in their aspirations. Shakespeare's are more flexible. They are not what they are. That is surely because Shakespeare was an actor and Marlowe was not. It is also one reason why Shakespeare's characters have a richer, more varied and continuous stage afterlife than Marlowe's. Only in his dreams does Richard stop acting. And when that happens, his identity collapses:

> Cold fearful drops stand on my trembling flesh.
> What? Do I fear myself? There's none else by.
> Richard loves Richard: that is, I am I.
> Is there a murderer here? No. Yes, I am.
> Then fly. What, from myself? Great reason why:

Lest I revenge. What? Myself upon myself?
Alack, I love myself. Wherefore? For any good
That I myself have done unto myself?
O no! Alas, I rather hate myself
For hateful deeds committed by myself!

Since he has forged his identity through acting, Richard denies the possibility of an essential being that is anterior to performance. He cannot sustain a language of being—"I am," "I am not"—because he keeps coming back to particular roles ("villain") and actions (murdering). The moment when an authentic self ought to be asserted, as in a deathbed repentance, becomes that when the self collapses. This is an actor-dramatist's way of looking at the nature of human being.

The Ghosts who appear to him in his dream the night before the last battle force him into the realization that actions have consequences: murder will bring him "to the bar" and a verdict of "guilty" will be pronounced. This final emphasis upon guilt is the pragmatic Shakespeare's correction of the blasphemous Marlowe toward religious and moral orthodoxy. Having been granted his earthly crown, Richard is defeated by Henry of Richmond, who has spent the night before the battle of Bosworth Field in pious prayer to the Christian God: "O thou, whose captain I account myself, / Look on my forces with a gracious eye." The fall of the overreacher is thus yoked to the Tudor myth of that providential scheme of history which combined the Houses of York and Lancaster and established the dynasty that brought unity, then Reformation and ambition for imperial glory to the nation.

Further selections from critical commentaries on the play, with linking narrative, are available on the edition website, www.therscshakespeare.com.

ABOUT THE TEXT

Shakespeare endures through history. He illuminates later times as well as his own. He helps us to understand the human condition. But he cannot do this without a good text of the plays. Without editions there would be no Shakespeare. That is why every twenty years or so throughout the last three centuries there has been a major new edition of his complete works. One aspect of editing is the process of keeping the texts up to date—modernizing the spelling, punctuation, and typography (though not, of course, the actual words), providing explanatory notes in the light of changing educational practices (a generation ago, most of Shakespeare's classical and biblical allusions could be assumed to be generally understood, but now they can't).

But because Shakespeare did not personally oversee the publication of his plays, editors also have to make decisions about the relative authority of the early printed editions. Half of the sum of his plays only appeared posthumously, in the elaborately produced First Folio text of 1623, the original "Complete Works" prepared for the press by Shakespeare's fellow actors, the people who knew the plays better than anyone else. The other half had appeared in print in his lifetime, in the more compact and cheaper form of "Quarto" editions, some of which reproduced good quality texts, others of which were to a greater or lesser degree garbled and error-strewn. In the case of *Richard III*, there are hundreds of differences between the two early editions, the Quarto of 1597 and the Folio.

Generations of editors have adopted a "pick and mix" approach, moving between Quarto and Folio readings, making choices on either aesthetic or bibliographic grounds, and creating a composite text that Shakespeare never actually wrote. Not until the 1980s did editors follow the logic of what ought to have been obvious to anyone who works in the theater: that the Quarto and the Folio texts represent two discrete moments in the life of *Richard III*; that plays change in the course of rehearsal, production, and revival, and that the major variants between the early printed versions almost certainly reflect this process.

If you look at printers' handbooks from the age of Shakespeare, you quickly discover that one of the first rules was that, whenever possible, compositors were recommended to set their type from existing printed books rather than manuscripts. This was the age before mechanical typesetting, when each individual letter had to be picked out by hand from the compositor's case and placed on a stick (upside down and back to front) before being laid on the press. It was an age of murky rushlight and of manuscripts written in a secretary hand that had dozens of different, hard-to-decipher forms. Printers' lives were a lot easier when they were reprinting existing books rather than struggling with handwritten copy. Easily the quickest way to have created the First Folio would have been simply to reprint those eighteen plays that had already appeared in Quarto and only work from manuscript on the other eighteen.

But that is not what happened. Whenever Quartos were used, playhouse "promptbooks" were also consulted and stage directions copied in from them. And in the case of several major plays where a reasonably well-printed Quarto was available, *Richard III* notable among them, the Folio printers were instructed to work from an alternative, playhouse-derived manuscript. This meant that the whole process of producing the first complete Shakespeare took months, even years, longer than it might have done. But for the men overseeing the project, John Hemings and Henry Condell, friends and fellow actors who had been remembered in Shakespeare's will, the additional labor and cost were worth the effort for the sake of producing an edition that was close to the practice of the theater. They wanted all the plays in print so that people could, as they wrote in their prefatory address to the reader, "read him and again and again," but they also wanted "the great variety of readers" to work from texts that were close to the theater life for which Shakespeare originally intended them. For this reason, the *RSC Shakespeare*, in both *Complete Works* and individual volumes, uses the Folio as base text wherever possible. Significant Quarto variants are, however, noted in the Textual Notes, and Quarto-only passages are appended after the text of *Richard III*.

The following notes highlight various aspects of the editorial process and indicate conventions used in the text of this edition:

Lists of Parts are supplied in the First Folio for only six plays, not including *Richard III*, so the list at the beginning of the play is provided by the editors, arranged by groups of characters. Capitals indicate that part of the name which is used for speech headings in the script. Thus "Lord Stanley, Earl of DERBY" indicates that lines spoken by this character are always headed "DERBY," even though he is sometimes addressed as "Stanley."

Locations are provided by the Folio for only two plays. Eighteenth-century editors, working in an age of elaborately realistic stage sets, were the first to provide detailed locations. Given that Shakespeare wrote for a bare stage and often an imprecise sense of place, we have relegated locations to the explanatory notes at the foot of the page, where they are given at the beginning of each scene where the imaginary location is different from the one before. We have emphasized broad geographical settings rather than specifics of the kind that suggest anachronistically realistic staging. We have therefore avoided such niceties as "another room in the palace."

Act and Scene Divisions were provided in the Folio in a much more thoroughgoing way than in the Quartos. Sometimes, however, they were erroneous or omitted; corrections and additions supplied by editorial tradition are indicated by square brackets. Five-act division is based on a classical model, and act breaks provided the opportunity to replace the candles in the indoor Blackfriars playhouse which the King's Men used after 1608, but Shakespeare did not necessarily think in terms of a five-part structure of dramatic composition. The Folio convention is that a scene ends when the stage is empty. Nowadays, partly under the influence of film, we tend to consider a scene to be a dramatic unit that ends with either a change of imaginary location or a significant passage of time within the narrative. Shakespeare's fluidity of composition accords well with this convention, so in addition to act and scene numbers we provide a *running scene* count in the right margin at the beginning of each new scene, in the typeface used for editorial directions. Where there is a scene break caused by a momentary bare stage, but the location does not change and extra time does not pass, we use the convention *running scene continues*. There is inevitably a degree of editorial judgment in making such calls, but the system is very valuable in suggesting the pace of the plays.

Speakers' Names are often inconsistent in Folio. We have regularized speech headings, but retained an element of deliberate inconsistency in entry directions, in order to give the flavor of Folio. For the sake of clarity, RICHARD is always so-called in his speech headings, though in the first half of the play he is sometimes addressed as "Gloucester" and in the Folio text of the second half some of his speeches are headed "*King.*"

Verse is indicated by lines that do not run to the right margin and by capitalization of each line. The Folio printers sometimes set verse as prose, and vice versa (either out of misunderstanding or for reasons of space). We have silently corrected in such cases, although in some instances there is ambiguity, in which case we have leaned toward the preservation of Folio layout. Folio sometimes uses contraction ("turnd" rather than "turned") to indicate whether or not the final "-ed" of a past participle is sounded, an area where there is variation for the sake of the five-beat iambic pentameter rhythm. We use the convention of a grave accent to indicate sounding (thus "turnèd" would be two syllables), but would urge actors not to overstress. In cases where one speaker ends with a verse half line and the next begins with the other half of the pentameter, editors since the late eighteenth century have indented the second line. We have abandoned this convention, since the Folio does not use it, and nor did actors' cues in the Shakespearean theater. An exception is made when the second speaker actively interrupts or completes the first speaker's sentence.

Spelling is modernized, but older forms are occasionally maintained where necessary for rhythm or aural effect.

Punctuation in Shakespeare's time was as much rhetorical as grammatical. "Colon" was originally a term for a unit of thought in an argument. The semicolon was a new unit of punctuation (some of the Quartos lack them altogether). We have modernized punctuation throughout, but have given more weight to Folio punctuation than many editors, since, though not Shakespearean, it reflects the usage of his period. In particular, we have used the colon far more than many editors: it is exceptionally useful as a way of indicating how many Shakespearean speeches unfold clause by clause in a developing argument that gives the illusion of enacting the process of thinking in the moment. We have also kept in mind the origin of punctuation in classical times as a way of assisting the actor and orator: the comma suggests the briefest of pauses for breath, the colon a middling one, and a full stop or period a longer pause. Semicolons, by contrast, belong to an era of punctuation that was only just coming in during Shakespeare's time and that is coming to an end now: we have accordingly only used them where they occur in our copy texts (and not always then). Dashes are sometimes used for parenthetical interjections where the Folio has brackets. They are also used for interruptions and changes in train of thought. Where a change of addressee occurs within a speech, we have used a dash preceded by a full stop (or occasionally another form of punctuation). Often the identity of the respective addressees is obvious from the context. When it is not, this has been indicated in a marginal stage direction.

Entrances and Exits are fairly thorough in Folio, which has accordingly been followed as faithfully as possible. Where characters are omitted or corrections are necessary, this is indicated by square brackets (e.g. "[*and Attendants*]"). *Exit* is sometimes silently normalized to *Exeunt* and *Manet* anglicized to "remains." We trust Folio positioning of entrances and exits to a greater degree than most editors.

Editorial Stage Directions such as stage business, asides, indications of addressee and of characters' position on the gallery stage are only used sparingly in Folio. Other editions mingle directions of this kind with original Folio and Quarto directions, sometimes marking them by means of square brackets. We have sought to distinguish what could be described as *directorial* interventions of this kind from Folio-style directions (either original or supplied) by placing them in the right margin in a different typeface. There is a degree of subjectivity about which directions are of which kind, but the procedure is intended as a reminder to the reader and the actor that Shakespearean stage directions are often dependent upon editorial inference alone and are not set in stone. We also depart from editorial tradition in sometimes admitting uncertainty and thus printing permissive stage directions, such as an ***Aside?*** (often a line may be equally effective as an aside or a direct address—it is for each production or reading to make its own decision) or a ***may exit*** or a piece of business placed between arrows to indicate that it may occur at various different moments within a scene.

Line Numbers in the left margin are editorial, for reference and to key the explanatory and textual notes.

Explanatory Notes at the foot of each page explain allusions and gloss obsolete and difficult words, confusing phraseology, occasional major textual cruces, and so on. Particular attention is given to nonstandard usage, bawdy innuendo, and technical terms (e.g. legal and military language). Where more than one sense is given, commas indicate shades of related meaning, slashes alternative or double meanings.

Textual Notes at the end of the play indicate major departures from the Folio. They take the following form: the reading of our text is given in bold and its source given after an equals sign, with "Q" indicating that it derives from the First Quarto and "Ed" that it derives from the editorial tradition. The rejected Folio ("F") reading is then given. Thus, for example, at 2.1.108 "**at** = Q. F = and" means that the Folio compositor erroneously printed "and," which does not make sense in context, so we have adopted Quarto "at."

KEY FACTS

MAJOR PARTS: (*with percentage of lines/number of speeches/scenes on stage*) Richard III/Duke of Gloucester (32%/301/14), Duke of Buckingham (10%/91/11), Queen Elizabeth (7%/98/6), Queen Margaret (6%/33/2), George, Duke of Clarence (5%/33/3), Lady Anne (5%/51/3), Lord Hastings (4%/47/8), Duchess of York (4%/43/4), Henry, Earl of Richmond (4%/14/3), Lord Stanley, Earl of Derby (3%/32/9), King Edward IV (2%/11/1), Sir William Catesby (2%/31/9), Earl Rivers (2%/24/5), Edward, Prince of Wales (1%/19/2), Richard, Duke of York (1%/21/2).

LINGUISTIC MEDIUM: 98% verse, 2% prose.

DATE: 1592? 1594? Must follow the *Henry VI* plays, so perhaps written shortly before the theaters were closed due to plague in June 1592. Alteration of the chronicle sources to flatter Lord Stanley, Earl of Derby, has led some scholars to suppose that the play was written for the acting company of Lord Strange's Men, active at this time, whose patron was Stanley's descendant. Alternatively, Shakespeare might have been writing for Pembroke's Men in 1592: the text also includes brief praise of the Pembroke family name. Some scholars, by contrast, suppose the play to be Shakespeare's first work for the Lord Chamberlain's Men, the company formed after the post-plague reopening of the theaters in summer 1594. Support for this view might come from the way in which the play was clearly written as a showcase for Richard Burbage, the Chamberlain's leading man.

SOURCES: The main source for the representation of Richard as a hunchbacked villain is Sir Thomas More's *History of King Richard III* (c.1513). Since More was writing at the court of King Henry VIII, son of Henry VII, who defeated Richard at Bosworth Field, he had a vested interest in portraying Richard as unfavorably as possible. He got much of his information from Bishop Morton of Ely, a bitter enemy of Richard. More's account was incorporated in the major Tudor chronicles; Shakespeare probably read it via Edward Hall's *Union of the Noble and Illustre Famelies of Lancastre and York* (1548). He may also have consulted Holinshed and one or more other chronicles. The historical poem sequence known as *The Mirror for Magistrates* (1559, expanded 1563) seems to have shaped Shakespeare's treatment of the Clarence plot. The relationship to an anonymous drama *The True Tragedie of Richard the Third* (registered for publication June 1594, poorly printed) is unclear: it seems to have been an older play, belonging to the Queen's Men, that was perhaps published to cash in on the success of Shakespeare's version.

TEXT: Quarto edition, 1597, with title advertising the content of the play: *The Tragedy of King Richard the third. Containing, His treacherous Plots against his brother Clarence: the pittiefull murther of his innocent nephewes: his tyrannicall vsurpation: with the whole course of his detested life, and most deserued death. As it hath beene lately Acted by the Right honorable the Lord Chamberlaine his seruants.* Reprinted 1598, with Shakespeare's name on the title page (one of the first printed plays to be so attributed), and again in 1602, 1605, 1612, 1622, 1629, 1634, indicating the play's popularity. Each Quarto was reprinted from the last, with some errors and occasional editorial correction. The 1623 Folio text derives from an independent manuscript that differed substantially from the Quarto tradition, though the Sixth Quarto and to a lesser extent the Third Quarto were consulted in its preparation. There has been much scholarly debate over the sources and relationship of the two texts: their relationship and relative authority has been justifiably described as the most difficult textual problem in all Shakespeare. It appears that the Folio, though printed much later, reflects an earlier version of the play. The Folio text is about 200 lines longer than the Quarto, a difference more probably due to Quarto cutting and streamlining than Folio expansion. The Quarto has just under 40 lines that are not in Folio. There are hundreds of variants of wording. The Folio text is generally more coherent; some of the difficulties of the Quarto have been attributed to "memorial reconstruction" by actors, but current scholarship questions this view. Though Folio has many deficiencies, some imported from the Quarto tradition and others introduced by the compositors, it requires less editorial intervention to render it comprehensible and theatrically workable. It has been the copy text for most, though not all, scholarly editions, as it is for ours, in accordance with our Folio-based policy.

THE TRAGEDY OF RICHARD THE THIRD:
With the Landing of Earl Richmond and the Battle at Bosworth Field

LIST OF PARTS

RICHARD, Duke of Gloucester, later King RICHARD III

Duke of CLARENCE, his brother

Duke of BUCKINGHAM

Lord HASTINGS, the Lord Chamberlain

Sir William CATESBY

Sir Richard RATCLIFFE

Lord LOVELL

BRACKENBURY, Lord Lieutenant of the Tower

Lord Stanley, Earl of DERBY (sometimes addressed as Derby and sometimes as Stanley, here given speech prefix Derby)

KING EDWARD IV, Gloucester's older brother

QUEEN ELIZABETH, his wife

PRINCE EDWARD, their older son

Duke of YORK, their younger son

Lord RIVERS, Elizabeth's brother

Lord GREY, Elizabeth's son by her first husband

Marquis of DORSET, his brother

Sir Thomas VAUGHAN

Lady ANNE, widow of Edward, Prince of Wales, later Duchess of Gloucester

QUEEN MARGARET, widow of Henry VI

DUCHESS OF YORK, mother to Gloucester, Clarence, Edward IV

BOY ⎫ Clar...
DAUGHTER ⎭ children

Earl of RICHMOND, later King Henry VII

Earl of OXFORD

Sir JAMES BLUNT

Sir WALTER HERBERT

Sir WILLIAM BRANDON

Duke of NORFOLK

Earl of SURREY

CARDINAL, Archbishop of Canterbury

ARCHBISHOP OF YORK

BISHOP OF ELY

SIR CHRISTOPHER, a priest

Sir John, a PRIEST

Lord MAYOR of London

Three CITIZENS

JAMES TYRRELL

Two MURDERERS

MESSENGERS

KEEPER

PURSUIVANT

PAGE

Ghost of KING HENRY VI

Ghost of EDWARD, his son

TWO BISHOPS, Soldiers, Halberdiers, Gentlemen, Lords, Citizens, Attendants

GREY . . . DORSET in the early scenes, these two may be treated as one figure widow historically she was betrothed, not married, to Prince Edward (son of King Henry VI), but in the play (following Hall's chronicle) she is described as his wife/widow *running scene 1*

Enter Richard, Duke of Gloucester, solus

RICHARD   Now is the winter of our discontent
Made glorious summer by this son of York:
And all the clouds that loured upon our house
In the deep bosom of the ocean buried.
5 Now are our brows bound with victorious wreaths,
Our bruisèd arms hung up for monuments,
Our stern alarums changed to merry meetings,
Our dreadful marches to delightful measures.
Grim-visaged war hath smoothed his wrinkled front,
10 And now, instead of mounting barbèd steeds
To fright the souls of fearful adversaries,
He capers nimbly in a lady's chamber
To the lascivious pleasing of a lute.
But I, that am not shaped for sportive tricks,
15 Nor made to court an amorous looking-glass:
I, that am rudely stamped, and want love's majesty
To strut before a wanton ambling nymph:
I, that am curtailed of this fair proportion,
Cheated of feature by dissembling nature,
20 Deformed, unfinished, sent before my time
Into this breathing world, scarce half made up,
And that so lamely and unfashionable

1.1 Location: near the Tower of London *solus* alone   2 son of York i.e. Edward IV,
whose father was Richard Duke of York (puns on "sun," the emblem of the House of York)
3 loured frowned threateningly   house family (of York)   6 arms armor, weapons   for as
7 alarums calls to arms/sudden attacks   8 dreadful fearsome, inspiring dread   measures
stately dances   9 front forehead   10 barbèd armored   11 fearful frightened (or possibly
"frightening")   12 capers dances with leaping movements/has sex   chamber plays on the
sense of "vagina"   13 pleasing attraction, delight   14 sportive pleasurable/amorous/sexual
tricks behavior, skills/sexual acts   15 court . . . looking-glass i.e. gaze lovingly at myself in a
mirror, flirt with my own reflection   16 rudely stamped crudely formed, roughly printed with
an image   want lack   17 wanton flirtatious, lascivious   ambling sauntering, walking with
a sexy rolling gait   18 curtailed deprived, cut short (literally refers to the docking of a dog's
tail)   19 feature a pleasing shape   dissembling cheating, deceitful   20 sent . . . time i.e.
born prematurely   21 made up fully formed   22 unfashionable odd-looking,
inelegant/poorly shaped

That dogs bark at me as I halt by them —
Why, I, in this weak piping time of peace,
25 Have no delight to pass away the time,
Unless to see my shadow in the sun
And descant on mine own deformity.
And therefore, since I cannot prove a lover,
To entertain these fair well-spoken days,
30 I am determinèd to prove a villain   *- predetermined by his shape - will it*
And hate the idle pleasures of these days.
Plots have I laid, inductions dangerous,
By drunken prophecies, libels and dreams,
To set my brother Clarence and the king
35 In deadly hate the one against the other.
And if King Edward be as true and just
As I am subtle, false and treacherous,
This day should Clarence closely be mewed up, *imprisoned*
About a prophecy, which says that 'G'
40 Of Edward's heirs the murderer shall be. *- Edward Dad & current King*
Dive, thoughts, down to my soul: here Clarence
    comes.—   *→ hide*

Enter Clarence, guarded, and Brackenbury

Brother, good day. What means this armèd guard
That waits upon your grace?
CLARENCE   His majesty, *- Edward*
45 Tend'ring my person's safety, hath appointed
This conduct to convey me to th'Tower. *- being locked up*
RICHARD   Upon what cause?
CLARENCE   Because my name is George.

- set bro G/C against Edward bro (current King)

23 **halt** limp   24 **piping** characterized by pastoral pipes, rather than warlike
instruments/shrill, weak, contemptible   27 **descant** improvise variations on (musical term),
i.e. ponder, comment   29 **entertain** pass enjoyably   **well-spoken** courteous, harmonious
30 **determinèd** resolved/destined   32 **inductions** initial steps, preparations   37 **subtle**
cunning, sly   **false** dishonest, disloyal   38 **mewed up** imprisoned, cooped up (like a caged
bird of prey)   39 **About** as a result of   **"G"** Clarence's first name is George; Richard, however,
is the Duke of Gloucester   43 **waits upon** attends   45 **Tend'ring** holding dear, being
concerned for (ironic)   46 **conduct** escort   **th'Tower** the Tower of London

RICHARD   Alack, my lord, that fault is none of yours.
50   He should, for that, commit your godfathers.
O, belike his majesty hath some intent
That you should be new-christened in the Tower.
But what's the matter, Clarence, may I know?
CLARENCE   Yea, Richard, when I know, but I protest
55   As yet I do not. But, as I can learn,
He hearkens after prophecies and dreams,
And from the cross-row plucks the letter G,
And says a wizard told him that by 'G'
His issue disinherited should be:
60   And, for my name of George begins with G,
It follows in his thought that I am he.
These, as I learn, and such like toys as these,
Hath moved his highness to commit me now.
RICHARD   Why, this it is when men are ruled by women:
65   'Tis not the king that sends you to the Tower,
My lady Grey his wife, Clarence, 'tis she
That tempts him to this harsh extremity.
Was it not she and that good man of worship,
Anthony Woodville, her brother there,
70   That made him send Lord Hastings to the Tower,
From whence this present day he is delivered?
We are not safe, Clarence, we are not safe.
CLARENCE   By heaven, I think there is no man secure
But the queen's kindred and night-walking heralds
75   That trudge betwixt the king and Mistress Shore.

---

50 commit imprison   **godfathers** sometimes responsible for the naming of the child at baptism   **51 belike** probably/perhaps   **52 new-christened** a grim anticipation of Clarence's death by drowning   **53 matter** reason   **54 protest** declare   **56 hearkens after** listens to **57 cross-row** alphabet (prefixed by a cross in children's primers)   **59 issue** children   **60 for** because   **62 toys** whims, trifles   **66 lady Grey** Elizabeth's title before her marriage to Edward; Richard is being contemptuous   **68 worship** repute, honor   **69 Anthony Woodville** i.e. Earl Rivers   **71 delivered** released   **74 night-walking heralds** secret, night-time messengers (a night-walker also meant a thief or a prostitute)   **75 trudge betwixt** go to and fro between   **Mistress Shore** Jane Shore, wife of a London goldsmith and Edward IV's lover; she later became Hastings' mistress   **Mistress** usual title for a woman; perhaps here with suggestive play on the sense of "lover" or even "female master"

Heard you not what an humble suppliant
Lord Hastings was to her, for his delivery?

RICHARD   Humbly complaining to her deity
Got my Lord Chamberlain his liberty.

80   I'll tell you what: I think it is our way,
If we will keep in favour with the king,
To be her men and wear her livery.
The jealous o'erworn widow and herself,
Since that our brother dubbed them gentlewomen,

85   Are mighty gossips in our monarchy.

BRACKENBURY   I beseech your graces both to pardon me:
His majesty hath straitly given in charge
That no man shall have private conference,
Of what degree soever, with your brother.

90   RICHARD   Even so, an please your worship, Brackenbury,
You may partake of anything we say.
We speak no treason, man: we say the king
Is wise and virtuous, and his noble queen
Well struck in years, fair and not jealous.

95   We say that Shore's wife hath a pretty foot,
A cherry lip, a bonny eye, a passing pleasing tongue,
And that the queen's kindred are made gentlefolks.
How say you sir? Can you deny all this?

BRACKENBURY   With this, my lord, myself have nought
to do.

100   RICHARD   Naught to do with Mistress Shore? I tell thee,
fellow,

---

76 **suppliant** petitioner   77 **delivery** release from prison   78 **complaining** appealing,
lamenting, pleading   **her deity** a mocking title for Mistress Shore   79 **Lord Chamberlain** i.e.
Hastings   82 **men** servants (perhaps with sexual connotations)   **livery** uniform indicating
whom one served (**wear her livery** may play on a sense of "have sex with her")   83 **o'erworn**
worn out (like old clothing/sexually)   **widow** i.e. Queen Elizabeth   84 **dubbed them**
conferred on them the rank of   85 **gossips** chatterers/godparents   87 **straitly . . . charge**
strictly ordered   89 **Of . . . soever** regardless of social rank   90 **an** if it   94 **Well . . . years**
well advanced in age (Richard seems to pretend to mean "mature, wise" or "well-preserved")
fair attractive/just   96 **passing** surpassingly, exceptionally

blackmails

threat

Richard has spies

He that doth naught with her, excepting one,
Were best to do it secretly, alone.

BRACKENBURY   What one, my lord?

RICHARD   Her husband, knave. Wouldst thou betray me?

105   BRACKENBURY   I do beseech your grace to pardon me,
and withal
Forbear your conference with the noble duke.

CLARENCE   We know thy charge, Brackenbury, and will
obey.

RICHARD   We are the queen's abjects, and must obey.—
Brother, farewell. I will unto the king,

110   And whatsoe'er you will employ me in,
dead
Were it to call King Edward's widow sister,
I will perform it to enfranchise you.
Meantime, this deep disgrace in brotherhood
Touches me deeper than you can imagine.   *Embraces him*

115   CLARENCE   I know it pleaseth neither of us well.

RICHARD   Well, your imprisonment shall not be long.
I will deliver you or else lie for you.
Meantime, have patience.

CLARENCE   I must perforce. Farewell.
                    Exit Clarence [led by Brackenbury and Guards]

120   RICHARD   Go, tread the path that thou shalt ne'er return.
Simple, plain Clarence, I do love thee so
That I will shortly send thy soul to heaven,
If heaven will take the present at our hands.
But who comes here? The new-delivered Hastings?

Enter Lord Hastings

125   HASTINGS   Good time of day unto my gracious lord.

---

101 **doth naught** Richard shifts the sense to "sexually penetrates her vagina"   104 **betray me**
i.e. by making me name the king as Shore's lover   105 **withal** moreover   106 **Forbear**
restrain, cease   107 **charge** duty, instructions   108 **abjects** varies "subjects" to incorporate
sense of "contemptible outcasts"   112 **enfranchise** free   114 **Touches** affects   117 **lie for**
you take your place in prison (playing on the sense of "lie about you")   119 **perforce** of
necessity ("patience perforce" was proverbial)   123 **present** gift   124 **new-delivered** recently
released

RICHARD   As much unto my good Lord Chamberlain.
Well are you welcome to this open air.
How hath your lordship brooked imprisonment?

HASTINGS   With patience, noble lord, as prisoners must.
130   But I shall live, my lord, to give them thanks
That were the cause of my imprisonment.

RICHARD   No doubt, no doubt. And so shall Clarence too,
For they that were your enemies are his,
And have prevailed as much on him as you.

135   HASTINGS   More pity that the eagles should be mewed,
Whiles kites and buzzards play at liberty.   *King's wife*

RICHARD   What news abroad?

HASTINGS   No news so bad abroad as this at home:
The <u>king is sickly</u>, weak and melancholy,
140   And his physicians fear him mightily.

RICHARD   Now, by Saint John, that news is bad indeed.
O, he hath kept an evil diet long,
And overmuch consumed his royal person.
'Tis very grievous to be thought upon.
145   Where is he, in his bed?

HASTINGS   He is.

RICHARD   Go you before, and I will follow you.

Exit Hastings

He cannot live, I hope, and must not die
fast
Till George be packed with post-horse up to heaven.

he can't die before George

150   I'll in to urge his hatred more to Clarence,
With lies well steeled with weighty arguments.
And, if I fail not in my deep intent,
Clarence hath not another day to live:
Which done, God take King Edward to his mercy,
155   And leave the world for me to bustle in.   — *wants activity*

---

128 brooked tolerated   **130 give them thanks** i.e. pay them back, have revenge   **135 mewed** caged   **136 kites and buzzards** inferior birds of prey   **137 abroad** in the world   **140 him** for him   **142 diet** lifestyle   **149 packed** packed off, dispatched   **post-horse** all possible speed   **151 steeled** strengthened with steel, reinforced   **152 deep** cunning/secret   **155 bustle** busy myself, be active

For then I'll marry Warwick's youngest daughter.
What though I killed her husband and her father?
The readiest way to make the wench amends
Is to become her husband and her father:
160   The which will I, <u>not all so much for love</u> ,
As for another secret close intent,
By marrying her which I must reach unto.
But yet I run before my horse to market:
Clarence still breathes, Edward still lives and reigns.
165   When they are gone, then must I count my gains.

Exit

Act 1 Scene 2   *running scene 1 continues*

*Enter the corpse of Henry the Sixth with [Gentlemen bearing] halberds
to guard it, Lady Anne being the mourner*

ANNE   Set down, set down your honourable load —
If honour may be shrouded in a hearse —
Whilst I awhile obsequiously lament
Th'untimely fall of virtuous Lancaster.   *They set down the coffin*
5   Poor key-cold figure of a holy king,
Pale ashes of the house of Lancaster,
Thou bloodless remnant of that royal blood,
Be it lawful that I invocate thy ghost,
To hear the lamentations of poor Anne,
10   Wife to thy Edward, to thy slaughtered son,

---

156 Warwick's youngest daughter i.e. Lady Anne Neville; having changed sides, the Earl of
Warwick died fighting against the House of York   **157 her husband** Anne Neville was not in
fact married to Prince Edward (Henry VI's son) although she had been betrothed to him before
his death   **father** father-in-law, i.e. Henry VI   **161 close** concealed   **162 reach unto** strive to
carry out   **163 run . . . market** i.e. get ahead of myself (proverbial)   **1.2 *Location: a
London street*   halberds** long-handled weapons with axelike heads   **2 shrouded**
concealed/wrapped in a shroud   **hearse** probably here an open coffin, or litter beneath a
frame supporting a funereal cloth   **3 obsequiously** in a manner proper to the dead
4 Lancaster i.e. Henry VI, former head of the House of Lancaster   **5 key-cold** cold as a metal
key (proverbial)   **6 ashes** i.e. remains, lifeless body   **8 Be it** let it be   **invocate** invoke, call
upon

Stabbed by the selfsame hand that made these
    wounds.
Lo, in these windows that let forth thy life,
I pour the helpless balm of my poor eyes.
O, cursèd be the hand that made these holes:

15 Cursed the heart that had the heart to do it:
Cursed the blood that let this blood from hence!
More direful hap betide that hated wretch
That makes us wretched by the death of thee
Than I can wish to wolves, to spiders, toads,

20 Or any creeping venomed thing that lives.
If ever he have child, abortive be it,
Prodigious, and untimely brought to light,
Whose ugly and unnatural aspect
May fright the hopeful mother at the view,

25 And that be heir to his unhappiness.
If ever he have wife, let her be made
More miserable by the death of him
Than I am made by my young lord and thee.—
Come, now towards Chertsey with your holy load,

30 Taken from Paul's to be interrèd there.   *They lift the coffin*
And still as you are weary of this weight,
Rest you, whiles I lament King Henry's corpse.

Enter Richard, Duke of Gloucester

RICHARD   Stay, you that bear the corpse, and set it down.
ANNE   What black magician conjures up this fiend,

35 To stop devoted charitable deeds?
RICHARD   Villains, set down the corpse, or, by Saint Paul,
I'll make a corpse of him that disobeys.

---

12 Lo look   windows vents, i.e. wounds   13 balm healing ointment/substance with which
the dead are anointed (i.e. tears)   17 direful hap dreadful fortune   betide befall, happen to
19 spiders, toads thought to be poisonous   21 abortive monstrous, deformed
22 Prodigious unnatural/ill-omened   23 aspect appearance   25 that may that (child)
unhappiness ill fortune/misery   29 Chertsey on the River Thames, in Surrey; site of a
famous monastery   30 Paul's St. Paul's Cathedral in London   31 still as whenever
35 devoted holy, devout

GENTLEMAN   My lord, stand back, and let the coffin pass.

RICHARD   Unmannered dog, stand'st thou when I
command.

40   Advance thy halberd higher than my breast,

Or, by Saint Paul, I'll strike thee to my foot,

And spurn upon thee, beggar, for thy boldness.   *They set down*

ANNE   What, do you tremble? Are you all afraid?   *the coffin*

Alas, I blame you not, for you are mortal,

45   And mortal eyes cannot endure the devil.—

Avaunt, thou dreadful minister of hell!

Thou hadst but power over his mortal body,

His soul thou canst not have: therefore be gone.

RICHARD   Sweet saint, for charity, be not so curst.

50   ANNE   Foul devil, for God's sake, hence, and trouble us
not,

For thou hast made the happy earth thy hell,

Filled it with cursing cries and deep exclaims.

If thou delight to view thy heinous deeds,

Behold this pattern of thy butcheries.—   *Uncovers the body*

55   O, gentlemen, see, see dead Henry's wounds

Open their congealed mouths and bleed afresh.—

Blush, blush, thou lump of foul deformity,

For 'tis thy presence that exhales this blood

From cold and empty veins, where no blood dwells.

60   Thy deeds, inhuman and unnatural,

Provokes this deluge most unnatural.—

O God, which this blood mad'st, revenge his death!

O earth, which this blood drink'st, revenge his death!

Either heav'n with lightning strike the murd'rer
dead,

65   Or earth gape open wide and eat him quick,

---

40 **Advance** raise   42 **spurn upon** kick   46 **Avaunt** be gone   49 **curst** ill-tempered/cursed,
damnable   50 **hence** get hence, go away   52 **exclaims** outcries, exclamations   54 **pattern**
example, model   58 **thy . . . blood** it was popularly believed that the wounds of a murder
victim would bleed in the presence of the murderer   **exhales** draws forth

As thou dost swallow up this good king's blood
Which his hell-governed arm hath butcherèd!
RICHARD   Lady, you know no rules of charity,
Which renders good for bad, blessings for curses.
70 ANNE   Villain, thou know'st nor law of God nor man:
No beast so fierce but knows some touch of pity.
RICHARD   But I know none, and therefore am no beast.
ANNE   O, wonderful, when devils tell the truth!
RICHARD   More wonderful, when angels are so angry.
75 Vouchsafe, divine perfection of a woman,
Of these supposèd crimes to give me leave,
By circumstance but to acquit myself.
ANNE   Vouchsafe, defused infection of man,
Of these known evils, but to give me leave,
80 By circumstance to curse thy cursèd self.
RICHARD   Fairer than tongue can name thee, let me have
Some patient leisure to excuse myself.
ANNE   Fouler than heart can think thee, thou canst make
No excuse current, but to hang thyself.
85 RICHARD   By such despair, I should accuse myself.
ANNE   And by despairing shalt thou stand excused
For doing worthy vengeance on thyself,
That didst unworthy slaughter upon others.
RICHARD   Say that I slew them not.
90 ANNE   Then say they were not slain.
But dead they are, and devilish slave, by thee.
RICHARD   I did not kill your husband.
ANNE   Why, then he is alive.
RICHARD   Nay, he is dead, and slain by Edward's hands.

---

71 **so** is so   73 **wonderful** extraordinary, astonishing   **devils . . . truth** Anne interprets
Richard's **am no beast** to mean that, as neither man nor beast, he must be a devil
75 **Vouchsafe** permit, consent   76 **leave** permission   77 **circumstance** detailed explanation
78 **defused** dispersed, spreading   82 **leisure** time, opportunity   84 **current** genuine, valid
85 **despair** spiritual hopelessness (thought to precede suicide)   87 **worthy . . . thyself** i.e.
committing suicide (a highly sinful act)   88 **unworthy** dishonorable, contemptible/causeless,
unjustified   91 **slave** villain, wretch

95 ANNE   In thy foul throat thou liest: Queen Margaret saw
                Thy murd'rous falchion smoking in his blood,
                The which thou once didst bend against her breast,
                But that thy brothers beat aside the point.

    RICHARD   I was provokèd by her sland'rous tongue,
100   That laid their guilt upon my guiltless shoulders.

    ANNE   Thou wast provokèd by thy bloody mind,
                That never dream'st on aught but butcheries.
                Didst thou not kill this king?

    RICHARD   I grant ye.

105 ANNE   Dost grant me, hedgehog? Then, God grant me too
                Thou mayst be damnèd for that wicked deed.
                O, he was gentle, mild and virtuous!

    RICHARD   The better for the king of heaven that hath
                him.

    ANNE   He is in heaven, where thou shalt never come.

110 RICHARD   Let him thank me, that holp to send him
                thither,
                For he was fitter for that place than earth.

    ANNE   And thou unfit for any place but hell.

    RICHARD   Yes, one place else, if you will hear me name it.

    ANNE   Some dungeon.

115 RICHARD   Your bedchamber.

    ANNE   Ill rest betide the chamber where thou liest.

    RICHARD   So will it, madam, till I lie with you.

    ANNE   I hope so.

    RICHARD   I know so. But, gentle Lady Anne,
120   To leave this keen encounter of our wits,
                And fall something into a slower method:
                Is not the causer of the timeless deaths

---

95 In . . . liest i.e. you lie outrageously   96 falchion curved sword   97 once at once
102 aught anything   105 hedgehog a contemptuous reference to Richard's crest, which
featured a wild boar   110 holp helped   115 bedchamber like hell, "chamber" could also be
euphemistic for the vagina   118 I hope so i.e. I certainly hope it will, as I shall never lie with
you (in an ironic anticipation of future events, however, the phrase may also be construed as "I
hope to lie with you")   120 keen sharp/eager   encounter . . . wits plays on the sense of
"sexual encounter of our genitals"   122 timeless untimely, premature

Of these Plantagenets, Henry and Edward,
As blameful as the executioner?

125 ANNE   Thou wast the cause and most accursed effect.

RICHARD   Your beauty was the cause of that effect.
Your beauty, that did haunt me in my sleep
To undertake the death of all the world,
So I might live one hour in your sweet bosom.

130 ANNE   If I thought that, I tell thee, homicide,
These nails should rend that beauty from my cheeks.

RICHARD   These eyes could never endure that beauty's
wreck.
You should not blemish it, if I stood by:
As all the world is cheerèd by the sun,

135 So I by that: it is my day, my life.

ANNE   Black night o'ershade thy day, and death thy life.

RICHARD   Curse not thyself, fair creature: thou art both.

ANNE   I would I were, to be revenged on thee.

RICHARD   It is a quarrel most unnatural

140 To be revenged on him that loveth thee.

ANNE   It is a quarrel just and reasonable
To be revenged on him that killed my husband.

RICHARD   He that bereft thee, lady, of thy husband,
Did it to help thee to a better husband.

145 ANNE   His better doth not breathe upon the earth.

RICHARD   He lives that loves thee better than he could.

ANNE   Name him.

RICHARD   Plantagenet.

ANNE   Why, that was he.

150 RICHARD   The selfsame name, but one of better nature.

ANNE   Where is he?

RICHARD   Here.   *Spits at him*
Why dost thou spit at me?

---

125 effect agent, perpetrator (Richard then shifts the sense to "outcome")   **130 homicide**
murderer   **137 thou art both** i.e. day and life   **138 would** wish   **146 He lives** i.e. there is a
man   **148 Plantagenet** the name was used by Richard Duke of York, Richard's father

	ANNE	Would it were mortal poison, for thy sake.
	RICHARD	Never came poison from so sweet a place.
155	ANNE	Never hung poison on a fouler toad.

Out of my sight, thou dost infect mine eyes.

	RICHARD	Thine eyes, sweet lady, have infected mine.
	ANNE	Would they were basilisks, to strike thee dead.
	RICHARD	I would they were, that I might die at once,

160 For now they kill me with a living death.
Those eyes of thine from mine have drawn salt tears,
Shamed their aspects with store of childish drops:
These eyes, which never shed remorseful tear —
No, when my father York and Edward wept,
165 To hear the piteous moan that Rutland made
When black-faced Clifford shook his sword at him,
Nor when thy warlike father, like a child,
Told the sad story of my father's death,
And twenty times made pause to sob and weep,
170 That all the standers-by had wet their cheeks
Like trees bedashed with rain: in that sad time,
My manly eyes did scorn an humble tear.
And what these sorrows could not thence exhale,
Thy beauty hath, and made them blind with
     weeping.
175 I never sued to friend nor enemy:
My tongue could never learn sweet smoothing word.
But now thy beauty is proposed my fee,
My proud heart sues, and prompts my tongue to speak.

She looks scornfully at him

Teach not thy lip such scorn, for it was made

---

157 infected mine both disease and love were thought to enter through the eyes
158 basilisks mythical reptiles whose gaze could kill   **159 die** plays on the sense of "achieve sexual orgasm"   **162 aspects** appearance/looks, gazes   **164 No, when** not even when
165 Rutland Richard's younger brother; his death is depicted in *3 Henry VI*, Act 1 Scene 3
166 black-faced evil, threatening, devilish   **167 father** i.e. the Earl of Warwick (originally a Yorkist, although he later changed sides)   **170 That** so that   **171 bedashed** splattered
172 humble lowly   **173 exhale** draw out   **175 sued** entreated, begged (for favor)
176 smoothing flattering   **177 fee** payment, reward

180   For kissing, lady, not for such contempt.
       If thy revengeful heart cannot forgive,
       Lo, here I lend thee this sharp-pointed sword,   *Gives her his sword*
       Which if thou please to hide in this true breast.   ↓*Kneels*↓
       And let the soul forth that adoreth thee,
185   I lay it naked to the deadly stroke
       And humbly beg the death upon my knee.
       He lays his breast open: she offers at [it] with his sword   *(confessing*
       Nay, do not pause, for I did kill King Henry —
       But 'twas thy beauty that provokèd me.
       Nay, now dispatch: 'twas I that stabbed young   *(she is devout)*
          Edward —
190   But 'twas thy heavenly face that set me on.
                                      She falls the sword
       Take up the sword again, or take up me. - *kill me or love me*

ANNE   Arise, dissembler. Though I wish thy death,
       I will not be thy executioner.

RICHARD   Then bid me kill myself, and I will do it.   *Takes his*
195 ANNE   I have already.   *sword back*

RICHARD   That was in thy rage:
       Speak it again, and even with the word,
       This hand, which for thy love did kill thy love,
       Shall for thy love kill a far truer love.
200   To both their deaths shalt thou be accessory.

ANNE   I would I knew thy heart. *if I knew you*
RICHARD   'Tis figured in my tongue. - *disfigured* (*lying*)
ANNE   I fear me both are false. - ♡ + *tongue*
RICHARD   Then never man was true.
205 ANNE   Well, well, put up your sword.
RICHARD   Say, then, my peace is made.

---

lays . . . open bares his chest   *offers* aims, makes to thrust   **190 set me on** this probably has
connotations of sexual arousal like **provokèd**   *falls* lets fall   **191 take up me** accept me
(perhaps with connotations of "possess me sexually/make my penis erect"; Anne interprets
"raise me from my kneeling position")   **192 dissembler** deceiver   **199 truer love** i.e.
Richard himself (supposedly a truer lover than the murdered Edward)   **202 figured in**
represented by

ANNE   That shalt thou know hereafter.

RICHARD   But shall I live in hope?

ANNE   All men, I hope, live so.   *general – dodges*

210 RICHARD   Vouchsafe to wear this ring.   *Puts a ring on her*

Look how my ring encompasseth thy finger.
Even so thy breast encloseth my poor heart:
Wear both of them, for both of them are thine.
And if thy poor devoted servant may
215 But beg one favour at thy gracious hand,
Thou dost confirm his happiness for ever.

ANNE   What is it?

RICHARD   That it may please you leave these sad designs
To him that hath most cause to be a mourner,
220 And presently repair to Crosby House,   *he thinks it's about love*
Where after I have solemnly interred
At Chertsey monast'ry this noble king,
And wet his grave with my repentant tears —
I will with all expedient duty see you.
225 For divers unknown reasons, I beseech you,   *she thinks forgiveness*
Grant me this boon. *favour*

ANNE   With all my heart, and much it joys me too,
To see you are become so penitent.—
Tressell and Berkeley, go along with me.

230 RICHARD   Bid me farewell.

ANNE   'Tis more than you deserve,
But since you teach me how to flatter you,
Imagine I have said farewell already.
                    Exeunt two [Tressell and Berkeley] with Anne

GENTLEMEN Towards Chertsey, noble lord?

235 RICHARD   No, to Whitefriars. There attend my coming.
                    Exit corpse [borne by the other gentlemen]

212 **Even so** in just such a way   220 **presently** immediately   **Crosby House** Richard's
London house, in Bishopsgate Street; later referred to as Crosby Place   224 **expedient duty**
dutiful haste   225 **divers** various, several   **unknown** private, that cannot be divulged
226 **boon** request, favor   229 **Tressell and Berkeley** minor characters, not mentioned again
in the play   235 **Whitefriars** a priory in London

Was ever woman in this humour wooed?
Was ever woman in this humour won?
I'll have her, but I will not keep her long.
What? I, that killed her husband and his father,
240   To take her in her heart's extremest hate,
With curses in her mouth, tears in her eyes,
The bleeding witness of my hatred by,
Having God, her conscience, and these bars against
    me,
And I no friends to back my suit withal,
245   But the plain devil and dissembling looks?
And yet to win her, all the world to nothing?
Ha!
Hath she forgot already that brave prince,
Edward, her lord, whom I, some three months since,
250   Stabbed in my angry mood at Tewkesbury?
A sweeter and a lovelier gentleman,
Framed in the prodigality of nature,
Young, valiant, wise, and, no doubt, right royal,
The spacious world cannot again afford.
255   And will she yet abase her eyes on me,
That cropped the golden prime of this sweet prince,
And made her widow to a woeful bed?
On me, whose all not equals Edward's moiety?
On me, that halts and am misshapen thus?
260   My dukedom to a beggarly denier!
I do mistake my person all this while.
Upon my life, she finds, although I cannot,
Myself to be a marv'llous proper man.

---

236 humour manner, style, way   **242 bleeding witness** i.e. Henry's body   **by** nearby
243 bars obstacles   **244 suit** courtship/formal supplication   **withal** with   **246 all . . .
nothing** i.e. against huge odds, with everything stacked against me   **248 brave** splendid, noble
250 mood fit of fury   **Tewkesbury** site of the Gloucestershire battle where the Lancastrians
were defeated; Edward's murder took place after the battle and is dramatized in *3 Henry VI*,
Act 5 Scene 5   **252 Framed . . . nature** created when nature was most generous, lavish
253 royal majestic, noble   **256 prime** youthful manhood/springtime   **258 whose . . . moiety**
the entirety of whom is not worth half of Edward   **259 halts** limps   **misshapen** deformed
260 denier small coin worth one tenth of a penny   **263 proper** handsome, fine

ll be at charges for a looking-glass,
And entertain a score or two of tailors
To study fashions to adorn my body.
Since I am crept in favour with myself,
I will maintain it with some little cost.
But first I'll turn yon fellow in his grave,
270 And then return lamenting to my love.
Shine out, fair sun, till I have bought a glass,
That I may see my shadow as I pass.

Exit

Act 1 Scene 3

Enter [Elizabeth] the Queen Mother, Lord Rivers and Lord Grey

RIVERS   Have patience, madam. There's no doubt his majesty
Will soon recover his accustomed health.

GREY   In that you brook it ill, it makes him worse: *To Queen*
Therefore, for God's sake, entertain good comfort,   *Elizabeth*
5   And cheer his grace with quick and merry eyes.

QUEEN ELIZABETH   If he were dead, what would betide on me?

GREY   No other harm but loss of such a lord.

QUEEN ELIZABETH   The loss of such a lord includes all harms.

GREY   The heavens have blessed you with a goodly son
10   To be your comforter when he is gone.

QUEEN ELIZABETH   Ah, he is young, and his minority
Is put unto the trust of Richard Gloucester,
A man that loves not me, nor none of you.

---

264 **be . . . for** buy, spend money on   265 **entertain** employ   **score . . . of** twenty or forty
269 **in** into   271 **glass** mirror, looking-glass   272 **shadow** also means "reflection"; the
shadow cast by the sun will substitute for the mirror's image   **1.3 *Location: the royal court,
London***   3 **brook it ill** endure it with difficulty, take it badly   4 **entertain good comfort** take
comfort, be cheerful   6 **betide on** happen to, befall   8 **includes** incorporates, is the sum of
9 **goodly** splendid, fine

RIVERS   Is it concluded he shall be Protector?

15 QUEEN ELIZABETH   It is determined, not concluded yet:
But so it must be, if the king miscarry.

Enter Buckingham and [Stanley, Earl of] Derby

GREY   Here come the lords of Buckingham and Derby.

BUCKINGHAM   Good time of day unto your royal grace.

DERBY   God make your majesty joyful as you have been.

20 QUEEN ELIZABETH   The Countess Richmond, good my
lord of Derby,
To your good prayer will scarcely say amen.
Yet, Derby, notwithstanding she's your wife,
And loves not me, be you, good lord, assured
I hate not you for her proud arrogance.

25 DERBY   I do beseech you either not believe
The envious slanders of her false accusers,
Or, if she be accused on true report,
Bear with her weakness, which I think proceeds
From wayward sickness and no grounded malice.

30 QUEEN ELIZABETH   Saw you the king today, my lord of
Derby?

DERBY   But now the Duke of Buckingham and I
Are come from visiting his majesty.

QUEEN ELIZABETH   What likelihood of his amendment,
lords?

BUCKINGHAM   Madam, good hope: his grace speaks
cheerfully.

35 QUEEN ELIZABETH   God grant him health. Did you confer
with him?

BUCKINGHAM   Ay, madam. He desires to make
atonement

---

14 concluded legally finalized   **Protector** guardian, who ruled on behalf of a king who was too young to do so   **16 miscarry** die   **20 Countess Richmond** Margaret Beaufort, Derby's wife; by her first husband, Edmund Tudor, she was mother to Henry, Earl of Richmond (later Henry VII)   **good my** my good   **26 envious** malicious   **29 wayward** obstinate, willful **36 atonement** reconciliation

Between the Duke of Gloucester and your brothers,

And between them and my Lord Chamberlain,

And sent to warn them to his royal presence.

40 QUEEN ELIZABETH   Would all were well! But that will
never be.

I fear our happiness is at the height.

Enter Richard [with Hastings and Dorset]

RICHARD   They do me wrong, and I will not endure it.

Who is it that complains unto the king

That I, forsooth, am stern and love them not?

45 By holy Paul, they love his grace but lightly

That fill his ears with such dissentious rumours.

Because I cannot flatter and look fair,

Smile in men's faces, smooth, deceive and cog,

Duck with French nods and apish courtesy,

50 I must be held a rancorous enemy.

Cannot a plain man live and think no harm,

But thus his simple truth must be abused

By silken, sly, insinuating jacks?

GREY   To who in all this presence speaks your grace?

55 RICHARD   To thee, that hast nor honesty nor grace.

When have I injured thee? When done thee wrong?

Or thee? Or thee? Or any of your faction?

A plague upon you all! His royal grace —

Whom God preserve better than you would wish —

60 Cannot be quiet scarce a breathing-while,

But you must trouble him with lewd complaints.

---

37 brothers only one brother, Anthony Woodville (Earl Rivers), appears in the play, but Shakespeare may have thought of him as two characters: Rivers and Woodville are listed separately in the opening stage directions at Act 2 Scene 1, and are addressed separately later in that scene   **39 warn** summon   **41 happiness** good fortune   **44 forsooth** indeed, in truth **stern** harsh, unfriendly   **45 lightly** little   **46 dissentious** inflammatory, quarrelsome **47 fair** pleasing, charming   **48 smooth** flatter   **cog** fawn, flatter, deceive   **49 Duck . . . nods** i.e. bow in an affected, courtly manner   **apish** idiotic/imitative   **51 plain** unaffected, simple, honest   **53 silken** smooth-tongued, ingratiating/elaborately dressed   **jacks** knaves, low-born men; plays on **Jack**, a common name   **54 presence** company/royal presence **55 nor** neither   **grace** virtue/propriety/nobility (picking up on **grace** as a form of address in the previous line)   **60 breathing-while** time to draw breath   **61 lewd** wicked/ignorant/ lowly

QUEEN ELIZABETH   Brother of Gloucester, you mistake the
    matter.
    The king, on his own royal disposition,
    And not provoked by any suitor else,
65   Aiming, belike, at your interior hatred,
    That in your outward action shows itself
    Against my children, brothers, and myself,
    Makes him to send, that he may learn the ground.
RICHARD   I cannot tell. The world is grown so bad
70   That wrens make prey where eagles dare not perch.
    Since every Jack became a gentleman,
    There's many a gentle person made a jack. — *lowly*
QUEEN ELIZABETH   Come, come, we know your meaning,
    brother Gloucester:
    You envy my advancement and my friends'.
75   God grant we never may have need of you.
RICHARD   Meantime, God grants that I have need of you.
    Our brother is imprisoned by your means,
    Myself disgraced, and the nobility
    Held in contempt, while great promotions
80   Are daily given to ennoble those
    That scarce some two days since were worth a noble.
QUEEN ELIZABETH   By him that raised me to this careful
    height
    From that contented hap which I enjoyed,
    I never did incense his majesty
85   Against the Duke of Clarence, but have been
    An earnest advocate to plead for him.
    My lord, you do me shameful injury,
    Falsely to draw me in these vile suspects.
RICHARD   You may deny that you were not the mean
90   Of my lord Hastings' late imprisonment.

---

65 **belike** probably/perhaps   68 **to send** summon (you)   70 **wrens** small, gentle birds (unlike large, predatory **eagles**)   74 **friends** relatives   77 **brother** i.e. George, Duke of Clarence 81 **noble** gold coin worth about a third of a pound (puns on **ennoble**)   82 **careful** full of cares 83 **hap** fortune   88 **draw me** implicate me/represent me   **suspects** suspicions   90 **late** recent

RIVERS   She may, my lord, for—

RICHARD   She may, Lord Rivers? Why, who knows not
        so?
    She may do more, sir, than denying that.
    She may help you to many fair preferments,
95 And then deny her aiding hand therein,
    And lay those honours on your high desert.
    What may she not? She may, ay, marry, may she—

RIVERS   What, marry, may she?

RICHARD   What, marry, may she? Marry with a king,
100 A bachelor and a handsome stripling too.
    Iwis your grandam had a worser match.

QUEEN ELIZABETH   My lord of Gloucester, I have too long
        borne
    Your blunt upbraidings and your bitter scoffs.
    By heaven, I will acquaint his majesty
105 Of those gross taunts that oft I have endured.
    I had rather be a country servant-maid
    Than a great queen, with this condition,
    To be so bated, scorned and stormèd at.   *hyperbole*

Enter old Queen Margaret [unseen by the others]
    Small joy have I in being England's queen.

110 QUEEN MARGARET   And lessened be that small, God,   *Speaks aside*
        I beseech him!   *throughout*
    Thy honour, state and seat is due to me.

RICHARD   What? Threat you me with telling of the king?   *To*
    I will avouch't in presence of the king.   *Queen Elizabeth*
    I dare adventure to be sent to th'Tower.
115 'Tis time to speak, my pains are quite forgot.

---

94 **preferments** promotions, advancements   96 **desert** deserving, merit   97 **marry** by the
Virgin Mary (Richard goes on to shift the sense to "wed")   100 **stripling** young man
101 **Iwis** indeed, certainly   **grandam** grandmother   105 **gross** base/wicked/excessive
Queen Margaret historically, the widow of Henry VI was imprisoned after the battle of
Tewkesbury, and later exiled to her native France   111 **state** rank   **seat** throne   112 **Threat**
threaten   113 **avouch't** affirm, declare it   114 **adventure** risk   115 **pains** efforts (made on
behalf of the king)

QUEEN MARGARET   Out, devil! I do remember them too well:
Thou kill'dst my husband Henry in the Tower,
And Edward, my poor son, at Tewkesbury.

RICHARD   Ere you were queen, ay, or your husband king,   *To*
120   I was a packhorse in his great affairs,   *Queen Elizabeth*
A weeder-out of his proud adversaries,   *did the work*
A liberal rewarder of his friends.   *dirty work*
To royalize his blood, I spent mine own.   *hitman*

QUEEN MARGARET   Ay, and much better blood than his
or thine.

125   RICHARD   In all which time you and your husband Grey
Were factious for the House of Lancaster.—
And, Rivers, so were you.— Was not your husband
In Margaret's battle at St Albans slain?
Let me put in your minds, if you forget,
130   What you have been ere this, and what you are:
Withal, what I have been, and what I am.

QUEEN MARGARET   A murd'rous villain, and so still thou
art.

RICHARD   Poor Clarence did forsake his father, Warwick,
Ay, and forswore himself — which Jesu pardon! —
135   QUEEN MARGARET   Which God revenge!

RICHARD   To fight on Edward's party for the crown.
And for his meed, poor lord, he is mewed up.
I would to God my heart were flint, like Edward's,
Or Edward's soft and pitiful, like mine.
140   I am too childish-foolish for this world.

---

116 Out exclamation of outrage and impatience   **119 Ere** before   **120 packhorse** workhorse
121 proud ambitious, arrogant   **126 factious for** on the side of, promoting dissent in the
interests of   **127 husband . . . slain** historically, Elizabeth's first husband, Sir John Grey, was
killed fighting for the Lancastrians, although in *3 Henry VI* (Act 3 Scene 2) he is depicted as
having fought for the Yorkists   **battle** army   **130 ere this** before now   **131 Withal** moreover
133 Clarence . . . Warwick Clarence and the Earl of Warwick deserted the Yorkists; Clarence
married Warwick's daughter, but later returned to the Yorkist cause, events that are depicted
in *3 Henry VI*   **father** father-in-law   **134 forswore himself** broke his oath (of loyalty)
137 meed reward   **139 pitiful** full of pity, compassionate   **140 childish-foolish** innocent,
inexperienced

QUEEN MARGARET   Hie thee to hell for shame, and leave
    this world,
Thou cacodemon! There thy kingdom is.
RIVERS   My lord of Gloucester, in those busy days
Which here you urge to prove us enemies,
145   We followed then our lord, our sovereign king.
So should we you, if you should be our king.
RICHARD   If I should be? I had rather be a pedlar.
Far be it from my heart, the thought thereof.
QUEEN ELIZABETH   As little joy, my lord, as you suppose
150   You should enjoy were you this country's king,
As little joy you may suppose in me,
That I enjoy, being the queen thereof.
QUEEN MARGARET   A little joy enjoys the queen thereof,
For I am she, and altogether joyless.
155   I can no longer hold me patient.—   *Comes forward*
Hear me, you wrangling pirates, that fall out
In sharing that which you have pilled from me.
Which of you trembles not that looks on me?
If not, that I am queen, you bow like subjects,
160   Yet that, by you deposed, you quake like rebels.
Ah, gentle villain, do not turn away.   *To Richard*
RICHARD   Foul wrinkled witch, what mak'st thou in my
    sight?
QUEEN MARGARET   But repetition of what thou hast
    marred,
That will I make before I let thee go.
165   RICHARD   Wert thou not banishèd on pain of death?
QUEEN MARGARET   I was, but I do find more pain in
    banishment
Than death can yield me here by my abode.

---

141 Hie hurry   142 cacodemon evil spirit   144 urge bring forward, offer as evidence
157 pilled pillaged, robbed   159 If . . . rebels Even if you do not bow to me as your queen,
then you tremble like the rebels who deposed me   161 gentle noble, high-born/kind   villain
low-born, rustic/scoundrel; the phrase is oxymoronic   162 mak'st thou are you doing
163 But repetition of merely recounting   marred destroyed   164 make do   167 abode
remaining

A husband and a son thou ow'st to me,

And thou a kingdom; all of you allegiance.

170 The sorrow that I have, by right is yours,

And all the pleasures you usurp are mine.

RICHARD   The curse my noble father laid on thee,

When thou didst crown his warlike brows with paper

And with thy scorns drew'st rivers from his eyes,

175 And then, to dry them, gav'st the duke a clout

Steeped in the faultless blood of pretty Rutland —

His curses then, from bitterness of soul

Denounced against thee, are all fall'n upon thee,

And God, not we, hath plagued thy bloody deed.

180 QUEEN ELIZABETH   So just is God, to right the innocent.

HASTINGS   O, 'twas the foulest deed to slay that babe,

And the most merciless that e'er was heard of!

RIVERS   Tyrants themselves wept when it was reported.

DORSET   No man but prophesied revenge for it.

185 BUCKINGHAM Northumberland, then present, wept to

see it.

QUEEN MARGARET   What? Were you snarling all before I

came,

Ready to catch each other by the throat,

And turn you all your hatred now on me?

Did York's dread curse prevail so much with heaven?

190 That Henry's death, my lovely Edward's death,

Their kingdom's loss, my woeful banishment,

Should all but answer for that peevish brat?

Can curses pierce the clouds and enter heaven?

Why then give way, dull clouds, to my quick curses.

195 Though not by war, by surfeit die your king,

[handwritten marginal notes: "He didn't pay them well — they had to kill a baby"; "Rutland" (next to "peevish brat")]

---

169 thou i.e. Elizabeth   **172 curse . . . paper** before his death, Richard Duke of York curses Margaret after she mockingly places a paper crown on his head (see *3 Henry VI*, Act 1 Scene 4) **175 clout** cloth   **176 pretty** youthful, fine-looking   **Rutland** York's young son; the episode with the cloth also appears in *3 Henry VI*, Act 1 Scene 4   **179 plagued** punished ceaselessly **181 that babe** i.e. Rutland   **184 No . . . prophesied** there was no man who did not prophesy **187 catch** seize   **192 but answer for** merely equal   **peevish** foolish, childish/obstinate **194 dull** thick, dark, sluggish   **quick** vigorous, lively, sharp   **195 surfeit** sickness resulting from overindulgence

As ours by murder, to make him a king.—
Edward thy son, that now is Prince of Wales,   *To Elizabeth*
For Edward our son, that was Prince of Wales,
Die in his youth by like untimely violence!
200   Thyself a queen, for me that was a queen,
Outlive thy glory, like my wretched self!
Long mayst thou live to wail thy children's death,
And see another, as I see thee now,
Decked in thy rights, as thou art stalled in mine.
205   Long die thy happy days before thy death,
And, after many lengthened hours of grief,
Die neither mother, wife, nor England's queen.—
Rivers and Dorset, you were standers-by,
And so wast thou, Lord Hastings, when my son
210   Was stabbed with bloody daggers: God, I pray him,
That none of you may live his natural age,
But by some unlooked accident cut off.

RICHARD   Have done thy charm, thou hateful withered
    hag.

QUEEN MARGARET   And leave out thee? Stay, dog, for
    thou shalt hear me.

215   If heaven have any grievous plague in store
Exceeding those that I can wish upon thee,
O, let them keep it till thy sins be ripe,
And then hurl down their indignation
On thee, the troubler of the poor world's peace.
220   The worm of conscience still begnaw thy soul.
Thy friends suspect for traitors while thou liv'st,
And take deep traitors for thy dearest friends.
No sleep close up that deadly eye of thine,
Unless it be while some tormenting dream
225   Affrights thee with a hell of ugly devils.

___

199 like the same   204 Decked adorned, dressed   stalled installed   208 standers-by
bystanders, lookers-on   212 unlooked unforeseen, unexpected   213 charm magic spell,
curse   hag witch   217 them i.e. the heavens   220 still constantly   begnaw eat away at,
gnaw   221 for to be   223 deadly murderous

Thou elvish-marked, abortive, rooting hog,
Thou that wast sealed in thy nativity
The slave of nature and the son of hell.
Thou slander of thy heavy mother's womb,
230   Thou loathèd issue of thy father's loins,
Thou rag of honour, thou detested—

RICHARD   Margaret.

QUEEN MARGARET   Richard.

RICHARD   Ha?

235   QUEEN MARGARET   I call thee not.

RICHARD   I cry thee mercy then, for I did think
That thou hadst called me all these bitter names.

QUEEN MARGARET   Why, so I did, but looked for no reply.
O, let me make the period to my curse.

240   RICHARD   'Tis done by me, and ends in 'Margaret'.

QUEEN ELIZABETH   Thus have you breathed your curse
against yourself.

QUEEN MARGARET   Poor painted queen, vain flourish of
my fortune.
Why strew'st thou sugar on that bottled spider,
Whose deadly web ensnareth thee about?
245   Fool, fool, thou whet'st a knife to kill thyself.
The day will come that thou shalt wish for me
To help thee curse this poisonous bunch-backed toad.

HASTINGS   False-boding woman, end thy frantic curse,
Lest to thy harm thou move our patience.

250   QUEEN MARGARET   Foul shame upon you! You have all
moved mine.

---

226 **elvish-marked** physically marked by evil elves at birth   **abortive** monstrous, deformed
rooting hog i.e. hunched and greedy; alludes to the boar on Richard's crest   **227 sealed . . .
nativity** branded at birth   **228 slave of nature** slave to bestial natural impulses/one
irredeemably marked out by nature   **229 slander** disgrace, shame   **heavy** pregnant,
weighty/sorrowful   **230 issue** offspring   **231 rag** discarded scrap   **232 Margaret** Richard
makes Margaret the subject of her insults to him   **236 cry thee mercy** beg your pardon
238 looked for expected   **239 period** end   **242 painted** artificial/made-up with cosmetics
vain flourish meaningless, frivolous adornment   **fortune** (rightful) position   **243 bottled**
swollen (with venom), rounded, bottle-shaped   **245 thou whet'st** you are sharpening
247 bunch-backed hunchbacked   **248 False-boding** falsely prophesying   **frantic**
deranged, mad

RIVERS   Were you well served, you would be taught your
  duty.

QUEEN MARGARET   To serve me well, you all should do
  me duty,
Teach me to be your queen, and you my subjects.
O, serve me well, and teach yourselves that duty.

255 DORSET   Dispute not with her, she is lunatic.

QUEEN MARGARET   Peace, Master Marquis, you are
  malapert:
Your fire-new stamp of honour is scarce current.
O, that your young nobility could judge
What 'twere to lose it, and be miserable.

260 They that stand high have many blasts to shake
  them,
And if they fall, they dash themselves to pieces.

RICHARD   Good counsel, marry. Learn it, learn it,
  marquis.

DORSET   It touches you, my lord, as much as me.

RICHARD   Ay, and much more. But I was born so high,

265 Our eyrie buildeth in the cedar's top,
And dallies with the wind and scorns the sun.

QUEEN MARGARET   And turns the sun to shade. Alas,
  alas!
Witness my son, now in the shade of death,
Whose bright out-shining beams thy cloudy wrath

270 Hath in eternal darkness folded up.
Your eyrie buildeth in our eyrie's nest.
O God, that see'st it, do not suffer it.
As it is won with blood, lost be it so!

---

251 **well served** treated as befits you (Margaret maintains the sense of "treated" and adds the
sense of "obeyed, paid respect to")   252 **duty** respect, deference   256 **Master Marquis**
Margaret contemptuously prefaces the aristocratic "marquis" with the form of address for an
untitled man   **malapert** impertinent   257 **fire-new** brand new, newly minted   **current**
valid, legitimate   258 **nobility** continues the coining imagery with a quibble on "noble" (a
gold coin)   264 **so high** this high (i.e. noble)   265 **eyrie** nest/brood of young birds of prey
(especially eagles, king of birds)/noble stock of children   266 **dallies with** teases, plays with
scorns the sun eagles were thought to be able to gaze unblinkingly into the sun   267 **sun**
puns on **son**   272 **suffer** endure, permit

BUCKINGHAM Peace, peace, for shame, if not for charity.

275 QUEEN MARGARET   Urge neither charity nor shame to
me:
Uncharitably with me have you dealt,
And shamefully my hopes by you are butchered.
My charity is outrage, life my shame,
And in that shame still live my sorrow's rage.

280 BUCKINGHAM Have done, have done.

QUEEN MARGARET   O princely Buckingham, I'll kiss thy
hand
In sign of league and amity with thee.
Now fair befall thee and thy noble house.
Thy garments are not spotted with our blood,

285 Nor thou within the compass of my curse.

BUCKINGHAM Nor no one here, for curses never pass
The lips of those that breathe them in the air.

QUEEN MARGARET   I will not think but they ascend the
sky,
And there awake God's gentle-sleeping peace.

290 O Buckingham, take heed of yonder dog:
Look when he fawns, he bites; and when he bites,
His venom tooth will rankle to the death.
Have not to do with him, beware of him.
Sin, death and hell have set their marks on him,

295 And all their ministers attend on him.

RICHARD   What doth she say, my lord of Buckingham?

BUCKINGHAM Nothing that I respect, my gracious lord.

QUEEN MARGARET   What, dost thou scorn me for my
gentle counsel?
And soothe the devil that I warn thee from?

---

278 My charity the charity I feel/the charity I am shown   outrage violence, hostility   life my
shame the only life I am allowed is a dishonorable one/I am ashamed to live   279 still
perpetually   283 fair good fortune   285 compass bounds   286 pass go any further than
288 but anything other than that   291 Look when whenever   292 venom poisonous
rankle inflict a festering wound   294 marks blemishes/identifying insignia/aims, sights
297 respect deem worthy of listening to   299 soothe flatter, humor

300   O, but remember this another day,
       When he shall split thy very heart with sorrow,
       And say poor Margaret was a prophetess.—
       Live each of you the subjects to his hate,
       And he to yours, and all of you to God's.   *Exit*

305   BUCKINGHAM My hair doth stand on end to hear her
           curses.
       RIVERS   And so doth mine. I muse why she's at liberty.
       RICHARD   I cannot blame her. By God's holy mother,
       She hath had too much wrong, and I repent
       My part thereof that I have done to her.

310   QUEEN ELIZABETH   I never did her any, to my knowledge.
       RICHARD   Yet you have all the vantage of her wrong.
       I was too hot to do somebody good,
       That is too cold in thinking of it now.
       Marry, as for Clarence, he is well repaid:

315   He is franked up to fatting for his pains —
       God pardon them that are the cause thereof!
       RIVERS   A virtuous and a Christian-like conclusion,
       To pray for them that have done scathe to us.
       RICHARD   So do I ever, being well advised.—

320   For had I cursed now, I had cursed myself.

                                                Speaks to himself

       Enter Catesby
       CATESBY   Madam, his majesty doth call for you,
       And for your grace, and yours, my gracious lord.
       QUEEN ELIZABETH   Catesby, I come. Lords, will you go
           with me?
       RIVERS   We wait upon your grace.

                           Exeunt all but [Richard of] Gloucester

---

311 **vantage** advantages, benefits (i.e. being queen)   **her wrong** the wrong done to her
312 **hot** eager   **do somebody good** i.e. help Edward to the crown   313 **cold** ungrateful,
indifferent   315 **franked . . . fatting** penned in to be fattened up (for slaughter)   318 **scathe**
harm   319 **well advised** cautious   324 **wait upon** attend

325 RICHARD   I do the wrong, and first begin to brawl.
    The secret mischiefs that I set abroach
    I lay unto the grievous charge of others.
    Clarence, who I indeed have cast in darkness,
    I do beweep to many simple gulls —
330   Namely, to Derby, Hastings, Buckingham —
    And tell them 'tis the queen and her allies
    That stir the king against the duke my brother.
    Now they believe it, and withal whet me
    To be revenged on Rivers, Dorset, Grey.
335   But then I sigh, and with a piece of scripture,
    Tell them that God bids us do good for evil:
    And thus I clothe my naked villainy
    With odd old ends stol'n forth of holy writ,
    And seem a saint when most I play the devil.

Enter two Murderers

340   But, soft, here come my executioners.—
    How now, my hardy, stout-resolvèd mates,
    Are you now going to dispatch this thing?

[Clarence depersonalizing dehumanizing]

    FIRST MURDERER   We are, my lord, and come to have the warrant
    That we may be admitted where he is.
345 RICHARD   Well thought upon. I have it here about me. *Gives the*
    When you have done, repair to Crosby Place. *warrant*
    But, sirs, be sudden in the execution,
    Withal obdurate, do not hear him plead;
    For Clarence is well-spoken, and perhaps
350   May move your hearts to pity if you mark him.
    FIRST MURDERER   Tut, tut! My lord, we will not stand to
    prate:

---

326 mischiefs wicked, evil deeds   **abroach** in motion   **327 lay . . . of** impose as a serious accusation against (i.e. blame on)   **328 cast in darkness** caused to be imprisoned (with connotations of death)   **329 beweep** cry over   **gulls** idiots, gullible people   **331 allies** supporters, relatives   **332 stir** incite, stir up   **333 whet** encourage, incite   **338 ends** scraps   **341 hardy** bold   **342 dispatch** carry out (plays on the sense of "kill")   **346 repair** make your way   **347 sudden** swift   **348 obdurate** inflexible, determined   **349 well-spoken** articulate, persuasive   **350 mark** pay attention to, listen to   **351 prate** chat

Talkers are no good doers. Be assured
We go to use our hands and not our tongues.

RICHARD   Your eyes drop millstones when fools' eyes fall
    tears.

355   I like you, lads. About your business straight.
Go, go, dispatch.

FIRST MURDERER   We will, my noble lord.   [*Exeunt*]

Act 1 Scene 4   *running scene 3*

Enter Clarence and Keeper

KEEPER   Why looks your grace so heavily today?

CLARENCE   O, I have passed a miserable night,
So full of fearful dreams, of ugly sights,
That, as I am a Christian faithful man,
5   I would not spend another such a night,
Though 'twere to buy a world of happy days,
So full of dismal terror was the time.

KEEPER   What was your dream, my lord? I pray you tell
    me.

CLARENCE   Methoughts that I had broken from the
    Tower,   , Belgium
10   And was embarked to cross to Burgundy,
And in my company my brother Gloucester,
Who from my cabin tempted me to walk
Upon the hatches: there we looked toward England,
And cited up a thousand heavy times,
15   During the wars of York and Lancaster
That had befall'n us. As we paced along
Upon the giddy footing of the hatches,
Methought that Gloucester stumbled, and in falling

---

354 **eyes drop millstones** proverbial image of hard-heartedness   **fall** let fall, drop
355 **straight** straightaway   **1.4 *Location: the Tower of London*   Keeper** guard (this role
could be conflated with Brackenbury)   **1 heavily** sadly   **5 spend** pass/expend (like money)
6 Though 'twere even if it were   **7 dismal** ominous, sinister   **13 hatches** deck   **14 cited up**
recalled   **17 giddy** swaying, unstable

help him

Struck me, that thought to stay him, overboard,

20   Into the tumbling billows of the main.
O lord, methought, what pain it was to drown!
What dreadful noise of water in mine ears,
What sights of ugly death within mine eyes.
Methoughts I saw a thousand fearful wrecks:

25   A thousand men that fishes gnawed upon:
Wedges of gold, great anchors, heaps of pearl,
Inestimable stones, unvalued jewels,
All scattered in the bottom of the sea.
Some lay in dead men's skulls, and in the holes

30   Where eyes did once inhabit, there were crept,
As 'twere in scorn of eyes, reflecting gems,
That wooed the slimy bottom of the deep,
And mocked the dead bones that lay scattered by.

KEEPER   Had you such leisure in the time of death

35   To gaze upon these secrets of the deep?

CLARENCE   Methought I had, and often did I strive
To yield the ghost. But still the envious flood
Stopped in my soul, and would not let it forth
To find the empty, vast and wand'ring air,

40   But smothered it within my panting bulk,
Which almost burst to belch it in the sea.

KEEPER   Awaked you not in this sore agony?

CLARENCE   No, no, my dream was lengthened after life.
O, then began the tempest to my soul,

45   I passed, methought, the melancholy flood,
With that sour ferryman which poets write of,
Unto the kingdom of perpetual night.
The first that there did greet my stranger soul,

---

19 stay steady, restrain   20 main sea   27 Inestimable impossible to count or value
unvalued priceless   37 yield the ghost die   envious flood malicious sea   38 Stopped in
shut up, blocked in   39 vast boundless/empty   40 bulk body   42 sore serious, extreme
45 melancholy flood the River Styx, which had to be crossed to get to Hades, the classical
underworld   46 sour ferryman Charon, who ferried souls to Hades   47 kingdom . . . night
Hades, the underworld   48 stranger foreign, newly arrived

Was my great father-in-law, renownèd Warwick,
50   Who spake aloud, 'What scourge for perjury
Can this dark monarchy afford false Clarence?'
And so he vanished. Then came wand'ring by
A shadow like an angel, with bright hair
Dabbled in blood, and he shrieked out aloud,
55   'Clarence is come: false, fleeting, perjured Clarence,
That stabbed me in the field by Tewkesbury.
Seize on him, Furies, take him unto torment!'
With that, methought, a legion of foul fiends
Environed me, and howlèd in mine ears
60   Such hideous cries, that with the very noise
I trembling waked, and for a season after
Could not believe but that I was in hell,
Such terrible impression made the dream.

KEEPER   No marvel, lord, though it affrighted you,
65   I am afraid, methinks, to hear you tell it.

CLARENCE   Ah, keeper, keeper, I have done these things,
That now give evidence against my soul,
For Edward's sake, and see how he requites me.
O God! If my deep prayers cannot appease thee,
70   But thou wilt be avenged on my misdeeds,
Yet execute thy wrath in me alone,
O, spare my guiltless wife and my poor children.
Keeper, I prithee sit by me awhile.
My soul is heavy, and I fain would sleep.

75   KEEPER   I will, my lord. God give your grace good rest. *Clarence*
Enter Brackenbury, the Lieutenant   *sleeps*

---

50 perjury oath-breaking; Clarence broke his oath of allegiance to Warwick by returning to
fight for the Yorkists after he and Warwick had changed sides to support the Lancastrians
51 monarchy kingdom (the underworld)   **afford** offer, give to   **53 shadow** ghost (of Prince
Edward, Henry VI's son)   **54 shrieked** ghosts were traditionally supposed to speak in shrill
voices   **55 fleeting** fickle, capricious   **56 field** battlefield   **57 Furies** in classical mythology,
three female spirits of vengeance   **58 legion** army   **59 Environed** surrounded   **61 season**
while, time   **64 though** if   **68 requites** rewards, repays   **73 prithee** beg you (literally "I pray
thee")   **74 heavy** oppressed, burdened, sorrowful

BRACKENBURY   Sorrow breaks seasons and reposing
    hours,
    Makes the night morning, and the noontide night.
    Princes have but their titles for their glories,
    An outward honour for an inward toil,
80   And, for unfelt imaginations,
    They often feel a world of restless cares:
    So that between their titles and low name,
    There's nothing differs but the outward fame.

Enter [the] two Murderers

FIRST MURDERER   Ho, who's here?

85   BRACKENBURY   What wouldst thou, fellow? And how
    cam'st thou hither?

SECOND MURDERER   I would speak with Clarence, and I came
    hither on my legs.

BRACKENBURY   What, so brief?

FIRST MURDERER   'Tis better, sir, than to be tedious. Let   *Gives*
90   him see our commission, and talk no more.   *Brackenbury a paper*

BRACKENBURY   I am in this commanded to deliver   *Reads*
    The noble Duke of Clarence to your hands.
    I will not reason what is meant hereby,
    Because I will be guiltless from the meaning.
95   There lies the duke asleep, and there the keys.
    I'll to the king and signify to him
    That thus I have resigned to you my charge.   *Exit*

FIRST MURDERER   You may, sir, 'tis a point of wisdom. Fare you
    well.

100   SECOND MURDERER   What, shall we stab him as he sleeps? *haha*

FIRST MURDERER   No: he'll say 'twas done cowardly, when he
    wakes.

---

76 **breaks** cracks, disrupts   **seasons** natural rhythms of time   **reposing hours** time for rest
77 **noontide** midday   78 **for** as   79 **for** at the cost of, as the result of   80 **for** in exchange for
unfelt imaginations abstract concepts that cannot actually be experienced, illusory glories
81 **cares** anxieties   82 **low name** those of ordinary humble status   83 **fame** reputation,
name   93 **reason** deduce, work out   94 **will** want to   96 **signify** to inform

SECOND MURDERER   Why he shall never wake until the great judgement day.

105 FIRST MURDERER   Why, then he'll say we stabbed him sleeping.

SECOND MURDERER   The urging of that word 'judgement' hath bred a kind of remorse in me.

FIRST MURDERER   What? Art thou afraid?

110 SECOND MURDERER   Not to kill him, having a warrant, but to be damned for killing him, from the which no warrant can defend me.

FIRST MURDERER   I thought thou hadst been resolute.

SECOND MURDERER   So I am, to let him live.

115 FIRST MURDERER   I'll back to the Duke of Gloucester and tell him so.

SECOND MURDERER   Nay, I prithee stay a little. I hope this passionate humour of mine will change. It was wont to hold me but while one tells twenty.   *They pause or count to twenty*

120 FIRST MURDERER   How dost thou feel thyself now?

SECOND MURDERER   Some certain dregs of conscience are yet within me.

FIRST MURDERER   Remember our reward, when the deed's done.

SECOND MURDERER   Come, he dies. I had forgot the reward.

125 FIRST MURDERER   Where's thy conscience now?

SECOND MURDERER   O, in the Duke of Gloucester's purse.

FIRST MURDERER   When he opens his purse to give us our reward, thy conscience flies out.

SECOND MURDERER   'Tis no matter, let it go. There's few or none
130 will entertain it.

FIRST MURDERER   What if it come to thee again?

SECOND MURDERER   I'll not meddle with it: it makes a man a coward. A man cannot steal, but it accuseth him: a man cannot swear, but it checks him: a man cannot lie with his

107 urging of bringing forth/emphasis on   117 stay wait   118 passionate humour emotional mood   It . . . me it usually lasts   119 tells twenty counts to twenty 130 entertain receive, be hospitable to   134 checks rebukes   lie have sex

135   neighbour's wife, but it detects him. 'Tis a blushing
shamefaced spirit that mutinies in a man's bosom: it fills a
man full of obstacles: it made me once restore a purse of gold
that, by chance, I found: it beggars any man that keeps it: it
is turned out of towns and cities for a dangerous thing: and
140   every man that means to live well endeavours to trust to
himself and live without it.

FIRST MURDERER   'Tis even now at my elbow, persuading me not
to kill the duke.

SECOND MURDERER   Take the devil in thy mind, and believe him
145   not: he would insinuate with thee but to make thee sigh.

FIRST MURDERER   I am strong-framed, he cannot prevail with
me.

SECOND MURDERER   Spoke like a tall man that respects thy
reputation. Come, shall we fall to work?

150   FIRST MURDERER   Take him on the costard with the hilts of thy
sword, and then throw him into the malmsey-butt in the
next room.

SECOND MURDERER   O, excellent device; and make a sop of him.

FIRST MURDERER   Soft, he wakes.

155   SECOND MURDERER   Strike!

FIRST MURDERER   No, we'll reason with him.

CLARENCE   Where art thou, keeper? Give me a cup of wine.

SECOND MURDERER   You shall have wine enough, my lord, anon.

CLARENCE   In God's name, what art thou?

160   FIRST MURDERER   A man, as you are.

CLARENCE   But not, as I am, royal.

FIRST MURDERER   Nor you, as we are, loyal.

CLARENCE   Thy voice is thunder, but thy looks are humble.

FIRST MURDERER   My voice is now the king's, my looks mine
own.

---

137 **restore** return   138 **keeps** retains/maintains, supports   139 **for** as   140 **well**
prosperously/virtuously   144 **him** i.e. conscience   145 **insinuate** ingratiate himself   148 **tall**
brave   150 **Take** strike   **costard** head (literally, a type of large apple)   151 **malmsey-butt**
barrel of strong, sweet wine from Greece   153 **device** plan   **sop** piece of bread soaked in
wine   156 **reason** converse, talk   158 **anon** soon

165   CLARENCE   How darkly and how deadly dost thou speak!
        Your eyes do menace me: why look you pale?
        Who sent you hither? Wherefore do you come?
      SECOND MURDERER   To, to, to—
      CLARENCE   To murder me?
170   BOTH   Ay, ay.
      CLARENCE   You scarcely have the hearts to tell me so,
        And therefore cannot have the hearts to do it.
        Wherein, my friends, have I offended you?
      FIRST MURDERER   Offended us you have not, but the
        king.
175   CLARENCE   I shall be reconciled to him again.
      SECOND MURDERER   Never, my lord: therefore prepare to
        die.
      CLARENCE   Are you drawn forth among a world of men
        To slay the innocent? What is my offence?
        Where is the evidence that doth accuse me?   _law_
180   What lawful quest have given their verdict up
        Unto the frowning judge? Or who pronounced
        The bitter sentence of poor Clarence' death,
        Before I be convict by course of law?
        To threaten me with death is most unlawful.
185   I charge you, as you hope for any goodness
        That you depart and lay no hands on me.
        The deed you undertake is damnable.   _religion_
      FIRST MURDERER   What we will do, we do upon
        command.
      SECOND MURDERER   And he that hath commanded is our
        king.
190   CLARENCE   Erroneous vassals, the great king of kings
        Hath in the table of his law commanded
        That thou shalt do no murder. Will you then

---

167 Wherefore why   **177 drawn forth** selected   **180 quest** inquest, those holding a judicial
inquiry   **183 convict** convicted   **185 charge** command   **190 Erroneous** misguided, erring
vassals servants, slaves   **king of kings** i.e. God   **191 table . . . law** i.e. the Ten
Commandments   **192 do no murder** the Sixth Commandment (Exodus 20:13)

Spurn at his edict and fulfil a man's?
Take heed, for he holds <u>vengeance</u> in his hand,

195 To hurl upon their heads that break his law.

SECOND MURDERER   And that same vengeance doth he
hurl on thee,
For false forswearing and for murder, too.
Thou didst receive the sacrament to fight
In quarrel of the house of Lancaster.

200 FIRST MURDERER   And, like a traitor to the name of God,
Didst break that vow, and with thy treacherous blade
Unripp'dst the bowels of thy sovereign's son.

SECOND MURDERER   Whom thou wast sworn to cherish
and defend.

FIRST MURDERER   How canst thou urge God's dreadful
law to us,

205 When thou hast broke it in such dear degree?

CLARENCE   Alas, for whose sake did I that ill deed?
For Edward, for my brother, for his sake.
He sends you not to murder me for this,
For in that sin he is as deep as I.

210 If God will be avengèd for the deed,
O, know you yet he doth it publicly.
Take not the quarrel from his powerful arm: *don't do–do*
He needs no indirect or lawless course   *(God's)*
To cut off those that have offended him.

215 FIRST MURDERER   Who made thee, then, a bloody
minister,
When gallant-springing brave Plantagenet,
That princely novice, was struck dead by thee?

---

193 **Spurn at** reject, scorn   197 **false forswearing** breaking your oath (forbidden by the Ninth
Commandment)   198 **receive the sacrament** take Communion as a means of affirming your
oath   199 **In quarrel of** in the cause of   202 **Unripp'dst** tore open   **bowels** intestines,
entrails   **sovereign's son** i.e. Prince Edward, son of Henry VI   204 **dreadful** inspiring dread
and awe   205 **dear** extreme, grievous (a)   212 **quarrel** (settling of the) dispute   213 **indirect**
devious, oblique   214 **cut off** kill   215 **bloody** violent, bloodthirsty   216 **gallant-springing**
gallant and youthful, growing promisingly   217 **novice** youth, beginner

CLARENCE   My brother's love, the devil and my rage.

FIRST MURDERER   Thy brother's love, our duty and thy
        faults,

220   Provoke us hither now to slaughter thee.

CLARENCE   If you do love my brother, hate not me.
    I am his brother and I love him well.
    If you are hired for meed, go back again,
    And I will send you to my brother Gloucester,

225   Who shall reward you better for my life
    Than Edward will for tidings of my death.

SECOND MURDERER   You are deceived, your brother
        Gloucester hates you.

CLARENCE   O no, he loves me, and he holds me dear.
    Go you to him from me.

230   FIRST MURDERER   Ay, so we will.

CLARENCE   Tell him, when that our princely father York
    Blessed his three sons with his victorious arm,
    He little thought of this divided friendship.
    Bid Gloucester think on this, and he will weep.

235   FIRST MURDERER   Ay, millstones, as he lessoned us to
        weep.

CLARENCE   O, do not slander him, for he is kind.

FIRST MURDERER   Right, as snow in harvest.
    Come, you deceive yourself:
    'Tis he that sends us to destroy you here.

240   CLARENCE   It cannot be, for he bewept my fortune,
    And hugged me in his arms, and swore, with sobs
    That he would labour my delivery.

FIRST MURDERER   Why, so he doth, when he delivers you
    From this earth's thraldom to the joys of heaven.

245   SECOND MURDERER   Make peace with God, for you must
        die, my lord.

---

218 My brother's love love for my brother   **223 meed** money, reward   **233 friendship** also
kinship   **235 lessoned** taught   **236 is kind** is gentle, well-meaning/has feelings of natural
kinship   **242 labour my delivery** strive to obtain my release   **244 thraldom** servitude,
enslavement

CLARENCE   Have you that holy feeling in your souls
To counsel me to make my peace with God,
And are you yet to your own souls so blind
That you will war with God by murd'ring me?
250   O, sirs, consider, they that set you on
To do this deed will hate you for the deed.

SECOND MURDERER   What shall we do?   *To First Murderer*

CLARENCE   Relent, and save your souls.
Which of you, if you were a prince's son,
255   Being pent from liberty, as I am now,
If two such murderers as yourselves came to you,
Would not entreat for life as you would beg,
Were you in my distress?

FIRST MURDERER   Relent? No: 'tis cowardly and womanish.

260   CLARENCE   Not to relent is beastly, savage, devilish.
My friend, I spy some pity in thy looks.   *To Second Murderer*
O, if thine eye be not a flatterer,
Come thou on my side, and entreat for me,
A begging prince what beggar pities not?

265   SECOND MURDERER   Look behind you, my lord.

FIRST MURDERER   Take that, and that: if all this will not do,

Stabs him

I'll drown you in the malmsey-butt within.

Exit [with the body]

SECOND MURDERER   A bloody deed, and desperately
dispatched.
How fain, like Pilate, would I wash my hands
270   Of this most grievous murder!

Enter First Murderer

FIRST MURDERER   How now? What mean'st thou, that
thou help'st me not?

---

246 feeling sensibility, awareness   **255 pent** shut up   **260 beastly** not human, lacking in
reason   **268 desperately dispatched** carried out in desperation, executed recklessly
(**desperately** has connotations of spiritual hopelessness)   **269 fain** willingly   **Pilate . . .
murder** Pontius Pilate, the Roman governor of Judaea involved in the crucifixion of Christ,
washed his hands before the discontented crowd as a means of exonerating himself from
blame

By heaven, the duke shall know how slack you have
    been!
SECOND MURDERER   I would he knew that I had saved
    his brother.
Take thou the fee, and tell him what I say,

275 For I repent me that the duke is slain.   *Exit*

FIRST MURDERER   So do not I. Go, coward as thou art.
Well, I'll go hide the body in some hole
Till that the duke give order for his burial.
And when I have my meed, I will away,

280 For this will out, and then I must not stay.   *Exit*

Act 2 Scene 1   *running scene 4*

Flourish. Enter the King, sick, the Queen, Lord Marquis Dorset, Rivers,
Hastings, Catesby, Buckingham, Woodville [and others]

KING EDWARD IV   Why, so. Now have I done a good day's
    work.
You peers, continue this united league.
I every day expect an embassage
From my redeemer to redeem me hence,

5 And more to peace my soul shall part to heaven,
Since I have made my friends at peace on earth.—
Dorset and Rivers, take each other's hand:
Dissemble not your hatred, swear your love.

RIVERS   By heaven, my soul is purged from grudging
    hate,

10 And with my hand I seal my true heart's love.   *Gives his hand*

HASTINGS   So thrive I, as I truly swear the like!   *to Hastings*

KING EDWARD IV   Take heed you dally not before your
    king,

---

280 **out** get out, be known ("murder will out" was proverbial)   **2.1 *Location: the royal***
court, London   ***Flourish*** trumpet fanfare signaling the arrival of a person in authority
3 **embassage** message   8 **Dissemble not** (in shaking hands) do not conceal, disguise
9 **from** of   10 **true** honest, faithful   11 **thrive I** may I thrive   12 **dally** trifle, feign, mock

Lest he that is the supreme king of kings
Confound your hidden falsehood, and award
15   Either of you to be the other's end.
HASTINGS   So prosper I, as I swear perfect love.
RIVERS   And I, as I love Hastings with my heart.
KING EDWARD IV   Madam, yourself is not exempt from
    this,
Nor you, son Dorset, Buckingham, nor you;
20   You have been factious one against the other.
Wife, love Lord Hastings: let him kiss your hand,
And what you do, do it unfeignedly.
QUEEN ELIZABETH   There, Hastings, I will never more
    remember
Our former hatred, so thrive I and mine.
25   KING EDWARD IV   Dorset, embrace him.— Hastings, love Lord
    Marquis.
DORSET   This interchange of love, I here protest,
Upon my part shall be inviolable.
HASTINGS   And so swear I.   *They embrace*
KING EDWARD IV   Now, princely Buckingham, seal thou this
    league
30   With thy embracements to my wife's allies,
And make me happy in your unity.
BUCKINGHAM   Whenever Buckingham doth turn his hate   *To the*
Upon your grace, but with all duteous love   *Queen*
Doth cherish you and yours, God punish me
35   With hate in those where I expect most love.
When I have most need to employ a friend,
And most assurèd that he is a friend,
Deep, hollow, treacherous, and full of guile
Be he unto me. This do I beg of heaven,
40   When I am cold in love to you or yours.   *Embrace*

---

13 king of kings i.e. God   14 Confound overthrow, catch out   award sentence, appoint
15 end (cause of) death   19 son i.e. stepson   20 factious divisive, generators of factions
22 unfeignedly sincerely, without deception   26 protest declare   30 allies relatives
33 but . . . Doth i.e. and does not, with all duteous love   38 Deep cunning   hollow insincere
guile cunning, deceit

KING EDWARD IV   A pleasing cordial, princely
    Buckingham,
  Is this thy vow unto my sickly heart.
  There wanteth now our brother Gloucester here,
  To make the blessèd period of this peace.
45 **BUCKINGHAM** And, in good time,
  Here comes Sir Richard Ratcliffe and the duke.
Enter Ratcliffe and [Richard, Duke of] Gloucester
RICHARD   Good morrow to my sovereign king and queen.
  And, princely peers, a happy time of day!
KING EDWARD IV   Happy, indeed, as we have spent the
    day.
50   Gloucester, we have done deeds of charity,
  Made peace of enmity, fair love of hate,
  Between these swelling wrong-incensèd peers.
RICHARD   A blessèd labour, my most sovereign lord.
  Among this princely heap, if any here,
55   By false intelligence, or wrong surmise,
  Hold me a foe, if I unwillingly, or in my rage,
  Have aught committed that is hardly borne
  To any in this presence, I desire
  To reconcile me to his friendly peace.
60   'Tis death to me to be at enmity:
  I hate it, and desire all good men's love.—
  First, madam, I entreat true peace of you,
  Which I will purchase with my duteous service.—
  Of you, my noble cousin Buckingham,
65   If ever any grudge were lodged between us.—
  Of you and you, Lord Rivers, and of Dorset,
  That all without desert have frowned on me.—

---

41 cordial heart-restoring medicine   **43 wanteth** only lacks   **44 period** end, completion
45 in good time right on time, at the perfect moment   **47 morrow** morning   **52 swelling**
proud, arrogant/incensed, angry   **wrong-incensèd** full of wrongly directed anger/enraged by
perceived wrongs   **54 heap** gathering, group (casual and demeaning term in this context)
55 intelligence information   **surmise** assumption, conjecture   **57 is hardly borne** has
caused offense, is resented   **67 desert** deserving, justification

Of you, Lord Woodville, and, Lord Scales, of you:
Dukes, earls, lords, gentlemen, indeed, of all.
70   I do not know that Englishman alive
With whom my soul is any jot at odds
More than the infant that is born tonight.
I thank my God for my humility.
QUEEN ELIZABETH   A holy day shall this be kept hereafter.
75   I would to God all strifes were well compounded.—
My sovereign lord, I do beseech your highness
To take our brother Clarence to your grace.
RICHARD   Why, madam, have I offered love for this
To be so flouted in this royal presence?
80   Who knows not that the gentle duke is dead?

                                        They all start

You do him injury to scorn his corpse.
KING EDWARD IV   Who knows not he is dead? Who knows
    he is?
QUEEN ELIZABETH   All-seeing heaven, what a world is
    this?
BUCKINGHAM   Look I so pale, Lord Dorset, as the rest?
85   DORSET   Ay, my good lord, and no man in the presence
But his red colour hath forsook his cheeks.
KING EDWARD IV   Is Clarence dead? The order was
    reversed.
RICHARD   But he, poor man, by your first order died,
And that a wingèd Mercury did bear:
90   Some tardy cripple bare the countermand,
That came too lag to see him burièd.
God grant that some, less noble and less loyal,

68 Lord Scales actually another title of Lord Rivers; Shakespeare erroneously supposes
another character; some editors omit the line   72 the . . . tonight a newborn baby   75 well
compounded settled as effectively   77 to your grace into your favor   79 flouted mocked
80 gentle kind, mild/noble   86 forsook abandoned   89 that i.e. that first order   Mercury
swift messenger of the Roman gods, usually depicted with wings on his cap and sandals
90 tardy slow   bare the countermand brought the order revoking the first   91 lag late,
slowly   92 God . . . suspicion I pray God there are none, less noble and loyal than Clarence,
more involved in treachery yet less closely related to the king, who deserve worse than
Clarence's fate yet go free from suspicion (a pointed remark aimed at Elizabeth and her
relatives)

Nearer in bloody thoughts, and not in blood,
Deserve not worse than wretched Clarence did,
95   And yet go current from suspicion.

Enter [Lord Stanley,] Earl of Derby

DERBY   A boon, my sovereign, for my service done.   *Kneels*
KING EDWARD IV   I prithee peace. My soul is full of sorrow.
DERBY   I will not rise, unless your highness hear me.
KING EDWARD IV   Then say at once what is it thou
    requests.
100   DERBY   The forfeit, sovereign, of my servant's life,   *Rises*
Who slew today a riotous gentleman
Lately attendant on the Duke of Norfolk.
KING EDWARD IV   Have I a tongue to doom my brother's
    death,
And shall that tongue give pardon to a slave?
105   My brother killed no man: his fault was thought,
And yet his punishment was bitter death.
Who sued to me for him? Who, in my wrath,
Kneeled at my feet, and bid me be advised?
Who spoke of brotherhood? Who spoke of love?
110   Who told me how the poor soul did forsake
The mighty Warwick and did fight for me?
Who told me, in the field at Tewkesbury
When Oxford had me down, he rescued me,
And said, 'Dear brother, live, and be a king'?
115   Who told me, when we both lay in the field,
Frozen almost to death, how he did lap me
Even in his garments, and did give himself,
All thin and naked, to the numb cold night?
All this from my remembrance brutish wrath
120   Sinfully plucked, and not a man of you

---

95 **go current** pass as legitimate coin   96 **boon** request for a favor   100 **forfeit . . . life**
revocation of the death penalty that his servant has incurred   103 **doom . . . death** sentence
(doom) my brother to death   107 **sued** pleaded   108 **be advised** to reconsider, reflect/to be
cautious   110 **forsake** abandon, renounce   112 **field** battlefield   113 **down** on the ground,
unhorsed/at his mercy   116 **lap** enfold, swathe   118 **thin** thinly dressed   **numb** numbing
119 **remembrance** memory

Had so much grace to put it in my mind.
But when your carters or your waiting vassals
Have done a drunken slaughter, and defaced
The precious image of our dear Redeemer,
125   You straight are on your knees for pardon, pardon,
And I, unjustly too, must grant it you.
But for my brother not a man would speak,
Nor I, ungracious, speak unto myself
For him, poor soul. The proudest of you all
130   Have been beholding to him in his life,
Yet none of you would once beg for his life.
O God, I fear thy justice will take hold
On me, and you, and mine, and yours for this!—
Come, Hastings, help me to my closet.
135   Ah, poor Clarence.

Exeunt some with King and Queen

RICHARD   This is the fruits of rashness. Marked you not
How that the guilty kindred of the queen
Looked pale when they did hear of Clarence' death?
O, they did urge it still unto the king!
140   God will revenge it. Come, lords, will you go
To comfort Edward with our company.

BUCKINGHAM We wait upon your grace.   *Exeunt*

Act 2 Scene 2   *running scene 4 continues*

Enter the old Duchess of York with the two children of Clarence

BOY   Good grandam, tell us, is our father dead?
DUCHESS OF YORK   No, boy.

---

122 **carters** cart drivers   **waiting vassals** attendant servants   123 **defaced . . . Redeemer**
i.e. committed murder (since man is made in God's image)   125 **straight** straightaway
127 **But** yet   128 **ungracious** wickedly, lacking divine grace   129 **proudest** most splendid,
eminent/most self-esteeming   130 **beholding** beholden, indebted   133 **On** of   **you** i.e. the
assembled company   134 **closet** private room/bedchamber   136 **Marked** observed, noticed
139 **still** constantly   **2.2 1 grandam** grandmother

DAUGHTER   Why do you weep so oft, and beat your
        breast,
    And cry 'O Clarence, my unhappy son'?
5 BOY   Why do you look on us, and shake your head,
    And call us orphans, wretches, castaways,
    If that our noble father were alive?
DUCHESS OF YORK   My pretty cousins, you mistake me
        both:
    I do lament the sickness of the king,
10   As loath to lose him, not your father's death.
    It were lost sorrow to wail one that's lost.
BOY   Then you conclude, my grandam, he is dead.
    The king mine uncle is to blame for it.
    God will revenge it, whom I will importune
15   With earnest prayers all to that effect.
DAUGHTER   And so will I.
DUCHESS OF YORK   Peace, children, peace. The king doth
        love you well.
    Incapable and shallow innocents,
    You cannot guess who caused your father's death.
20 BOY   Grandam, we can, for my good uncle Gloucester
    Told me the king, provoked to it by the queen,
    Devised impeachments to imprison him;
    And when my uncle told me so, he wept,
    And pitied me, and kindly kissed my cheek,
25   Bade me rely on him as on my father,
    And he would love me dearly as a child.
DUCHESS OF YORK   Ah, that deceit should steal such
        gentle shape,
    And with a virtuous visor hide deep vice!

---

6 **wretches** exiles/miserable people   **castaways** rejected ones   8 **cousins** a general term for
relatives   10 **As** being   11 **lost** wasted, pointless (sense then shifts to "gone")   14 **importune**
urge, entreat persistently   18 **Incapable** inexperienced, unknowing   **shallow** naive
22 **impeachments** accusations, charges   24 **kindly** gently, benevolently/as a family member
27 **gentle shape** an appearance of nobility, a benevolent guise   28 **visor** mask

He is my son — ay, and therein my shame.

30   Yet from my dugs he drew not this deceit.

BOY   Think you my uncle did dissemble, grandam?

DUCHESS OF YORK   Ay, boy.

BOY   I cannot think it. Hark, what noise is this? *Wailing within*

Enter the Queen with her hair about her ears, Rivers and Dorset after her

QUEEN ELIZABETH   Ah, who shall hinder me to wail and
         weep,

35   To chide my fortune, and torment myself?

I'll join with black despair against my soul,

And to myself become an enemy.

DUCHESS OF YORK   What means this scene of rude
         impatience?

QUEEN ELIZABETH   To make an act of tragic violence.

40   Edward, my lord, thy son, our king, is dead.

Why grow the branches when the root is gone?

Why wither not the leaves that want their sap?

If you will live, lament: if die, be brief,

That our swift-wingèd souls may catch the king's,

45   Or, like obedient subjects, follow him

To his new kingdom of ne'er-changing night.

DUCHESS OF YORK   Ah, so much interest have I in thy
         sorrow

As I had title in thy noble husband.

I have bewept a worthy husband's death,

50   And lived with looking on his images:

But now two mirrors of his princely semblance

Are cracked in pieces by malignant death,

---

30 dugs breasts (breast milk was popularly thought to convey some of the qualities of the mother)   **hair . . . ears** disheveled and loose hair was a theatrical convention signifying distress   **35 chide** berate, chastise   **36 black** profound, dark, hellish   **37 to . . . enemy** i.e. commit suicide   **38 rude impatience** uncontrolled outburst, violent want of endurance   **39 act** deed/division of a play (continuing the theatrical image begun with **scene**)   **42 want** lack   **43 brief** quick   **44 catch** catch up with   **47 interest** right, entitlement   **48 title** in claim on (as Edward's mother)   **50 his images** i.e. his sons   **51 mirrors** i.e. images, reflections   **semblance** likeness

And I for comfort have but one false glass,
That grieves me when I see my shame in him.
55   Thou art a widow, yet thou art a mother,
And hast the comfort of thy children left.
But death hath snatched my husband from mine
        arms,
And plucked two crutches from my feeble hands,
Clarence and Edward. O, what cause have I,
60   Thine being but a moiety of my moan,
To overgo thy woes and drown thy cries.

BOY   Ah, aunt, you wept not for our father's death: *To the*
How can we aid you with our kindred tears?   *Queen*

DAUGHTER   Our fatherless distress was left unmoaned.
65   Your widow-dolour likewise be unwept.   *To the Queen*

QUEEN ELIZABETH   Give me no help in lamentation,
I am not barren to bring forth complaints.
All springs reduce their currents to mine eyes,
That I, being governed by the watery moon,
70   May send forth plenteous tears to drown the world.
Ah, for my husband, for my dear lord Edward!

CHILDREN   Ah, for our father, for our dear lord Clarence!

DUCHESS OF YORK   Alas for both, both mine, Edward and
        Clarence!

QUEEN ELIZABETH   What stay had I but Edward? And he's
        gone.

75   CHILDREN   What stay had we but Clarence? And he's
        gone.

DUCHESS OF YORK   What stays had I but they? And they are
        gone.

QUEEN ELIZABETH   Was never widow had so dear a loss.

CHILDREN   Were never orphans had so dear a loss!

---

53 false glass i.e. Richard, a distorted, false image of his father   **60 moiety** small portion
61 overgo exceed   **63 kindred** similar, belonging to relatives   **64 unmoaned** unlamented,
not grieved for   **65 widow-dolour** widow's grief   **be** shall be   **67 barren to** so infertile that I
cannot   **complaints** grief, lamentations   **68 reduce** return, bring together   **69 watery**
moon i.e. the moon, which controls the tides   **74 stay** support   **77 Was never widow** there
was never a widow who   **dear** grievous/costly

DUCHESS OF YORK   Was never mother had so dear a loss.
80   Alas, I am the mother of these griefs!
    Their woes are parcelled, mine is general.
    She for an Edward weeps, and so do I:
    I for a Clarence weep, so doth not she:
    These babes for Clarence weep, and so do I:
85   I for an Edward weep, so do not they.
    Alas, you three, on me, threefold distressed,
    Pour all your tears! I am your sorrow's nurse,
    And I will pamper it with lamentation.
DORSET   Comfort, dear mother. God is much displeased   *To the*
90   That you take with unthankfulness, his doing.   *Queen*
    In common worldly things, 'tis called ungrateful,
    With dull unwillingness to repay a debt
    Which with a bounteous hand was kindly lent,
    Much more to be thus opposite with heaven,
95   For it requires the royal debt it lent you.
RIVERS   Madam, bethink you, like a careful mother
    Of the young prince your son: send straight for him
    Let him be crowned. In him your comfort lives.
    Drown desperate sorrow in dead Edward's grave
100   And plant your joys in living Edward's throne.
Enter Richard, Buckingham, [Stanley, Earl of] Derby, Hastings and
Ratcliffe
RICHARD   Sister, have comfort. All of us have cause   *To the Queen*
    To wail the dimming of our shining star,
    But none can help our harms by wailing them.—
    Madam, my mother, I do cry you mercy: *Kneels*
105   I did not see your grace. Humbly on my knee
    I crave your blessing.

---

81 **parcelled** in specific parts, divided between them   **general** all-encompassing   87 **nurse**
nourisher, feeder   88 **pamper** cram, feed luxuriously   92 **dull** sluggish, reluctant
94 **opposite** antagonistic, adversarial   95 **For it requires** because it reclaims   96 **careful**
caring   104 **cry you mercy** beg your pardon

DUCHESS OF YORK   God bless thee, and put meekness in thy
       breast,
     Love, charity, obedience and true duty.   ↓*Richard rises*↓

RICHARD   Amen.— And make me die a good old man.   *Aside*

110   That is the butt-end of a mother's blessing;
     I marvel that her grace did leave it out.

BUCKINGHAM   You cloudy princes and heart-sorrowing
       peers,
     That bear this heavy mutual load of moan,
     Now cheer each other in each other's love.

115   Though we have spent our harvest of this king,
     We are to reap the harvest of his son.
     The broken rancour of your high-swoll'n hates,
     But lately splintered, knit, and joined together,
     Must gently be preserved, cherished, and kept.

120   Meseemeth good, that, with some little train,
     Forthwith from Ludlow the young prince be fet
     Hither to London, to be crowned our king.

RIVERS   Why with some little train, my lord of
       Buckingham?

BUCKINGHAM   Marry, my lord, lest by a multitude,

125   The new-healed wound of malice should break out,
     Which would be so much the more dangerous
     By how much the estate is green and yet
       ungoverned.
     Where every horse bears his commanding rein,
     And may direct his course as please himself,

---

107 **meekness** humility   110 **butt-end** concluding part   111 **grace** quibbling on the
duchess' title and on the sense of "religious virtue"   112 **cloudy** gloomy   113 **moan** sorrow,
grief   117 **broken rancour** divisive animosity (**broken** begins an image of an injured limb)
high-swoll'n very inflamed/proud   118 **But lately splintered** only recently splinted, reset
(though at the same time continuing the imagery of fragmentation)   119 **kept** looked after
120 **Meseemeth** it seems to me   **little train** small retinue of attendants and accompanying
nobles   121 **Forthwith** immediately   **Ludlow** Ludlow Castle, in Shropshire, near the Welsh
border   **fet** fetched   124 **multitude** large group   127 **estate** state, kingdom   **green** new,
vulnerable (with suggestions of the prince's youth)   128 **Where . . . himself** when each horse
is in control of his own reins and may go where he pleases (i.e. in the absence of a strong rider
to govern)

130   As well the fear of harm, as harm apparent,
       In my opinion, ought to be prevented.
       RICHARD   I hope the king made peace with all of us,
       And the compact is firm and true in me.
       RIVERS   And so in me, and so, I think, in all.
135   Yet since it is but green, it should be put
       To no apparent likelihood of breach,
       Which haply by much company might be urged:
       Therefore I say with noble Buckingham,
       That it is meet so few should fetch the prince.
140   HASTINGS   And so say I.
       RICHARD   Then be it so, and go we to determine
       Who they shall be that straight shall post to Ludlow.
       Madam, and you my sister, will you go
       To give your censures in this business?

                              Exeunt. Buckingham and Richard remain

145   BUCKINGHAM My lord, whoever journeys to the prince,
       For God's sake, let not us two stay at home.
       For by the way I'll sort occasion,
       As index to the story we late talked of,
       To part the queen's proud kindred from the prince.
150   RICHARD   My other self, my counsel's consistory,
       My oracle, my prophet, my dear cousin,
       I, as a child, will go by thy direction.
       Towards Ludlow then, for we'll not stay behind.

                                                    Exeunt

---

130 As . . . apparent both the fear of possible harm as well as actual harm   133 with between
134 compact agreement, contract   135 green new, not tested   136 apparent evident, real
breach breakage, rupture   137 haply perhaps/probably   urged encouraged   139 meet
appropriate, suitable   142 post hasten   144 censures opinions   147 by on   sort occasion
arrange an opportunity   148 index preface   story plan, business   late recently
150 counsel's innermost thoughts' (puns on advisory "council")   consistory council
chamber, meeting place   152 direction instruction, guidance

Act 2 Scene 3

Enter one Citizen at one door, and another at the other

FIRST CITIZEN   Good morrow, neighbour. Whither away
so fast?

SECOND CITIZEN   I promise you, I scarcely know myself.
Hear you the news abroad?

FIRST CITIZEN   Yes, that the king is dead.

5   SECOND CITIZEN   Ill news, by'r lady, seldom comes the
better:
I fear, I fear 'twill prove a giddy world.

Enter another Citizen

THIRD CITIZEN   Neighbours, God speed.

FIRST CITIZEN   Give you good morrow, sir.

THIRD CITIZEN   Doth the news hold of good King Edward's
death?

10   SECOND CITIZEN   Ay, sir, it is too true, God help the
while.

THIRD CITIZEN   Then, masters, look to see a troublous
world.

FIRST CITIZEN   No, no. By God's good grace his son shall
reign.

THIRD CITIZEN   Woe to that land that's governed by a
child.

SECOND CITIZEN   In him there is a hope of government,

15   Which in his nonage, council under him,
And in his full and ripened years, himself,
No doubt shall then, and till then govern well.

FIRST CITIZEN   So stood the state when Henry the Sixth
Was crowned in Paris but at nine months old.

2.3 *Location: a London street*   3 abroad at large, in the outside world   **5 by'r lady** by Our
Lady (the Virgin Mary)   **seldom . . . better** is rarely followed by better things   **6 giddy**
inconstant, unstable   **7 God speed** God be with you; a standard greeting   **8 Give . . .
morrow** God give you good day; a standard greeting   **9 Doth . . . hold** is the news true
10 God . . . while i.e. God help us   **while** age, times   **11 masters** sirs   **look** expect
15 nonage minority, youth   **council under him** the Privy Council, a group of the king's
ministers, governing for him

20   THIRD CITIZEN   Stood the state so? No, no, good friends,
         God wot,
      For then this land was famously enriched
      With politic grave counsel; then the king
      Had virtuous uncles to protect his grace.
     FIRST CITIZEN   Why, so hath this, both by his father and
         mother.
25   THIRD CITIZEN   Better it were they all came by his father,
      Or by his father there were none at all.
      For emulation, who shall now be nearest,
      Will touch us all too near, if God prevent not.
      O, full of danger is the Duke of Gloucester,
30   And the queen's sons and brothers haught and
         proud:
      And were they to be ruled, and not to rule,
      This sickly land might solace as before.
     FIRST CITIZEN   Come, come, we fear the worst. All will be
         well.
     THIRD CITIZEN   When clouds are seen, wise men put on
         their cloaks;
35   When great leaves fall, then winter is at hand;
      When the sun sets, who doth not look for night?
      Untimely storms makes men expect a dearth.
      All may be well; but, if God sort it so,
      'Tis more than we deserve or I expect.
40   SECOND CITIZEN   Truly, the hearts of men are full of fear.
      You cannot reason almost with a man
      That looks not heavily and full of dread.
     THIRD CITIZEN   Before the days of change, still is it so.
      By a divine instinct men's minds mistrust
45   Pursuing danger. As by proof, we see

20 so in the same condition   wot knows   22 politic grave counsel wise and reverend
guidance   23 protect act as formal guardians for   27 emulation rivalry   nearest most
closely related to the king/most influential over the king   28 touch . . . near affect us all too
closely   30 haught haughty, aspiring   32 solace take comfort, be happy   36 look for expect
37 dearth famine, shortage   38 sort ordain, arrange   41 cannot reason almost can scarcely
reason   42 heavily gravely, anxiously   43 still always   44 mistrust suspect   45 proof
experience

The water swell before a boist'rous storm.
But leave it all to God. Whither away?

SECOND CITIZEN   Marry, we were sent for to the justices.

THIRD CITIZEN   And so was I. I'll bear you company.

Exeunt

Act 2 Scene 4

Enter [the] Archbishop, young York, the Queen and the Duchess

ARCHBISHOP OF YORK   Last night, I heard, they lay at
    Stony Stratford
And at Northampton they do rest tonight.
Tomorrow, or next day, they will be here.

DUCHESS OF YORK   I long with all my heart to see the
    prince.

5   I hope he is much grown since last I saw him.

QUEEN ELIZABETH   But I hear, no. They say my son of
    York
Has almost overta'en him in his growth.

YORK   Ay, mother, but I would not have it so.

DUCHESS OF YORK   Why, my good cousin, it is good to
    grow.

10   YORK   Grandam, one night as we did sit at supper,
My uncle Rivers talked how I did grow
More than my brother. 'Ay', quoth my uncle
    Gloucester,
'Small herbs have grace, great weeds do grow apace.'
And since, methinks, I would not grow so fast,
15   Because sweet flowers are slow and weeds make haste.

---

46 boist'rous violent   47 Whither away? Where are you going?   48 justices justices of the peace; the reason for this is never stated   2.4 *Location: the royal court, London*   1 lay spent the night   Stony Stratford small town in Buckinghamshire   2 Northampton Northamptonshire town twelve miles farther from London than Stony Stratford, an apparent confusion explained by Shakespeare's sources: Richard and Buckingham met the Prince at Stony Stratford, then (Rivers, Vaughan, and Grey having been arrested) took him back to Northampton before resuming the journey to London   9 cousin general term for a relative   13 grace virtuous qualities; possibly Richard quibbles on "herb of grace" or rue, an herb with medicinal qualities whose name means "sorrow"   apace quickly

DUCHESS OF YORK   Good faith, good faith, the saying did
not hold
In him that did object the same to thee.
He was the wretched'st thing when he was young,
So long a-growing and so leisurely,

20   That, if his rule were true, he should be gracious.
ARCHBISHOP OF YORK   And so no doubt he is, my
gracious madam.
DUCHESS OF YORK   I hope he is, but yet let mothers
doubt.
YORK   Now, by my troth, if I had been remembered,
I could have given my uncle's grace a flout,

25   To touch his growth nearer than he touched mine.
DUCHESS OF YORK   How, my young York? I prithee let
me hear it.
YORK   Marry, they say my uncle grew so fast
That he could gnaw a crust at two hours old.
'Twas full two years ere I could get a tooth.

30   Grandam, this would have been a biting jest.
DUCHESS OF YORK   I prithee, pretty York, who told thee
this?
YORK   Grandam, his nurse.
DUCHESS OF YORK   His nurse? Why, she was dead ere
thou wast born.
YORK   If 'twere not she, I cannot tell who told me.

35   **QUEEN ELIZABETH**   A parlous boy. Go to, you are too
shrewd.
DUCHESS OF YORK   Good madam, be not angry with the
child.
QUEEN ELIZABETH   Pitchers have ears.
Enter a Messenger

---

16 hold apply, prove true   **17 object the same** suggest it, apply it   **23 troth** faith   **been
remembered** remembered   **24 flout** taunt, mocking insult   **25 touch . . . mine** mock his
growth more pointedly than he mocked mine   **28 gnaw . . . old** various historical accounts
claim that Richard was born with teeth, something considered abnormal and ominous
30 biting sharp/to do with teeth   **35 parlous** mischievous, wily   **Go to** expression of
dismissive impatience   **shrewd** sharp-tongued, cheeky   **37 Pitchers have ears** proverbial;
pitchers were jugs with large handles ("ears")—Elizabeth means that the boy has been
eavesdropping on adult conversation

ARCHBISHOP OF YORK   Here comes a messenger. What
    news?

MESSENGER   Such news, my lord, as grieves me to report.

40 QUEEN ELIZABETH   How doth the prince?

MESSENGER   Well, madam, and in health.

DUCHESS OF YORK   What is thy news?

MESSENGER   Lord Rivers and Lord Grey are sent to
    Pomfret,
    And with them Sir Thomas Vaughan, prisoners.

45 DUCHESS OF YORK   Who hath committed them?

MESSENGER   The mighty dukes, Gloucester and
    Buckingham.

ARCHBISHOP OF YORK   For what offence?

MESSENGER   The sum of all I can, I have disclosed.
    Why or for what the nobles were committed
50   Is all unknown to me, my gracious lord.

QUEEN ELIZABETH   Ay me, I see the ruin of my house.
    The tiger now hath seized the gentle hind, *deer*
    Insulting tyranny begins to jut
    Upon the innocent and aweless throne.
55   Welcome, destruction, blood and massacre.
    I see, as in a map, the end of all.

DUCHESS OF YORK   Accursèd and unquiet wrangling
    days,
    How many of you have mine eyes beheld?
    My husband lost his life to get the crown,
60   And often up and down my sons were tossed,
    For me to joy and weep their gain and loss.
    And being seated, and domestic broils
    Clean overblown, themselves the conquerors,
    Make war upon themselves, brother to brother,
65   Blood to blood, self against self. O, preposterous

---

43 **Pomfret** Pontefract castle, in Yorkshire   48 **can** know, can say   51 **house** family
52 **hind** female deer   53 **Insulting** threatening, harmful/exulting scornfully   **jut** thrust,
shove/project, encroach   54 **aweless** inspiring no awe or dread   **throne** i.e. Prince Edward
56 **map** chart of the world/diagram/summary, epitome   62 **seated** in power, having gained
the throne   **broils** turmoil   63 **overblown** blown over   65 **preposterous** unnatural
(literally, in reverse order)

And frantic outrage, end thy damnèd spleen,
Or let me die, to look on earth no more!

QUEEN ELIZABETH   Come, come, my boy, we will to   *To young York*
sanctuary.—
Madam, farewell.   *To the Duchess*

70   DUCHESS OF YORK   Stay, I will go with you.

QUEEN ELIZABETH   You have no cause.

ARCHBISHOP OF YORK   My gracious lady, go,
And thither bear your treasure and your goods.
For my part, I'll resign unto your grace

75   The seal I keep: and so betide to me
As well I tender you and all of yours!
Go, I'll conduct you to the sanctuary.   *Exeunt*

Act 3 Scene 1   *running scene 7*

*The trumpets sound. Enter young Prince [Edward], the Dukes of
Gloucester [Richard] and Buckingham, Lord Cardinal with others*

BUCKINGHAM   Welcome, sweet prince, to London, to
your chamber.

RICHARD   Welcome, dear cousin, my thoughts'
sovereign.
The weary way hath made you melancholy.

PRINCE EDWARD   No, uncle, but our crosses on the way

5   Have made it tedious, wearisome, and heavy.
I want more uncles here to welcome me.

RICHARD   Sweet prince, the untainted virtue of your
years
Hath not yet dived into the world's deceit.

---

66 **frantic outrage** insane violence   **spleen** fury (the spleen was thought to be the seat of
extreme emotion)   68 **sanctuary** churches and their precincts provided sanctuary from
arrest; Elizabeth went to Westminster Abbey   75 **seal** great seal of England, used by the king
to authenticate documents; the Archbishop was its official keeper   **so . . . you** may my
fortunes depend on the care I show you   **3.1 *Location: London; exact location
unspecified, possibly a street***   1 **chamber** London was known as the *camera regis*, Latin for
the "king's chamber"   2 **my thoughts' sovereign** my chief concern/head of my thoughts
4 **crosses** troubles (i.e. the arrests of Rivers, Vaughan, and Grey)   5 **heavy** laborious,
burdensome, sorrowful   6 **want** lack/desire

No more can you distinguish of a man
10   Than of his outward show, which — God he knows —
Seldom or never jumpeth with the heart.
Those uncles which you want were dangerous:
Your grace attended to their sugared words,
But looked not on the poison of their hearts.
15   God keep you from them, and from such false friends.

PRINCE EDWARD   God keep me from false friends, but they
were none.

RICHARD   My lord, the Mayor of London comes to greet
you.

Enter Lord Mayor

LORD MAYOR   God bless your grace with health and
happy days.

PRINCE EDWARD   I thank you, good my lord, and thank
you all.—
20   I thought my mother, and my brother York,
Would long ere this have met us on the way.
Fie, what a slug is Hastings, that he comes not
To tell us whether they will come or no.

Enter Lord Hastings

BUCKINGHAM   And, in good time, here comes the sweating
lord.

25   PRINCE EDWARD   Welcome, my lord. What, will our
mother come?

HASTINGS   On what occasion, God he knows, not I,
The queen your mother, and your brother York,
Have taken sanctuary. The tender prince
Would fain have come with me to meet your grace,
30   But by his mother was perforce withheld.

BUCKINGHAM   Fie, what an indirect and peevish course
Is this of hers?— Lord Cardinal, will your grace

---

11 jumpeth accords, agrees   13 attended paid attention, listened   21 ere before   22 slug
sluggard, lazy fellow   26 On what occasion for what reason   28 tender young   prince i.e.
Edward's younger brother, Richard   29 fain willingly   30 perforce forcibly   31 indirect
devious/oblique, lengthy/erroneous   peevish obstinate/perverse

Persuade the queen to send the Duke of York
Unto his princely brother presently?—
35   If she deny, Lord Hastings, go with him,
And from her jealous arms pluck him perforce.
CARDINAL   My lord of Buckingham, if my weak oratory
Can from his mother win the Duke of York,
Anon expect him here. But if she be obdurate
40   To mild entreaties, God forbid
We should infringe the holy privilege
Of blessèd sanctuary. Not for all this land
Would I be guilty of so great a sin.
BUCKINGHAM You are too senseless obstinate, my lord,
45   Too ceremonious and traditional.
Weigh it but with the grossness of this age,
You break not sanctuary in seizing him.
The benefit thereof is always granted
To those whose dealings have deserved the place,
50   And those who have the wit to claim the place:
This prince hath neither claimed it nor deserved it,
And therefore, in mine opinion, cannot have it.
Then, taking him from thence that is not there,
You break no privilege nor charter there.
55   Oft have I heard of sanctuary men,
But sanctuary children ne'er till now.
CARDINAL   My lord, you shall o'er-rule my mind for
once.—
Come on, Lord Hastings, will you go with me?
HASTINGS   I go, my lord.   *Exeunt Cardinal and Hastings*
60   PRINCE EDWARD   Good lords, make all the speedy haste
you may.—

---

34 presently immediately   36 jealous suspicious, mistrustful, overprotective   37 oratory
rhetorical skill   39 Anon shortly   obdurate inflexible, determined   44 senseless
unreasonably, foolishly   46 Weigh . . . with if you only judge it by   grossness low standards,
coarseness   48 benefit protection   49 dealings actions, conduct   50 wit intelligence,
mature judgment   53 thence . . . there a place that cannot really be considered as sanctuary
in his case   54 charter privilege, legal right

Say, uncle Gloucester, if our brother come,
Where shall we sojourn till our coronation?

RICHARD   Where it think'st best unto your royal self.
If I may counsel you, some day or two

65   Your highness shall repose you at the Tower:
Then where you please, and shall be thought most fit
For your best health and recreation.

PRINCE EDWARD   I do not like the Tower, of any place.—
Did Julius Caesar build that place, my lord?   *To Buckingham*

70   BUCKINGHAM   He did, my gracious lord, begin that place,
Which, since, succeeding ages have re-edified.

PRINCE EDWARD   Is it upon record? Or else reported
Successively from age to age, he built it?

BUCKINGHAM   Upon record, my gracious lord.

75   PRINCE EDWARD   But say, my lord, it were not registered,
Methinks the truth should live from age to age,
As 'twere retailed to all posterity,
Even to the general ending day.

RICHARD   So wise so young, they say, do never live long.   *Aside*

80   PRINCE EDWARD   What say you, uncle?

RICHARD   I say, without characters, fame lives long.—
Thus, like the formal Vice, Iniquity,   *Aside*
I moralize two meanings in one word.

PRINCE EDWARD   That Julius Caesar was a famous man.

85   With what his valour did enrich his wit,
His wit set down to make his valour live.
Death makes no conquest of his conqueror,

---

62 **sojourn** stay, reside   65 **repose you** settle yourself, rest   **Tower** a royal residence as well as a much-feared prison   68 **any place** all places   71 **re-edified** rebuilt, developed   72 **upon record** written down   75 **registered** recorded   77 **retailed** recounted, retold   78 **general ending day** universal doomsday, the end of the world   79 **So . . . long** proverbial: "too soon wise to live long"   81 **characters** written records   82 **formal Vice** conventional Vice figure of morality plays, an allegorical character named after a particular sin and known for wordplay and grim humor   **Iniquity** sinfulness; a stock name for a Vice figure   83 **moralize** interpret (perhaps playing on the idea of expounding God's word for the purpose of moral teaching)   85 **With . . . live** i.e. he used his intellect to write down the courageous military exploits that had enriched it, in order to ensure that his reputation lived on   87 **his conqueror** the one who conquers death

For now he lives in fame, though not in life.

I'll tell you what, my cousin Buckingham—

90 BUCKINGHAM What, my gracious lord?

PRINCE EDWARD   An if I live until I be a man,

I'll win our ancient right in France again,

Or die a soldier, as I lived a king.

RICHARD   Short summers lightly have a forward spring.   *Aside*

Enter young York, Hastings and Cardinal

95 BUCKINGHAM Now, in good time, here comes the Duke of
York.

PRINCE EDWARD   Richard of York, how fares our noble
brother?

YORK   Well, my dear lord, so must I call you now.

PRINCE EDWARD   Ay, brother, to our grief, as it is yours:

Too late he died that might have kept that title,

100 Which by his death hath lost much majesty.

RICHARD   How fares our cousin, noble lord of York?

YORK   I thank you, gentle uncle. O, my lord,

You said that idle weeds are fast in growth:

The prince my brother hath outgrown me far.

105 RICHARD   He hath, my lord.

YORK   And therefore is he idle?   useless

RICHARD   O, my fair cousin, I must not say so.

YORK   Then he is more beholding to you than I.

RICHARD   He may command me as my sovereign,

110 But you have power in me as in a kinsman.

YORK   I pray you, uncle, give me this dagger.

RICHARD   My dagger, little cousin? With all my heart.

PRINCE EDWARD   A beggar, brother?

YORK   Of my kind uncle, that I know will give,

115 And being but a toy, which is no grief to give.

---

91 An if if   94 lightly usually   forward early   98 grief Edward refers to the death of his
father   99 late recently   103 idle useless   108 beholding beholden, indebted   110 as in in
that I am   111 dagger perhaps maintaining the link between Richard and the medieval Vice
figure, who traditionally carried a dagger   112 With . . . heart very willingly (but also
implying that he would gladly stab York with it)   115 toy trifle   grief hardship

RICHARD	A greater gift than that I'll give my cousin.
YORK	A greater gift? O, that's the sword to it.
RICHARD	Ay, gentle cousin, were it light enough.
YORK	O, then, I see, you will part but with light gifts.

120   In weightier things you'll say a beggar nay.

RICHARD	It is too weighty for your grace to wear.
YORK	I weigh it lightly, were it heavier.
RICHARD	What, would you have my weapon, little lord?
YORK	I would, that I might thank you as you call me.

125   RICHARD   How?

YORK   Little.

PRINCE EDWARD   My lord of York will still be cross in talk.
Uncle, your grace knows how to bear with him.

YORK   You mean to bear me, not to bear with me.—
130   Uncle, my brother mocks both you and me,
Because that I am little, like an ape,
He thinks that you should bear me on your
      shoulders.

BUCKINGHAM With what a sharp-provided wit he
      reasons!   *Aside*
To mitigate the scorn he gives his uncle,
135   He prettily and aptly taunts himself.
So cunning and so young is wonderful.

RICHARD   My lord, will't please you pass along?
Myself and my good cousin Buckingham
Will to your mother, to entreat of her
140   To meet you at the Tower and welcome you.

YORK   What, will you go unto the Tower, my lord?

PRINCE EDWARD   My Lord Protector will have it so.

---

117 to it that goes with it   118 light not heavy (York shifts the sense to "trifling, cheap")
120 a beggar nay no to a beggar   122 weigh it lightly consider it a trifle/do not think it weighs
very much   122 were it even if it were   123 have continues the grim play on "receive as a
gift/receive in death"   127 still always   cross contrary, perverse   131 like . . . shoulders
professional fools or tame bears carried apes on their backs at fairs; attention is drawn here to
Richard's hunched back   bear puns on the name of the animal   133 sharp-provided quick
and ready   134 mitigate moderate, lessen   135 prettily cleverly, charmingly   136 cunning
crafty, clever

	YORK	I shall not sleep in quiet at the Tower.
	RICHARD	Why, what should you fear?
145	YORK	Marry, my uncle Clarence' angry ghost.

My grandam told me he was murdered there.

PRINCE EDWARD   I fear no uncles dead.

RICHARD   Nor none that live, I hope.

PRINCE EDWARD   An if they live, I hope I need not fear.

150   But come, my lord and with a heavy heart,

Thinking on them, go I unto the Tower.

A sennet.

Exeunt Prince, York, Hastings and Dorset.
Richard, Buckingham and Catesby remain

BUCKINGHAM   Think you, my lord, this little prating York

Was not incensèd by his subtle mother

To taunt and scorn you thus opprobriously?

155   RICHARD   No doubt, no doubt. O, 'tis a perilous boy:

Bold, quick, ingenious, forward, capable.

He is all the mother's, from the top to toe.

BUCKINGHAM   Well, let them rest.— Come hither,

Catesby.

Thou art sworn as deeply to effect what we intend

160   As closely to conceal what we impart.

Thou know'st our reasons urged upon the way,

What think'st thou? Is it not an easy matter

To make William Lord Hastings of our mind,

For the instalment of this noble duke

165   In the seat royal of this famous isle?

CATESBY   He for his father's sake so loves the prince,

That he will not be won to aught against him.

---

sennet trumpet call signaling the continuation of a procession   **152 prating** chattering, prattling   **153 incensèd** urged on, incited   **subtle** cunning   **154 opprobriously** scornfully, insultingly   **155 perilous** wily, dangerous, mischievous   **156 forward** spirited, ready **capable** responsive, receptive   **157 all the mother's** exactly like his mother   **158 let them rest** enough of them, leave them for the moment; or perhaps literally "let them take their rest" **159 deeply** profoundly, solemnly   **160 closely** secretly   **161 urged** proposed, discussed **way** i.e. the journey from Ludlow to London   **163 of . . . For** share our opinion and intention regarding   **166 He . . . father's** Hastings for Edward IV's   **167 won to aught** persuaded to do anything

BUCKINGHAM What think'st thou, then, of Stanley? Will
   not he?

CATESBY   He will do all in all as Hastings doth.

170 BUCKINGHAM Well, then, no more but this: go, gentle
   Catesby,
   And, as it were far off sound thou Lord Hastings,
   How he doth stand affected to our purpose,
   And summon him tomorrow to the Tower,
   To sit about the coronation.

175   If thou dost find him tractable to us,
   Encourage him, and tell him all our reasons.
   If he be leaden, icy-cold, unwilling,
   Be thou so too, and so break off the talk,
   And give us notice of his inclination,

180   For we tomorrow hold divided councils,
   Wherein thyself shalt highly be employed.

RICHARD   Commend me to Lord William. Tell him,
   Catesby,
   His ancient knot of dangerous adversaries
   Tomorrow are let blood at Pomfret Castle,

185   And bid my lord, for joy of this good news,
   Give Mistress Shore one gentle kiss the more.

BUCKINGHAM Good Catesby, go effect this business
   soundly.

CATESBY   My good lords both, with all the heed I can.

RICHARD   Shall we hear from you, Catesby, ere we sleep?

190 CATESBY   You shall, my lord.

RICHARD   At Crosby House, there shall you find us both.

Exit Catesby

---

171 as . . . off in a roundabout way, indirectly   **sound** sound out, probe   **172 affected to**
disposed toward   **174 sit** confer, sit in council   **180 divided councils** two separate meetings
181 highly crucially   **182 Lord William** i.e. Hastings   **183 ancient knot** long-standing group
(**knot** may play on the sense of "tumor")   **184 are let blood** i.e. will be executed; literally,
refers to surgical bloodletting   **186 Mistress Shore** Hastings' mistress Jane Shore (formerly
mistress of Edward IV)   **188 heed** care

BUCKINGHAM Now my lord, what shall we do if we
    perceive
    Lord Hastings will not yield to our complots?
RICHARD <u>Chop off his head</u>: something we will
    determine:
195   And look when I am king, claim thou of me
    The earldom of Hereford, and all the movables
    Whereof the king my brother was possessed.
BUCKINGHAM I'll claim that promise at your grace's
    hand.
RICHARD   And look to have it yielded with all kindness.
200   Come, let us sup betimes, that afterwards
    We may digest our complots in some form.   *Exeunt*

Act 3 Scene 2

Enter a Messenger to the door of Hastings

MESSENGER My lord, my lord!
HASTINGS Who knocks?   *Within*
MESSENGER One from the lord Stanley.
HASTINGS What is't o'clock?   *Within*
5 MESSENGER Upon the stroke of four.
Enter Lord Hastings
HASTINGS Cannot my lord Stanley sleep these tedious
    nights?
MESSENGER So it appears by that I have to say.
    First, he commends him to your noble self.
HASTINGS What then?
10 MESSENGER Then certifies your lordship that this night
    He dreamt the boar had razèd off his helm.
    Besides, he says there are two councils kept,
    And that may be determined at the one

193 **complots** conspiracies, schemes   196 **movables** portable property   200 **sup betimes** have supper early   201 **digest** arrange (plays on the sense of literal digestion)   **form** good order   **3.2 *Location: outside Hastings' house***   6 **tedious** weary, long   11 **boar** Richard's heraldic emblem   **razèd** pulled, torn   **helm** helmet   13 **that . . . determined** decisions may be taken

Which may make you and him to rue at th'other:

15   Therefore he sends to know your lordship's pleasure,

If you will presently take horse with him,

And with all speed post with him toward the north,

To shun the danger that his soul divines.

HASTINGS   Go, fellow, go, return unto thy lord,

20   Bid him not fear the separated council:

His honour and myself are at the one,

And at the other is my good friend Catesby,

Where nothing can proceed that toucheth us

Whereof I shall not have intelligence.

25   Tell him his fears are shallow, without instance.

And for his dreams, I wonder he's so simple

To trust the mock'ry of unquiet slumbers.

To fly the boar before the boar pursues,

Were to incense the boar to follow us

30   And make pursuit where he did mean no chase.

Go, bid thy master rise and come to me

And we will both together to the Tower,

Where he shall see the boar will use us kindly.

MESSENGER   I'll go, my lord, and tell him what you say.

Exit

Enter Catesby

35   CATESBY   Many good morrows to my noble lord.

HASTINGS   Good morrow, Catesby. You are early stirring.

What news, what news, in this our tott'ring state?

CATESBY   It is a reeling world, indeed, my lord,

And I believe will never stand upright

40   Till Richard wear the garland of the realm.

HASTINGS   How? Wear the garland? Dost thou mean the

crown?

---

14 to rue grieve   15 pleasure will, inclination   16 presently immediately   17 post ride
swiftly   21 His honour Lord Stanley   23 toucheth affects, relates to   24 have intelligence
be informed   25 without instance lacking evidence   27 mock'ry foolish delusions, false
images   28 fly flee   29 Were would be   30 mean (originally) intend   33 use treat   kindly
gently, courteously (plays on the sense of "according to his [boarlike] nature")   40 garland i.e.
crown (with connotations of a victor's garland)

CATESBY   Ay, my good lord.

HASTINGS   I'll have this crown of mine cut from my
shoulders

Before I'll see the crown so foul misplaced.

45   But canst thou guess that he doth aim at it?

CATESBY   Ay, on my life, and hopes to find you forward

Upon his party for the gain thereof:

And thereupon he sends you this good news,

That this same very day your enemies,

50   The kindred of the queen, must die at Pomfret.

HASTINGS   Indeed, I am no mourner for that news,

Because they have been still my adversaries.

But that I'll give my voice on Richard's side

To bar my master's heirs in true descent,

55   God knows I will not do it, to the death.

CATESBY   God keep your lordship in that gracious mind.

HASTINGS   But I shall laugh at this a twelvemonth hence,

That they which brought me in my master's hate,

I live to look upon their tragedy.

60   Well, Catesby, ere a fortnight make me older,

I'll send some packing that yet think not on't.

CATESBY   'Tis a vile thing to die, my gracious lord,

When men are unprepared and look not for it.

HASTINGS   O, monstrous, monstrous! And so falls it out

65   With Rivers, Vaughan, Grey: and so 'twill do

With some men else, that think themselves as safe

As thou and I — who, as thou know'st, are dear

To princely Richard and to Buckingham.

CATESBY   The princes both make high account of you.—

70   For they account his head upon the bridge.   *Aside*

---

43 **crown** head   44 **foul** wickedly, wrongfully/in an ugly manner (perhaps recalling Richard's
appearance)   46 **forward . . . party** ready to support him, eagerly on his side   54 **master's** i.e.
Edward IV's   58 **they** i.e. the queen's relatives   **in** into   64 **monstrous** unnatural   **falls it
out** it has happened   69 **make high account** hold you in high estimation (in the context of
the following line, **high** plays on the sense of "high up, aloft")   70 **account** consider, expect
the bridge London Bridge, on which traitors' heads were displayed on poles

HASTINGS   I know they do, and I have well deserved it.

Enter Lord Stanley [Earl of Derby]

Come on, come on, where is your boar-spear, man?   *To Derby*

Fear you the boar, and go so unprovided?

DERBY   My lord, good morrow.— Good morrow, Catesby.

75   You may jest on, but, by the holy rood,

I do not like these several councils, I.

HASTINGS   My lord, I hold my life as dear as yours,

And never in my days, I do protest,

Was it so precious to me as 'tis now.

80   Think you, but that I know our state secure,

I would be so triumphant as I am?

DERBY   The lords at Pomfret, when they rode from London,

Were jocund and supposed their states were sure,

And they indeed had no cause to mistrust:

85   But yet you see how soon the day o'ercast.

This sudden stab of rancour I misdoubt:

Pray God, I say, I prove a needless coward.

What, shall we toward the Tower? The day is spent.

HASTINGS   Come, come, have with you. Wot you what, my lord?

90   Today the lords you talk of are beheaded.

LORD DERBY   They, for their truth, might better wear their heads

Than some that have accused them wear their hats.

But come, my lord, let's away.

Enter a Pursuivant

---

73 **unprovided** unprepared, ill-equipped   75 **rood** (Christ's) cross   76 **several** separate
78 **protest** declare   81 **triumphant** cheerful/exultant (over my enemies' deaths)   83 **jocund**
merry, cheerful   **states were sure** positions were secure   84 **mistrust** doubt, suspect
86 **This . . . misdoubt** i.e. this sudden hostile attack has made me fearful, mistrustful
88 **spent** coming to an end (although the scene begins at 4 a.m.; perhaps Stanley refers
figuratively to his own "time," i.e. life)   89 **have with you** literally "I'll join you" or as a
reprimand "come along now"   **Wot** know   91 **truth** loyalty, honesty   92 **hats** i.e. official
positions (Stanley has Richard's role as royal Protector in mind)   *Pursuivant* state messenger
with the power to execute warrants

HASTINGS   Go on before: I'll talk with this good fellow.—

Exeunt Derby and Catesby

95   How now, sirrah? How goes the world with thee?

PURSUIVANT   The better that your lordship please to ask.

HASTINGS   I tell thee, man, 'tis better with me now

Than when thou met'st me last where now we meet:

Then was I going prisoner to the Tower,

100   By the suggestion of the queen's allies.

But now, I tell thee — keep it to thyself —

This day those enemies are put to death,

And I in better state than e'er I was.

PURSUIVANT   God hold it to your honour's good content.

105   HASTINGS   Gramercy, fellow. There, drink that for me.

Throws him his purse

PURSUIVANT   I thank your honour.   *Exit*

Enter a Priest

PRIEST   Well met, my lord. I am glad to see your honour.

HASTINGS   I thank thee, good Sir John, with all my heart.

I am in your debt for your last exercise:

110   Come the next Sabbath, and I will content you. *Whispers in his ear*

PRIEST   I'll wait upon your lordship.

Enter Buckingham

BUCKINGHAM What, talking with a priest, Lord

Chamberlain?

Your friends at Pomfret, they do need the priest:

Your honour hath no shriving work in hand.

115   HASTINGS   Good faith, and when I met this holy man,

The men you talk of came into my mind.

What, go you toward the Tower?

BUCKINGHAM I do, my lord, but long I cannot stay there.

I shall return before your lordship thence.

---

94 before ahead   **95 sirrah** sir (used to inferiors)   **100 suggestion** instigation, prompting
103 state prosperity, position, circumstances   **104 hold** keep, maintain   **105 Gramercy** great
thanks   **108 Sir** conventional title for a clergyman   **109 I . . . exercise** Hastings apologizes
for not attending the last church service (during which he was in prison) **exercise** religious
service   **110 content** recompense   **114 shriving work** business of saying confession and
receiving absolution   **119 thence** from there

120 HASTINGS   Nay, like enough, for I stay dinner there.

BUCKINGHAM And supper too, although thou know'st it   *Aside*
   not.—

Come, will you go?

HASTINGS   I'll wait upon your lordship.   *Exeunt*

Act 3 Scene 3   *running scene 9*

Enter Sir Richard Ratcliffe with Halberds, carrying the nobles [Rivers, Grey and Vaughan] to death at Pomfret

RIVERS   Sir Richard Ratcliffe, let me tell thee this:
   Today shalt thou behold a subject die
   For truth, for duty, and for loyalty.

GREY   God bless the prince from all the pack of you.

5   A knot you are of damnèd blood-suckers!

VAUGHAN   You live that shall cry woe for this hereafter.

RATCLIFFE   Dispatch. The limit of your lives is out.

RIVERS   O Pomfret, Pomfret! O thou bloody prison!
   Fatal and ominous to noble peers!

10   Within the guilty closure of thy walls
   Richard the Second here was hacked to death.
   And, for more slander to thy dismal seat,
   We give to thee our guiltless blood to drink.

GREY   Now Margaret's curse is fall'n upon our heads,

15   When she exclaimed on Hastings, you and I,
   For standing by when Richard stabbed her son.

RIVERS   Then cursed she Richard, then cursed she
   Buckingham,
   Then cursed she Hastings. O, remember, God,
   To hear her prayer for them, as now for us:

20   And for my sister and her princely sons,

---

120 stay stay for   **3.3 Location: Pomfret (Pontefract) castle, Yorkshire**   5 knot tight group   7 Dispatch get on with it   10 closure enclosure   12 for . . . seat to add to the disgrace associated with this place   dismal seat ominous position   15 exclaimed on cried out against, condemned   Hastings . . . I in fact, Margaret does not mention Grey (see Act 1 Scene 3)   20 for instead of

Be satisfied, dear God, with our true blood,
Which, as thou know'st, unjustly must be spilt.

RATCLIFFE   Make haste: the hour of death is expiate.

RIVERS   Come, Grey, come, Vaughan, let us here
   embrace.

25   Farewell, until we meet again in heaven.   *Exeunt*

Act 3 Scene 4   *running scene 10*

*Enter Buckingham, Derby, Hastings, Bishop of Ely, Norfolk, Ratcliffe,
Lovell, with others. [They take their seats] at a table*

HASTINGS   Now, noble peers, the cause why we are met
Is to determine of the coronation.
In God's name speak: when is the royal day?

BUCKINGHAM   Is all things ready for the royal time?

5   DERBY   It is, and wants but nomination.

BISHOP OF ELY   Tomorrow, then, I judge a happy day.

BUCKINGHAM   Who knows the Lord Protector's mind
   herein?
Who is most inward with the noble duke?

BISHOP OF ELY   Your grace, we think, should soonest know his
   mind.

10   BUCKINGHAM   We know each other's faces: for our
   hearts,
He knows no more of mine, than I of yours,
Or I of his, my lord, than you of mine.—
Lord Hastings, you and he are near in love.

HASTINGS   I thank his grace, I know he loves me well.

15   But, for his purpose in the coronation,
I have not sounded him, nor he delivered
His gracious pleasure any way therein:

---

23 expiate reached, fully come   **3.4 *Location: council chamber, the Tower of London***
2 of about   **5 wants but nomination** requires only the appointing of the date   **6 happy**
auspicious, favorable   **8 inward** intimate   **9 mind** temperament/opinion on the
coronation/intentions in general   **10 for** as for   **13 near in love** close, intimate
16 sounded questioned, sounded out

But you, my honourable lords, may name the time,
And in the duke's behalf I'll give my voice,
20   Which I presume he'll take in gentle part.

Enter [Richard of] Gloucester

BISHOP OF ELY   In happy time, here comes the duke
      himself.

RICHARD   My noble lords and cousins all, good morrow.
      I have been long a sleeper: but I trust
      My absence doth neglect no great design
25   Which by my presence might have been concluded.

BUCKINGHAM   Had you not come upon your cue, my
      lord,
      William Lord Hastings had pronounced your part —
      I mean your voice — for crowning of the king.

RICHARD   Than my lord Hastings no man might be
      bolder:
30   His lordship knows me well, and loves me well.—
      My lord of Ely, when I was last in Holborn,
      I saw good strawberries in your garden there:
      I do beseech you send for some of them.

BISHOP OF ELY   Marry, and will, my lord, with all my
      heart.   *Exit Bishop*

35   RICHARD   Cousin of Buckingham, a word with you.
      Catesby hath sounded Hastings in our business,   *They speak*
      And finds the testy gentleman so hot   *aside*
      That he will lose his head ere give consent
      His master's child, as worshipfully he terms it,
40   Shall lose the royalty of England's throne.

BUCKINGHAM   Withdraw yourself a while. I'll go with
      you.   *Exeunt [Richard and Buckingham]*

---

19 in on   **voice** vote   **20 take . . . part** accept in a gracious manner   **22 cousins** term of
address between nobles   **24 neglect** cause the neglect of   **27 part** role (continues the
theatrical language begun with **cue**)   **29 bolder** more confident   **37 testy** headstrong, short-
tempered   **hot** angry/impetuous   **38 head** plays on the etymology of **testy**, i.e. *teste*, Old
French for "head"   **39 worshipfully** respectfully

DERBY   We have not yet set down this day of triumph.

Tomorrow, in my judgement, is too sudden,

For I myself am not so well provided

45   As else I would be, were the day prolonged.

Enter the Bishop of Ely

BISHOP OF ELY   Where is my lord, the Duke of

Gloucester?

I have sent for these strawberries.

HASTINGS   His grace looks cheerfully and smooth this

morning:

There's some conceit or other likes him well,

50   When that he bids good morrow with such spirit.

I think there's never a man in Christendom

Can lesser hide his love or hate than he,

For by his face straight shall you know his heart.

DERBY   What of his heart perceive you in his face

55   By any livelihood he showed today?

HASTINGS   Marry, that with no man here he is offended:

For, were he, he had shown it in his looks.

Enter Richard and Buckingham

RICHARD   I pray you all, tell me what they deserve

That do conspire my death with devilish plots

60   Of damnèd witchcraft, and that have prevailed

Upon my body with their hellish charms.

HASTINGS   The tender love I bear your grace, my lord,

Makes me most forward in this princely presence

To doom th'offenders, whosoe'er they be:

65   I say, my lord, they have deservèd death.

RICHARD   Then be your eyes the witness of their evil.

Look how I am bewitched: behold, mine arm   *Points to his arm*

Is like a blasted sapling, withered up:

---

42 set down confirmed   **44 provided** prepared   **45 prolonged** postponed, delayed
48 smooth seemingly amiable or friendly   **49 conceit** idea, fancy   **likes** pleases   **53 straight**
instantly   **55 livelihood** liveliness   **61 charms** magic spells   **64 doom** sentence   **68 blasted**
shriveled, blighted by supernatural means

And this is Edward's wife, that monstrous witch,
70   Consorted with that harlot, strumpet Shore,
That by their witchcraft thus have markèd me.
HASTINGS   If they have done this deed, my noble lord—
RICHARD   If? Thou protector of this damnèd strumpet—
Talk'st thou to me of 'ifs'? Thou art a traitor.
75   Off with his head! Now, by Saint Paul I swear,
I will not dine until I see the same. —
Lovell and Ratcliffe, look that it be done.
The rest that love me, rise and follow me.

Exeunt. Lovell and Ratcliffe with
the Lord Hastings remain

HASTINGS   Woe, woe for England! Not a whit for me,
80   For I, too fond, might have prevented this.
Stanley did dream the boar did rouse our helms;
And I did scorn it and disdain to fly.
Three times today my foot-cloth horse did stumble,
And started, when he looked upon the Tower,
85   As loath to bear me to the slaughter-house.
O, now I need the priest that spake to me:
I now repent I told the pursuivant,
As too triumphing how mine enemies
Today at Pomfret bloodily were butchered,
90   And I myself secure in grace and favour.
O Margaret, Margaret, now thy heavy curse
Is lighted on poor Hastings' wretched head!
RATCLIFFE   Come, come, dispatch. The duke would be at
dinner.
Make a short shrift: he longs to see your head.
95   HASTINGS   O, momentary grace of mortal men,
Which we more hunt for than the grace of God!

---

69 is i.e. is the doing of   **monstrous** unnatural   **70 Consorted** associated, in conjunction
Shore Jane Shore, Hastings' mistress and formerly Edward IV's   **76 the same** i.e. Hastings'
beheading accomplished   **80 fond** foolish   **81 rouse** move violently, pull from our heads
83 foot-cloth horse horse with a long ornate cloth draped over its back   **84 started** shied,
moved suddenly   **85 As** as if   **loath** reluctant, unwilling   **88 triumphing** exulting
victoriously   **94 shrift** confession (to a priest)   **95 grace** fortune, favor (in the next line, the
sense shifts to "divine grace, mercy")

Who builds his hope in air of your good looks,

Lives like a drunken sailor on a mast,

Ready with every nod to tumble down

100   Into the fatal bowels of the deep.

LOVELL   Come, come, dispatch: 'tis bootless to exclaim.

HASTINGS   O bloody Richard! Miserable England!

I prophesy the fearful'st time to thee

That ever wretched age hath looked upon.

105   Come, lead me to the block: bear him my head.

They smile at me who shortly shall be dead.   *Exeunt*

[Act 3 Scene 5]   *running scene 11*

Enter Richard and Buckingham, in rotten armour, marvellous
ill-favoured

RICHARD   Come, cousin, canst thou quake and change

thy colour,

be an actor?

Murder thy breath in middle of a word,

And then again begin, and stop again,

As if thou were distraught and mad with terror?

5   BUCKINGHAM   Tut, I can counterfeit the deep tragedian,

Speak and look back, and pry on every side,

Tremble and start at wagging of a straw:

Intending deep suspicion, ghastly looks

Are at my service, like enforcèd smiles,

10   And both are ready in their offices

At any time to grace my stratagems.

But what, is Catesby gone?

---

97 Who he who   **in air** on the insubstantial foundation, in the emptiness   **good** favoring,
approving   **101 bootless** useless   **exclaim** protest, cry out   **3.5 *Location: within the
walls of the Tower of London*   rotten** rusty/old, decaying   ***marvellous ill-favoured***
(looking) extremely unsightly   **1 change thy colour** i.e. make yourself look pale with fear
2 Murder i.e. cut off, catch   **5 counterfeit** imitate   **deep** artful, cunning   **tragedian** tragic
actor   **6 back** behind me, over my shoulder (presumably in alarm or distrust)   **pry** peer
(nervously or suspiciously)   **7 at wagging** at the mere stirring, shaking   **8 Intending**
expressing, pretending   **ghastly** full of fear   **9 service** command   **enforcèd** false, deliberate
10 offices roles, tasks

RICHARD   He is, and see, he brings the mayor along.

Enter the Mayor and Catesby

BUCKINGHAM Lord Mayor—

15 RICHARD   Look to the drawbridge there!

BUCKINGHAM Hark, a drum!

RICHARD   Catesby, o'erlook the walls.

BUCKINGHAM Lord Mayor, the reason we have sent—

RICHARD   Look back, defend thee, here are enemies.

20 BUCKINGHAM God and our innocency defend and guard
            us!

Enter Lovell and Ratcliffe, with Hastings' head

RICHARD   Be patient, they are friends: Ratcliffe and
            Lovell.

LOVELL   Here is the head of that ignoble traitor,
            The dangerous and unsuspected Hastings.

RICHARD   So dear I loved the man that I must weep.
25   I took him for the plainest harmless creature
            That breathed upon the earth a Christian,
            Made him my book, wherein my soul recorded
            The history of all her secret thoughts.
            So smooth he daubed his vice with show of virtue
30   That, his apparent open guilt omitted —
            I mean, his conversation with Shore's wife —
            He lived from all attainder of suspects.

BUCKINGHAM Well, well, he was the covert'st sheltered
            traitor
            That ever lived.
35   Would you imagine, or almost believe,
            Were't not that, by great preservation
            We live to tell it, that the subtle traitor

---

17 o'erlook look over (seems to suggest that the scene takes place on the battlements)
21 patient calm   **25 plainest** most honest   **27 book** i.e. diary, personal notebook   **28 history** narrative, record   **29 smooth** plausibly   **30 his . . . omitted** apart from his manifest guilt
31 conversation sexual relationship   **32 from** free from   **attainder of suspects** stain of suspicion   **33 covert'st sheltered** most secretly concealed   **35 almost** even   **37 subtle** cunning

This day had plotted, in the council house,
To murder me and my good lord of Gloucester?

40 MAYOR   Had he done so?

RICHARD   What? Think you we are Turks or infidels?
Or that we would, against the form of law,
Proceed thus rashly in the villain's death,
But that the extreme peril of the case,
45 The peace of England and our person's safety,
Enforced us to this execution?

MAYOR   Now fair befall you! He deserved his death,
And your good graces, both have well proceeded
To warn false traitors from the like attempts.

50 BUCKINGHAM I never looked for better at his hands,
After he once fell in with Mistress Shore.
Yet had we not determined he should die
Until your lordship came to see his end,
Which now the loving haste of these our friends,
55 Something against our meanings, have prevented;
Because, my lord, I would have had you heard
The traitor speak, and timorously confess
The manner and the purpose of his treasons,
That you might well have signified the same
60 Unto the citizens, who haply may
Misconster us in him and wail his death.

MAYOR   But, my good lord, your grace's words shall serve
As well as I had seen and heard him speak:
And do not doubt, right noble princes both,
65 But I'll acquaint our duteous citizens
With all your just proceedings in this case.

---

41 Turks i.e. barbarians, non-Christians   **42 form** order, code   **43 rashly** hastily   **47 fair** good fortune   **48 proceeded** acted (perhaps with connotations of "taken legal proceedings")   **50 looked for** expected   **51 fell in** plays on the sense of "penetrated sexually"   **52 had . . . die** we had determined that he should not die   **53 see** attend to, manage   **57 timorously** with fear, tremblingly   **60 haply** perhaps   **61 Misconster** misconstrue   **us in him** our role in or motives for his death   **63 as** as if

RICHARD   And to that end we wished your lordship here,
　　　T'avoid the censures of the carping world.
BUCKINGHAM Which since you come too late of our
　　　intent,
70　　Yet witness what you hear we did intend.
　　　And so, my good Lord Mayor, we bid farewell.

Exit Mayor

RICHARD   Go, after, after, cousin Buckingham.
　　　The mayor towards Guildhall hies him in all post:
　　　There, at your meetest vantage of the time,
75　　Infer the bastardy of Edward's children:
　　　Tell them how Edward put to death a citizen
　　　Only for saying he would make his son
　　　Heir to the crown, meaning indeed his house,
　　　Which, by the sign thereof was termèd so.
80　　Moreover, urge his hateful luxury
　　　And bestial appetite in change of lust,
　　　Which stretched unto their servants, daughters,
　　　wives,
　　　Even where his raging eye or savage heart,
　　　Without control, lusted to make a prey.
85　　Nay, for a need, thus far come near my person:
　　　Tell them, when that my mother went with child
　　　Of that insatiate Edward, noble York
　　　My princely father then had wars in France,
　　　And by true computation of the time,
90　　Found that the issue was not his begot —
　　　Which well appearèd in his lineaments,
　　　Being nothing like the noble duke my father.

---

68 **carping** fault-finding, dissatisfied   69 **of** regarding   70 **witness** testify to   73 **Guildhall** central building in which civic affairs were conducted   **hies . . . post** hurries as quickly as possible   74 **meetest vantage** best opportunity   75 **Infer** allege   78 **house** both home and either shop or inn   79 **sign** i.e. sign bearing the name (The Crown) of the shop or inn   80 **luxury** lechery, lust   81 **change of lust** constantly requiring new sexual partners   83 **Even where** wherever   85 **for a need** if necessary   **come . . . person** i.e. tell a tale that will affect me too   86 **went . . . Of** was pregnant with   89 **true** exact, accurate   90 **his begot** conceived by him   91 **well . . . lineaments** was obvious in Edward's features, appearance

Yet touch this sparingly, as 'twere far off,
Because, my lord, you know my mother lives.

95 BUCKINGHAM Doubt not, my lord, I'll play the orator
As if the golden fee for which I plead
Were for myself. And so, my lord, adieu.

RICHARD   If you thrive well, bring them to Baynard's
Castle,
Where you shall find me well accompanied
100 With reverend fathers and well-learnèd bishops.

BUCKINGHAM I go: and towards three or four o'clock
Look for the news that the Guildhall affords.

Exit Buckingham

RICHARD   Go, Lovell, with all speed to Doctor Shaw.—
Go thou to Friar Penker: bid them both   *To Catesby or Ratcliffe*
105 Meet me within this hour at Baynard's Castle.

Exeunt [all but Richard]

Now will I go to take some privy order
To draw the brats of Clarence out of sight,
And to give order that no manner person
Have any time recourse unto the princes.   *Exit*

[Act 3 Scene 6]   *running scene 12*

Enter a Scrivener

SCRIVENER   Here is the indictment of the good Lord
Hastings,   *Shows a paper*
Which in a set hand fairly is engrossed,

---

93 **sparingly** carefully, discreetly, with restraint   96 **golden fee** i.e. the crown (**fee** perhaps
plays on the legal sense of "inherited estate"; the sense of "payment" anticipates the reward
Buckingham expects for his services)   98 **thrive well** are successful   **Baynard's Castle**
London residence owned by the Duchess of York, situated by the River Thames near Blackfriars
103 **Shaw . . . Penker** both clergymen who supported Richard   106 **take . . . order** make
some secret arrangements   108 **manner** manner of   109 **recourse** means of access
3.6 Location: London   **Scrivener** professional scribe, particularly of legal documents
1 **indictment** formal statement of charges   2 **a set hand** formal handwriting   **fairly** elegantly
engrossed written in large characters appropriate for legal documents ("gross" in its sense of
"wicked, reprehensible" may pick up on its moral opposite, "fair")

That it may be today read o'er in Paul's.

And mark how well the sequel hangs together:

5   Eleven hours I have spent to write it over,

For yesternight by Catesby was it sent me,

The precedent was full as long a-doing.

And yet within these five hours Hastings lived,

Untainted, unexamined, free, at liberty.

10   Here's a good world the while! Who is so gross

That cannot see this palpable device?

Yet who so bold, but says he sees it not?

Bad is the world, and all will come to nought

When such ill dealing must be seen in thought.

Exit

[Act 3 Scene 7]   *running scene 13*

Enter Richard and Buckingham, at several doors

RICHARD   How now, how now? What say the citizens?

BUCKINGHAM Now, by the holy mother of our lord,

The citizens are mum, say not a word.

RICHARD   Touched you the bastardy of Edward's   *spreading rumours*

children?

5   BUCKINGHAM I did: with his contract with Lady Lucy,

And his contract by deputy in France,

Th'unsatiate greediness of his desire,

And his enforcement of the city wives,

---

3 **Paul's** St. Paul's Cathedral (where public proclamations were often made)   4 **the sequel** the following/the sequence of events/subsequent scribal copy he produced   7 **precedent** preceding document, first draft (from which the final copy has been made)   9 **Untainted** unstained by accusation   **unexamined** not questioned, interrogated   **free** at liberty/innocent/untroubled   10 **the while** these days   **gross** stupid   11 **palpable device** obvious contrivance   14 **seen in thought** i.e. not acknowledged openly
3.7 Location: Baynard's Castle, London   *several* separate   3 **mum** silent   4 **Touched you** did you mention   5 **contract** betrothal   6 **contract . . . France** in *3 Henry VI* (Act 3 Scene 3) the Earl of Warwick goes to France as Edward's **deputy** to secure a betrothal with the King of France's sister-in-law; he and the French king are furious and humiliated when word comes that Edward has abruptly married Elizabeth instead   8 **enforcement** coercion/rape

His tyranny for trifles, his own bastardy,
10   As being got, your father then in France,
And his resemblance, being not like the duke.
Withal I did infer your lineaments,
Being the right idea of your father,
Both in your form and nobleness of mind:
15   Laid open all your victories in Scotland,
Your discipline in war, wisdom in peace,
Your bounty, virtue, fair humility:
Indeed, left nothing fitting for your purpose
Untouched, or slightly handled, in discourse.
20   And when my oratory drew toward end,
I bid them that did love their country's good
Cry 'God save Richard, England's royal king!'
RICHARD   And did they so?
BUCKINGHAM No, so God help me, they spake not a
        word,
25   But, like dumb statues or breathing stones,
Stared each on other and looked deadly pale:
Which when I saw, I reprehended them,
And asked the mayor what meant this wilful silence:
His answer was, the people were not used
30   To be spoke to but by the recorder.
Then he was urged to tell my tale again:
'Thus saith the duke, thus hath the duke inferred' —
But nothing spoke in warrant from himself.
When he had done, some followers of mine own,
35   At lower end of the hall, hurled up their caps,
And some ten voices cried, 'God save King Richard!'
And thus I took the vantage of those few:
'Thanks, gentle citizens and friends,' quoth I,

---

9 tyranny for trifles severe punishment of minor crimes/oppressive behavior even with regard
to trivialities   10 got begot, conceived   15 Laid open revealed/described/elaborated on
16 discipline strategic skill   17 bounty generosity   fair honorable   18 fitting for relevant to
19 slightly neglectfully   30 recorder civic official in the City of London   32 inferred alleged
33 in . . . himself on his own authority   35 hall i.e. the Guildhall   37 the vantage advantage

'This general applause and cheerful shout

40   Argues your wisdom and your love to Richard.'

And even here brake off, and came away.

RICHARD   What tongueless blocks were they? Would they
not speak?

Will not the mayor then and his brethren come?

BUCKINGHAM The mayor is here at hand. Intend some
fear:

45   Be not you spoke with, but by mighty suit.

And look you get a prayer-book in your hand,

And stand between two churchmen, good my lord,

For on that ground I'll make a holy descant:

And be not easily won to our requests.

50   Play the maid's part: still answer nay, and take it.

RICHARD   I go. And if you plead as well for them

As I can say nay to thee for myself,

No doubt we bring it to a happy issue.

BUCKINGHAM Go, go, up to the leads. The Lord Mayor
knocks.   [*Exit Richard*]

Enter the Mayor and Citizens

55   Welcome, my lord. I dance attendance here:

I think the duke will not be spoke withal.

Enter Catesby

Now, Catesby, what says your lord to my request.

CATESBY   He doth entreat your grace, my noble lord,

To visit him tomorrow or next day:

60   He is within, with two right reverend fathers,

Divinely bent to meditation,

---

39 general public/widespread   40 Argues demonstrates   41 even here at this point
brake broke   42 blocks blockheads, idiots   43 brethren members of the town corporation
44 Intend pretend, feign   fear an intimidating manner/religious veneration/fearfulness
45 suit request, entreaty   46 look make sure   48 ground base melody   descant
accompaniment to or improvised variation on the ground, or underlying melody   49 won
persuaded   50 maid's young woman's/virgin's   still constantly, repeatedly   and take it yet
have sex all the same   52 for myself on my own behalf/for my own advantage   53 issue
outcome   54 leads lead-covered flat roof   55 dance attendance am being kept waiting, am
eager to be seen   61 bent occupied, concerned/bent over (in prayer)

And in no worldly suits would he be moved,
To draw him from his holy exercise.

BUCKINGHAM Return, good Catesby, to the gracious
duke:
65 Tell him myself, the Mayor and Alderman,
In deep designs, in matter of great moment,
No less importing than our general good,
Are come to have some conference with his grace.

CATESBY   I'll signify so much unto him straight.   *Exit*

70 BUCKINGHAM Ah, ha, my lord, this prince is not an
Edward!
He is not lulling on a lewd love-bed,
But on his knees at meditation:
Not dallying with a brace of courtesans,
But meditating with two deep divines:
75 Not sleeping, to engross his idle body,
But praying, to enrich his watchful soul.
Happy were England, would this virtuous prince
Take on his grace the sovereignty thereof:
But sure I fear we shall not win him to it.

80 MAYOR   Marry, God defend his grace should say us nay!

BUCKINGHAM I fear he will. — Here Catesby comes
again.

Enter Catesby

Now, Catesby, what says his grace?

CATESBY   He wonders to what end you have assembled
Such troops of citizens to come to him,
85 His grace not being warned thereof before.
He fears, my lord, you mean no good to him.

BUCKINGHAM Sorry I am my noble cousin should
Suspect me that I mean no good to him.

62 **suits** affairs, petitions (especially legal)   63 **exercise** prayers   66 **deep** very important, profound   **moment** significance   67 **No less importing** concerning no less a matter   71 **lulling** lolling, reclining   73 **dallying** toying sexually, having sex   **brace** pair   74 **deep** learned, profoundly wise   **divines** priests   75 **engross** fatten   76 **watchful** alert/awake   77 **Happy** fortunate   78 **his grace** plays on the ducal title and on the sense of "divine grace" (suggesting a God-given right to the crown)   80 **defend** forbid

By heaven, we come to him in perfect love,
90   And so once more return and tell his grace.

Exit [*Catesby*]

When holy and devout religious men
Are at their beads, 'tis hard to draw them thence,
So sweet is zealous contemplation.

Enter Richard aloft, between two Bishops. [*Catesby returns*]

MAYOR   See, where his grace stands 'tween two
    clergymen.
95   BUCKINGHAM Two props of virtue for a Christian prince,
    To stay him from the fall of vanity:
    And, see, a book of prayer in his hand,
    True ornaments to know a holy man.—   *indictator*
    Famous Plantagenet, most gracious prince,
100   Lend favourable ear to our requests,
    And pardon us the interruption
    Of thy devotion and right Christian zeal.
RICHARD   My lord, there needs no such apology:
    I do beseech your grace to pardon me,
105   Who, earnest in the service of my God,
    Deferred the visitation of my friends.
    But, leaving this, what is your grace's pleasure?
BUCKINGHAM Even that, I hope, which pleaseth God
    above,
    And all good men of this ungoverned isle.
110   RICHARD   I do suspect I have done some offence
    That seems disgracious in the city's eye,
    And that you come to reprehend my ignorance.
BUCKINGHAM You have, my lord: would it might please
    your grace,
    On our entreaties, to amend your fault.

---

89 perfect complete   **92 beads** rosary beads   **93 zealous** pious, devout   *aloft* i.e. on the
upper staging level, or gallery   **95 props** supports   **96 stay** keep   **fall of** moral fall caused by
102 right rightful/genuine, true/extremely   **106 visitation** visit (especially by an ecclesiastical
body); Richard is deliberately employing language with religious connotations
111 disgracious disliked   **112 reprehend my ignorance** rebuke me for the fault I am
unaware of

115   RICHARD   Else wherefore breathe I in a Christian land?

      BUCKINGHAM Know then, it is your fault that you resign

        The supreme seat, the throne majestical,

        The sceptred office of your ancestors,

        Your state of fortune and your due of birth,

120   The lineal glory of your royal house,

        To the corruption of a blemished stock;

        Whiles, in the mildness of your sleepy thoughts,

        Which here we waken to our country's good,

        The noble isle doth want his proper limbs:

125   His face defaced with scars of infamy,

        His royal stock graft with ignoble plants,

        And almost shouldered in the swallowing gulf

        Of dark forgetfulness and deep oblivion.

        Which to recure, we heartily solicit

130   Your gracious self to take on you the charge

        And kingly government of this your land —

        Not as Protector, steward, substitute,

        Or lowly factor for another's gain;

        But as successively from blood to blood,

135   Your right of birth, your empery, your own.

        For this, consorted with the citizens,

        Your very worshipful and loving friends,

        And by their vehement instigation,

        In this just cause come I to move your grace.

140   RICHARD   I cannot tell if to depart in silence,

        Or bitterly to speak in your reproof

---

115 **Else . . . land?** Why else do I live as a Christian (if not to amend my faults)?
118 **sceptred** involving the bearing of a royal scepter   119 **state** position, rank/kingship   **of fortune** to which fortune entitles you   120 **lineal** hereditary   121 **blemished** morally tainted (through illegitimacy)   **stock** family tree (sense subsequently shifts to "tree trunk")
124 **want** lack   **proper** rightful, own   125 **infamy** bad reputation, disgrace   126 **graft** grafted, i.e. united (as in horticulture)   **plants** may pun on "Plantagenet"   127 **shouldered** shoved (possibly "immersed up to the shoulders")   **gulf** abyss/whirlpool   129 **recure** redress, cure   133 **factor** agent   134 **successively** by right of succession   135 **empery** sovereign dominions   136 **consorted** united, in league   137 **worshipful** honorable/respectful
139 **move** persuade

Best fitteth my degree or your condition.
If not to answer, you might haply think
Tongue-tied ambition, not replying, yielded
145 To bear the golden yoke of sovereignty,
Which fondly you would here impose on me.
If to reprove you for this suit of yours,
So seasoned with your faithful love to me,
Then on the other side I checked my friends.
150 Therefore, to speak, and to avoid the first,
And then, in speaking, not to incur the last,
Definitively thus I answer you:
Your love deserves my thanks, but my desert
Unmeritable shuns your high request.
155 First, if all obstacles were cut away,
And that my path were even to the crown,
As the ripe revenue and due of birth,
Yet so much is my poverty of spirit,
So mighty and so many my defects,
160 That I would rather hide me from my greatness —
Being a bark to brook no mighty sea —
Than in my greatness covet to be hid,
And in the vapour of my glory smothered.
But, God be thanked, there is no need of me,
165 And much I need to help you, were there need.
The royal tree hath left us royal fruit,
Which, mellowed by the stealing hours of time,
Will well become the seat of majesty,
And make, no doubt, us happy by his reign.
170 On him I lay that you would lay on me,

142 **degree** rank or perhaps "spiritual condition"   **condition** social status   143 **not to** I do not   **haply** perhaps   144 **yielded** consented   146 **fondly** foolishly   149 **checked** (would have) rebuked   153 **desert Unmeritable** unworthiness   155 **cut away** with sinister connotations of "cut off, killed"   156 **even** direct, smooth   157 **revenue** possession/yield, income   160 **greatness** i.e. kingship   161 **bark** ship   **brook** endure, withstand   162 **in . . . hid** desire to be enveloped by greatness   163 **vapour** mist/spray   165 **much I need** I would need a great deal (i.e. I am inadequate)   166 **royal tree** i.e. King Edward IV   167 **mellowed** matured   **stealing** creeping (forward)   168 **become** suit, befit   **seat** throne   170 **that** what

The right and fortune of his happy stars,

Which God defend that I should wring from him!

BUCKINGHAM My lord, this argues conscience in your
grace,

But the respects thereof are nice and trivial,

175 All circumstances well considerèd.

You say that Edward is your brother's son:

So say we too, but not by Edward's wife,

For first was he contract to Lady Lucy —

Your mother lives a witness to his vow —

180 And afterward by substitute betrothed

To Bona, sister to the King of France.

These both put off, a poor petitioner,

A care-crazed mother to a many sons,

A beauty-waning and distressèd widow,

185 Even in the afternoon of her best days,

Made prize and purchase of his wanton eye,

Seduced the pitch and height of his degree

To base declension and loathed bigamy.

By her, in his unlawful bed, he got

190 This Edward, whom our manners call the prince.

More bitterly could I expostulate,

Save that, for reverence to some alive,

I give a sparing limit to my tongue.

Then, good my lord, take to your royal self

195 This proffered benefit of dignity:

If not to bless us and the land withal,

---

171 happy auspicious, favorable   172 defend forbid   wring wrench   173 argues shows, is
evidence of   174 respects thereof factors in your argument   nice unimportant, trifling
178 contract . . . vow the verbal contract entered into at betrothal was considered binding
180 substitute deputy, delegate   181 sister sister-in-law   182 petitioner Elizabeth Grey
catches Edward's eye when she entreats him for the return of her dead husband's lands (see
3 Henry VI, Act 3 Scene 2)   183 care-crazed fraught, worn out with anxiety   186 purchase
booty, plunder   wanton lustful   187 pitch height (literally, the highest point in a falcon's
flight)   188 base declension descent to baseness   bigamy i.e. because Edward had been
engaged to two other women previously   190 our manners courtesy   191 expostulate
expound on, argue about   192 some alive i.e. Richard and Edward's mother, the Duchess of
York   193 sparing considerate, forbearing   195 benefit benevolent bestowal   dignity
honor, high rank, kingship

Yet to draw forth your noble ancestry
From the corruption of abusing times,
Unto a lineal true-derivèd course.

200 MAYOR   Do, good my lord: your citizens entreat you. *To Richard*

BUCKINGHAM Refuse not, mighty lord, this proffered
      love.

CATESBY   O, make them joyful, grant their lawful suit!

RICHARD   Alas, why would you heap this care on me?
I am unfit for state and majesty.

fake humble

205 I do beseech you, take it not amiss:
I cannot nor I will not yield to you.

BUCKINGHAM If you refuse it — as, in love and zeal,
Loath to depose the child, your brother's son,
As well we know your tenderness of heart

210 And gentle, kind, effeminate remorse,
Which we have noted in you to your kindred
And equally indeed to all estates —
Yet know, whe'er you accept our suit or no,
Your brother's son shall never reign our king,

215 But we will plant some other in the throne
To the disgrace and downfall of your house:
And in this resolution here we leave you.—
Come, citizens, we will entreat no more.

              Exeunt [Buckingham with Citizens]

CATESBY   Call him again, sweet prince. Accept their suit.

220 If you deny them all the land will rue it.

RICHARD   Will you enforce me to a world of cares?
Call them again. I am not made of stones,
But penetrable to your kind entreaties,
Albeit against my conscience and my soul.

Enter Buckingham and the rest

225 Cousin of Buckingham, and sage, grave men,
Since you will buckle fortune on my back,

---

199 true-derivèd legitimate, directly descended   **203 care** duty, trouble, source of anxiety
207 as being, because (you are)   **zeal** devotion   **210 effeminate** tender, gentle   **212 estates**
social ranks   **226 buckle** i.e. like armor; **my back** draws attention to Richard's hunched back

To bear her burden, whe'er I will or no,
I must have patience to endure the load:
But if black scandal or foul-faced reproach
230 Attend the sequel of your imposition,
Your mere enforcement shall acquittance me
From all the impure blots and stains thereof;
For God doth know, and you may partly see,
How far I am from the desire of this.

235 MAYOR   God bless your grace! We see it and will say it.
RICHARD   In saying so, you shall but say the truth.
BUCKINGHAM Then I salute you with this royal title:
Long live King Richard, England's worthy king!
ALL   Amen.
240 BUCKINGHAM Tomorrow may it please you to be
crowned?
RICHARD   Even when you please, for you will have it so.
BUCKINGHAM Tomorrow, then, we will attend your
grace.
And so most joyfully we take our leave.
RICHARD   Come, let us to our holy work again.   *To the Bishops*
245 Farewell, my cousins: farewell, gentle friends.
Exeunt

Act 4 Scene 1   *running scene 14*

Enter the Queen, Anne Duchess of Gloucester [leading a girl], the
Duchess of York and Marquis Dorset

DUCHESS OF YORK   Who meets us here? My niece
Plantagenet
Led in the hand of her kind aunt of Gloucester?

---

230 **sequel** consequences   231 **Your . . . me** the fact that you forced me shall acquit me
mere absolute   241 **Even** just, exactly   **4.1 *Location: outside the Tower of London***
Anne . . . Gloucester i.e. Lady Anne, who has married Richard at some point since his
wooing of her in Act 1 Scene 2   ***leading a girl*** probably Clarence's daughter   1 **niece**
granddaughter

Now, for my life, she's wand'ring to the Tower,
On pure heart's love to greet the tender prince.

5   Daughter, well met.

ANNE   God give your graces both
A happy and a joyful time of day.

QUEEN ELIZABETH   As much to you, good sister. Whither
away?

ANNE   No further than the Tower, and, as I guess,
10   Upon the like devotion as yourselves,
To gratulate the gentle princes there.

QUEEN ELIZABETH   Kind sister, thanks: we'll enter all
together.

Enter the Lieutenant [Brackenbury]

And, in good time, here the lieutenant comes.
Master Lieutenant, pray you, by your leave,
15   How doth the prince, and my young son of York?

BRACKENBURY   Right well, dear madam. By your
patience,
I may not suffer you to visit them:
The king hath strictly charged the contrary.

QUEEN ELIZABETH   The king? Who's that?

20   BRACKENBURY   I mean the Lord Protector.

QUEEN ELIZABETH   The lord protect him from that kingly
title!
Hath he set bounds between their love and me?
I am their mother: who shall bar me from them?

DUCHESS OF YORK   I am their father's mother: I will see
them.

25   ANNE   Their aunt I am in law, in love their mother:
Then bring me to their sights. I'll bear thy blame
And take thy office from thee, on my peril.

BRACKENBURY   No, madam, no; I may not leave it so:
I am bound by oath, and therefore pardon me.   *Exit*

---

4 tender young   **10 like devotion** same devoted purpose   **11 gratulate** greet, welcome
17 suffer allow   **22 bounds** boundaries   **25 in law** i.e. by marriage   **27 office** responsibility,
official duty

Enter Stanley [Earl of Derby]

30 DERBY   Let me but meet you, ladies, one hour hence,
And I'll salute your grace of York as mother,
And reverend looker-on, of two fair queens.—
Come, madam, you must straight to Westminster,   *To Anne*
There to be crownèd Richard's royal queen.

35 QUEEN ELIZABETH   Ah, cut my lace asunder,
That my pent heart may have some scope to beat,
Or else I swoon with this dead-killing news!

ANNE   Despiteful tidings! O, unpleasing news!

DORSET   Be of good cheer. Mother, how fares your grace?

40 QUEEN ELIZABETH   O Dorset, speak not to me, get thee
gone!
Death and destruction dogs thee at thy heels:
Thy mother's name is ominous to children.
If thou wilt outstrip death, go cross the seas,
And live with Richmond, from the reach of hell.

45 Go, hie thee, hie thee from this slaughter-house,
Lest thou increase the number of the dead
And make me die the thrall of Margaret's curse,
Nor mother, wife, nor England's counted queen.

DERBY   Full of wise care is this your counsel, madam.—

50 Take all the swift advantage of the hours.   *To Dorset*
You shall have letters from me to my son
In your behalf, to meet you on the way.
Be not ta'en tardy by unwise delay.

DUCHESS OF YORK   O ill-dispersing wind of misery!

55 O my accursèd womb, the bed of death!

---

31 mother mother-in-law (of Elizabeth and Anne)   **32 looker-on** beholder   **two fair queens**
i.e. Elizabeth and Anne (as wife of Richard, who is shortly to be crowned)   **33 straight** (go)
straightaway   **35 lace** cords that fastened the tightly laced bodice (often cut when a woman
became faint)   **36 pent** confined, penned in   **38 Despiteful** cruel, malicious   **44 Richmond**
i.e. Henry Tudor, Earl of Richmond (later Henry VII), who had sought refuge in Brittany
from away from   **45 hie** hurry   **47 thrall** slave   **48 Nor** neither   **counted** accounted,
acknowledged   **51 letters . . . way** i.e. the letters will be sent to Dorset while en route/the
letters will ask George Stanley to meet Dorset on the way and assist his journey/the letters will
enable Dorset to be introduced to and assisted by Richmond when he reaches Brittany   **son**
stepson (Richmond), or possibly Stanley's own son George   **53 ta'en tardy** caught by surprise
54 ill-dispersing evil-spreading

A cockatrice hast thou hatched to the world,
Whose unavoided eye is murderous.

DERBY   Come, madam, come: I in all haste was sent.   *To Anne*

ANNE   And I with all unwillingness will go.

60   O, would to God that the inclusive verge
Of golden metal that must round my brow
Were red-hot steel, to sear me to the brains!
Anointed let me be with deadly venom,
And die, ere men can say, 'God save the queen!'

65   QUEEN ELIZABETH   Go, go, poor soul, I envy not thy glory:
To feed my humour wish thyself no harm.

ANNE   No? Why? When he that is my husband now
Came to me, as I followed Henry's corpse,
When scarce the blood was well washed from his
          hands

70   Which issued from my other angel husband
And that dear saint which then I weeping
          followed —
O, when I say I looked on Richard's face,
This was my wish: 'Be thou', quoth I, 'accursed
For making me, so young, so old a widow!

75   And, when thou wed'st, let sorrow haunt thy bed;
And be thy wife — if any be so mad —
More miserable by the life of thee
Than thou hast made me by my dear lord's death!'
Lo, ere I can repeat this curse again,

80   Within so small a time, my woman's heart
Grossly grew captive to his honey words
And proved the subject of mine own soul's curse,

---

56 **cockatrice** basilisk, a mythical reptile that could kill with its gaze   57 **unavoided**
unavoidable   60 **inclusive** enclosing   **verge** band, rim   63 **Anointed** anointing with holy oil
was a key part of the coronation   66 **To . . . harm** Do not wish yourself harm just to satisfy my
mood   70 **other angel husband** my other (first) husband, who was an angel/my first
husband, who was a different (i.e. good) type of angel (implying that Richard is the fallen angel
Lucifer)   74 **old** experienced/worn-out   81 **Grossly** stupidly/excessively/coarsely

Which hitherto hath held mine eyes from rest,
For never yet one hour in his bed
85   Did I enjoy the golden dew of sleep,
But with his timorous dreams was still awaked.
Besides, he hates me for my father Warwick,
And will, no doubt, shortly be rid of me.

QUEEN ELIZABETH   Poor heart, adieu! I pity thy
    complaining.
90   ANNE   No more than with my soul I mourn for yours.

DORSET   Farewell, thou woeful welcomer of glory.

ANNE   Adieu, poor soul, that tak'st thy leave of it.

DUCHESS OF YORK   Go thou to Richmond, and good fortune
    guide thee.—   *To Dorset*
    Go thou to Richard, and good angels tend thee.—   *To Anne*
95   Go thou to sanctuary, and good thoughts possess   *To Queen*
    thee.—   *Elizabeth*
    I to my grave, where peace and rest lie with me.
    Eighty odd years of sorrow have I seen,
    And each hour's joy wrecked with a week of teen.   *She starts to*

QUEEN ELIZABETH   Stay, yet look back with me unto the   *leave*
    Tower.
100   Pity, you ancient stones, those tender babes
    Whom envy hath immured within your walls,
    Rough cradle for such little pretty ones,
    Rude ragged nurse, old sullen playfellow
    For tender princes: use my babies well.
105   So foolish sorrows bids your stones farewell.   *Exeunt*

---

86 timorous full of fear   87 Warwick with Clarence, the Earl of Warwick deserted the Yorkist
cause   89 complaining lamentations   98 teen grief, suffering   101 immured imprisoned,
closed in   103 Rude harsh, rough   ragged rugged, eroded   sullen dismal, melancholy
105 So such/thus   foolish fond, doting

Act 4 Scene 2

Sound a sennet. Enter Richard in pomp, Buckingham, Catesby,
Ratcliffe, Lovell, [a Page and others. A throne is brought forth]

RICHARD   Stand all apart.— Cousin of Buckingham.

BUCKINGHAM My gracious sovereign?

RICHARD   Give me thy hand.   *Sound [trumpets]*

He ascends the throne

        Thus high, by thy advice and thy assistance,   *Richard and*
5   Is King Richard seated.   *Buckingham speak aside*
        But shall we wear these glories for a day?
        Or shall they last, and we rejoice in them?

BUCKINGHAM Still live they and forever let them last!

RICHARD   Ah, Buckingham, now do I play the touch,
10   To try if thou be current gold indeed:
        Young Edward lives. Think now what I would speak.

BUCKINGHAM Say on, my loving lord.

RICHARD   Why, Buckingham, I say I would be king,

BUCKINGHAM Why, so you are, my thrice-renownèd
        lord.

15 RICHARD   Ha? Am I king? 'Tis so: but Edward lives.

BUCKINGHAM True, noble prince.

RICHARD   O, bitter consequence,
        That Edward still should live — true noble prince.
        Cousin, thou wast not wont to be so dull.
20   Shall I be plain? I wish the bastards dead,
        And I would have it suddenly performed.
        What say'st thou now? Speak suddenly, be brief.

BUCKINGHAM Your grace may do your pleasure.

RICHARD   Tut, tut, thou art all ice: thy kindness freezes.
25   Say, have I thy consent that they shall die?

4.2 Location: *the royal court, London*   *pomp* ceremony, splendor, celebration   **1 apart**
aside   **9 play the touch** act the touchstone (used to test the validity of gold)   **10 try** test
current genuine   **17 consequence** outcome   **18 true noble prince** Richard adapts
Buckingham's phrase so that it applies to Edward   **19 wont . . . dull** accustomed to be so
stupid   **21 suddenly** immediately

BUCKINGHAM Give me some little breath, some pause,
    dear lord,
  Before I positively speak in this:
  I will resolve you herein presently.   *Exit*

CATESBY   The king is angry: see, he gnaws his lip.   *Aside*

30 RICHARD   I will converse with iron-witted fools
  And unrespective boys: none are for me
  That look into me with considerate eyes.
  High-reaching Buckingham grows circumspect.—
  Boy!

35 PAGE   My lord?   *Comes forward*

RICHARD   Know'st thou not any whom corrupting gold
  Will tempt unto a close exploit of death?

PAGE   I know a discontented gentleman,
  Whose humble means match not his haughty spirit:
40   Gold were as good as twenty orators,
  And will, no doubt, tempt him to anything.

RICHARD   What is his name?

PAGE   His name, my lord, is Tyrrell.

RICHARD   I partly know the man. Go, call him hither,
    boy.   *Exit [Page]*
45   The deep-revolving witty Buckingham
  No more shall be the neighbour to my counsels.
  Hath he so long held out with me untired,
  And stops he now for breath? Well, be it so.

Enter Stanley

  How now, Lord Stanley, what's the news?

50 DERBY   Know, my loving lord, the marquis Dorset
  As I hear, is fled to Richmond,
  In the parts where he abides.   *Stands apart*

---

26 **breath** breathing space   27 **positively** definitively, directly   28 **resolve** answer   30 **iron-witted** dull-witted, stupid, obtuse   31 **unrespective** inattentive, disrespectful   32 **considerate** thoughtful   33 **High-reaching** ambitious   37 **close** secret   39 **haughty** proud, aspiring   40 **orators** persuasive speakers   45 **deep-revolving** deeply thoughtful, musing **witty** sharp, clever   46 **counsels** secrets, confidences   47 **held out** kept up

RICHARD   Come hither, Catesby. Rumour it abroad
That Anne, my wife, is very grievous sick:
55   I will take order for her keeping close.
Inquire me out some mean poor gentleman,
Whom I will marry straight to Clarence' daughter:
The boy is foolish, and I fear not him.
Look, how thou dream'st! I say again, give out
60   That Anne my queen is sick and like to die:
About it, for it stands me much upon,
To stop all hopes whose growth may damage me.

                                           [*Exit Catesby*]

I must be married to my brother's daughter,
Or else my kingdom stands on brittle glass.
65   Murder her brothers, and then marry her:
Uncertain way of gain! But I am in
So far in blood that sin will pluck on sin:
Tear-falling pity dwells not in this eye.

Enter [Page, with] Tyrrell

    Is thy name Tyrrell?
70   TYRRELL   James Tyrrell, and your most obedient subject.
RICHARD   Art thou, indeed?
TYRRELL   Prove me, my gracious lord.   *King Richard and Tyrrell*
RICHARD   Dar'st thou resolve to kill a friend of mine? *speak aside*
TYRRELL   Please you:
75   But I had rather kill two enemies.
RICHARD   Why, then thou hast it: two deep enemies,
Foes to my rest and my sweet sleep's disturbers
Are they that I would have thee deal upon —
Tyrrell, I mean those bastards in the Tower.
80   TYRRELL   Let me have open means to come to them,
And soon I'll rid you from the fear of them.

---

55 take order make arrangements   **close** shut away   **56 mean** humble, low-ranking
58 The boy i.e. Clarence's son   **59 how thou dream'st** i.e. pay attention (perhaps Catesby is
shocked)   **give out** make it known   **61 it . . . upon** it is very important for me   **63 brother's
daughter** i.e. Edward IV's daughter Elizabeth   **67 pluck on** draw on   **68 Tear-falling pity**
mercy, compassion that induces weeping   **72 Prove** test, try   **73 friend** plays on the sense of
"relative"   **78 deal upon** deal with, act against   **80 open** unrestricted

RICHARD   Thou sing'st sweet music. Hark, come hither,
 Tyrrell
 Go, by this token: rise, and lend thine ear.   *Gives a token*
 There is no more but so: say it is done,   *Whispers*
85 And I will love thee, and prefer thee for it.
TYRRELL I will dispatch it straight.

        Exit [Tyrrell, with the Page]

Enter Buckingham

BUCKINGHAM My lord, I have considered in my mind
 The late request that you did sound me in.
RICHARD   Well, let that rest. Dorset is fled to Richmond.
90 BUCKINGHAM I hear the news, my lord.
RICHARD   Stanley, he is your wife's son. Well, look unto
 it.
BUCKINGHAM My lord, I claim the gift, my due by
 promise,
 For which your honour and your faith is pawned:
 Th'earldom of Hereford and the movables
95 Which you have promisèd I shall possess.
RICHARD   Stanley, look to your wife: if she convey
 Letters to Richmond, you shall answer it.
BUCKINGHAM What says your highness to my just
 request?
RICHARD   I do remember me, Henry the Sixth
100 Did prophesy that Richmond should be king,
 When Richmond was a little peevish boy.
 A king, perhaps—
BUCKINGHAM May it please you to resolve me in my suit.
RICHARD   Thou troublest me: I am not in the vein. *Exit*
105 BUCKINGHAM And is it thus? Repays he my deep service
 With such contempt? Made I him king for this?

---

83 **token** some symbol of authority, perhaps a ring 84 **There . . . so** that is all there is to it
85 **prefer** advance, promote 88 **late** recent **sound me in** ask me about 91 **he** i.e.
Richmond 93 **pawned** pledged 94 **movables** portable property 96 **look to** beware, watch
97 **answer** be answerable for 101 **peevish** foolish, childish 103 **resolve** answer, satisfy
104 **vein** mood

O, let me think on Hastings, and be gone
To Brecknock, while my fearful head is on!   *Exit*

[Act 4 Scene 3]   *running scene 15 continues*

Enter Tyrrell

TYRRELL   The tyrannous and bloody act is done,
The most arch deed of piteous massacre
That ever yet this land was guilty of.
Dighton and Forrest, who I did suborn
5   To do this piece of ruthful butchery,
Albeit they were fleshed villains, bloody dogs,
Melted with tenderness and mild compassion,
Wept like to children in their deaths' sad story.
'O, thus', quoth Dighton, 'lay the gentle babes.'
10   'Thus, thus', quoth Forrest, 'girdling one another
Within their alabaster innocent arms.
Their lips were four red roses on a stalk,
And in their summer beauty kissed each other.
A book of prayers on their pillow lay,
15   Which one', quoth Forrest, 'almost changed my
        mind.
But O! The devil'— there the villain stopped.
When Dighton thus told on: 'We smotherèd
The most replenishèd sweet work of nature,
That from the prime creation e'er she framed.'
20   Hence both are gone with conscience and remorse:
They could not speak, and so I left them both,
To bear this tidings to the bloody king.
Enter Richard

---

108 **Brecknock** Brecon in Wales, Buckingham's family seat   **4.3 2 arch** extreme, foremost
4 suborn bribe   **5 ruthful** lamentable, sad   **6 fleshed** experienced (hunting term referring to
feeding hounds with raw meat to excite them for the chase)   **8 their . . . story** in telling the sad
story of their deaths   **10 girdling** hugging, encircling   **11 alabaster** i.e. white (the substance
was often used for human figures that formed part of funeral monuments)   **15 Which one**
which, which thing   **18 replenishèd** complete, perfect   **19 prime** first   **framed** created
20 gone overcome   **22 bloody** bloodthirsty

And here he comes.—

All health, my sovereign lord!

25 RICHARD   Kind Tyrrell, am I happy in thy news?

TYRRELL   If to have done the thing you gave in charge

Beget your happiness, be happy then,

For it is done.

RICHARD   But didst thou see them dead?

30 TYRRELL   I did, my lord.

RICHARD   And buried, gentle Tyrrell?

TYRRELL   The chaplain of the Tower hath buried them,

But where, to say the truth, I do not know.

RICHARD   Come to me, Tyrrell, soon and after supper,

35 When thou shalt tell the process of their death.

Meantime, but think how I may do thee good,

And be inheritor of thy desire.

Farewell till then.

TYRRELL   I humbly take my leave.   [*Exit*]

40 RICHARD   The son of Clarence have I pent up close,

His daughter meanly have I matched in marriage,

The sons of Edward sleep in Abraham's bosom,

And Anne my wife hath bid the world good night.

Now, for I know the Breton Richmond aims

45 At young Elizabeth, my brother's daughter,

And by that knot looks proudly on the crown,

To her go I, a jolly thriving wooer.

Enter Ratcliffe

RATCLIFFE   My lord!

RICHARD   Good or bad news, that thou com'st in so

blutly?

50 RATCLIFFE   Bad news, my lord: Morton is fled to

Richmond,

---

26 gave in charge ordered   34 soon and i.e. soon   35 process account, story   37 be . . .
desire you shall get what you wish   40 close securely, privately   41 meanly . . . marriage
I have married to a low-ranking man   42 Abraham's bosom i.e. heaven   44 for because
Breton from Brittany (where Richmond is taking refuge)   46 by that knot through that
marriage   49 bluntly unceremoniously, abruptly   50 Morton John Morton, Bishop of Ely
(whom Richard asks for strawberries in Act 3 Scene 4)

And Buckingham, backed with the hardy Welshmen,
Is in the field, and still his power increaseth.

RICHARD   Ely with Richmond troubles me more near
Than Buckingham and his rash-levied strength.

55 Come, I have learned that fearful commenting
Is leaden servitor to dull delay:
Delay leads impotent and snail-paced beggary.
Then fiery expedition be my wing,
Jove's Mercury, and herald for a king!

60 Go, muster men. My counsel is my shield:
We must be brief when traitors brave the field.

Exeunt

[Act 4 Scene 4]   *running scene 16*

Enter old Queen Margaret

QUEEN MARGARET   So, now prosperity begins to mellow
And drop into the rotten mouth of death.
Here in these confines slyly have I lurked,
To watch the waning of mine enemies.

5 A dire induction am I witness to,
And will to France, hoping the consequence
Will prove as bitter, black, and tragical.
Withdraw thee, wretched Margaret. Who comes
here?

Enter Duchess [of York] and Queen [Elizabeth]

QUEEN ELIZABETH   Ah, my poor princes! Ah, my tender
babes!

51 **hardy** bold, resolute   52 **power** army   53 **near** deeply   54 **rash-levied** rapidly mustered   55 **fearful commenting** nervous talk   56 **leaden servitor** the slow servant   57 **leads** precedes, generates   **beggary** ruin   58 **expedition** speed, quick action   59 **Jove's Mercury** swift messenger of Jove, king of the Roman gods   60 **My . . . shield** the best advice is to arm myself/arms shall be my advisers (i.e. let us not waste time discussing matters)   61 **brief** swift   **brave the field** challenge us on the battlefield   **4.4** *Location: unspecified; probably somewhere near the royal court*   1 **mellow** ripen   3 **confines** regions, territories (of England)   5 **induction** introduction, opening scene   6 **consequence** unfolding events and their conclusion

10 My unblowed flowers, new-appearing sweets!
   If yet your gentle souls fly in the air
   And be not fixed in doom perpetual,
   Hover about me with your airy wings
   And hear your mother's lamentation!

15 QUEEN MARGARET Hover about her: say that right for *Aside*
   right
   Hath dimmed your infant morn to agèd night.

  DUCHESS OF YORK So many miseries have crazed my
   voice,
   That my woe-wearied tongue is still and mute.
   Edward Plantagenet, why art thou dead?

20 QUEEN MARGARET Plantagenet doth quit Plantagenet: *Aside*
   Edward for Edward pays a dying debt.

  QUEEN ELIZABETH Wilt thou, O God, fly from such gentle
   lambs,
   And throw them in the entrails of the wolf?
   When didst thou sleep when such a deed was done?

25 QUEEN MARGARET When holy Harry died, and my sweet
   son.   *Aside*

  DUCHESS OF YORK Dead life, blind sight, poor mortal
   living ghost,
   Woe's scene, world's shame, grave's due by life
   usurped,
   Brief abstract and record of tedious days,
   Rest thy unrest on England's lawful earth, *Sits down*
30 Unlawfully made drunk with innocent blood!

  QUEEN ELIZABETH Ah, that thou wouldst as soon afford a
   grave
   As thou canst yield a melancholy seat!

---

10 **unblowed** young and unopened, not yet in bloom **sweets** flowers/dear ones **12 in doom perpetual** eternally in the place appointed for you **15 right for right** even-handed justice **17 crazed** cracked **19 Edward Plantagenet** could refer to Edward IV or his son **20 quit** requite, repay **21 Edward for Edward** probably refers to Elizabeth's son and Margaret's (with Henry VI) **23 entrails** insides, intestines **25 Harry** Henry VI (Margaret's husband) **27 grave's . . . usurped** i.e. one who should have died but remains living **28 abstract** summary/epitome **29 lawful** own proper, that is rightfully England's **31 thou** i.e. the earth **afford** offer

Then would I hide my bones, not rest them here.
Ah, who hath any cause to mourn but we?   *Sits with her*

35   QUEEN MARGARET   If ancient sorrow be most reverend,   *Comes*
Give mine the benefit of seniory,   *forward*
And let my griefs frown on the upper hand.
If sorrow can admit society,   *Sits with them*
I had an Edward, till a Richard killed him:
40   I had a husband, till a Richard killed him:
Thou hadst an Edward, till a Richard killed him:
Thou hadst a Richard, till a Richard killed him.

DUCHESS OF YORK   I had a Richard too, and thou didst
kill him;
I had a Rutland too, thou holp'st to kill him.

45   QUEEN MARGARET   Thou hadst a Clarence too, and
Richard killed him.
From forth the kennel of thy womb hath crept
A hell-hound that doth hunt us all to death:
That dog, that had his teeth before his eyes,
To worry lambs and lap their gentle blood,
50   That foul defacer of God's handiwork,
That reigns in gallèd eyes of weeping souls,
That excellent grand tyrant of the earth,
Thy womb let loose, to chase us to our graves.
O upright, just, and true-disposing God,
55   How do I thank thee, that this carnal cur
Preys on the issue of his mother's body,
And makes her pew-fellow with others' moan!

---

36 seniory seniority   **37 on . . . hand** from the superior position   **38 admit society** permit
company   **39 Edward** Margaret's son with Henry VI (murdered by Richard, Edward IV and
Clarence; see *3 Henry VI*, Act 5 Scene 5)   **40 husband** Henry VI (murdered by Richard; see
3 Henry VI, Act 5 Scene 6)   **41 Edward** Elizabeth's eldest son with Edward IV   **42 Richard**
Elizabeth's second son, the young Duke of York   **43 Richard** the Duke of York, the Duchess'
husband (killed by Margaret and Clifford; see *3 Henry VI*, Act 1 Scene 4)   **44 Rutland** the
Duchess' youngest son (murdered by Clifford; see *3 Henry VI*, Act 1 Scene 3)   **holp'st** helped
48 teeth . . . eyes i.e. could bite before he could see properly; Richard was born with teeth
49 worry seize by the throat   **50 defacer . . . handiwork** i.e. murderer (perhaps also alludes to
Richard's own deformed physique)   **51 gallèd** irritated, swollen (from weeping)
52 excellent supreme   **54 upright** righteous, just   **true-disposing** arranging all justly
55 carnal cur flesh-eating dog   **56 issue** offspring, children   **57 pew-fellow** fellow mourner
moan lamentations, grief

DUCHESS OF YORK   O Harry's wife, triumph not in my
    woes!
God witness with me, I have wept for thine.
60 QUEEN MARGARET   Bear with me: I am hungry for
    revenge,
And now I cloy me with beholding it.
Thy Edward he is dead, that killed my Edward:
The other Edward dead, to quit my Edward:
Young York he is but boot, because both they
65 Matched not the high perfection of my loss.
Thy Clarence he is dead that stabbed my Edward,
And the beholders of this frantic play,
Th'adulterate Hastings, Rivers, Vaughan, Grey,
Untimely smothered in their dusky graves.
70 Richard yet lives, hell's black intelligencer,
Only reserved their factor to buy souls
And send them thither. But at hand, at hand,
Ensues his piteous and unpitied end:
Earth gapes, hell burns, fiends roar, saints pray,
75 To have him suddenly conveyed from hence.
Cancel his bond of life, dear God, I pray,
That I may live and say, 'The dog is dead!'
QUEEN ELIZABETH   O, thou didst prophesy the time would
    come
That I should wish for thee to help me curse
80 That bottled spider, that foul bunch-backed toad!
QUEEN MARGARET   I called thee then vain flourish of my
    fortune:

---

58 triumph glory, exult   61 cloy me gorge myself   62 Thy Edward Edward IV   my Edward
Margaret's son with Henry VI   63 other Edward Elizabeth's eldest son with Edward IV
64 Young York Elizabeth's second son, the young Duke of York   but boot merely added to
make up the total   both they Edward IV and his eldest son   65 perfection . . . loss
completeness, extent of the loss I experience/excellence of the people I have lost   67 frantic
mad, frenzied   68 Th'adulterate the adulterous (Hastings; refers to his affair with Jane Shore)
70 intelligencer spy, secret agent   71 Only reserved solely kept alive (to be)/exclusively
selected (as)   factor agent, representative   80 bottled swollen (with venom), rounded,
bottle-shaped   bunch-backed hunchbacked   81 vain flourish meaningless, frivolous
adornment

I called thee then poor shadow, painted queen,
The presentation of but what I was,
The flattering index of a direful pageant,
One heaved a-high, to be hurled down below,
A mother only mocked with two fair babes,
A dream of what thou wast, a garish flag,
To be the aim of every dangerous shot;
A sign of dignity, a breath, a bubble;
A queen in jest, only to fill the scene.
Where is thy husband now? Where be thy brothers?
Where be thy two sons? Wherein dost thou joy?
Who sues, and kneels and says, 'God save the queen'?
Where be the bending peers that flattered thee?
Where be the thronging troops that followed thee?
Decline all this, and see what now thou art:
For happy wife, a most distressèd widow:
For joyful mother, one that wails the name:
For one being sued to, one that humbly sues:
For queen, a very caitiff crowned with care:
For she that scorned at me, now scorned of me:
For she being feared of all, now fearing one:
For she commanding all, obeyed of none.
Thus hath the course of justice whirled about,
And left thee but a very prey to time,
Having no more but thought of what thou wast,
To torture thee the more, being what thou art.
Thou didst usurp my place, and dost thou not
Usurp the just proportion of my sorrow?

---

82 **shadow** illusory, fragile image/actor   **painted** artificial/made-up with cosmetics
83 **presentation** imitation   84 **flattering index** deceptively attractive prologue   **pageant** play
86 **mocked** taunted/imitated, play-acted   87 **dream** mere image   **flag** army's identifying
banner, highly visible in battle/type of flower belonging to the iris family   89 **sign** mere
symbol/military banner   **dignity** monarchy   90 **in jest** for entertainment/pretend   **fill the**
fulfill the requirements of/make up numbers in   93 **sues** pays court, entreats   94 **bending**
bowing/yielding   95 **troops** retinues   96 **Decline** go through in order (grammatical term)
97 **For** instead of   98 **name** i.e. of mother   100 **caitiff** wretch   **care** troubles, grief   101 **of**
by   104 **course . . . about** an image that recalls the popular conception of fortune as a wheel
that raised humans up and cast them down as it came full circle   105 **very** absolute
106 **thought** i.e. memory

110   Now thy proud neck bears half my burdened yoke,
From which even here I slip my wearied head,
And leave the burden of it all on thee.
Farewell, York's wife, and queen of sad mischance:
These English woes shall make me smile in France. *Starts to leave*

115 QUEEN ELIZABETH   O thou well skilled in curses, stay
     awhile,
   And teach me how to curse mine enemies!
QUEEN MARGARET   Forbear to sleep the night, and fast
     the day:
   Compare dead happiness with living woe:
   Think that thy babes were sweeter than they were,
120   And he that slew them fouler than he is.
   Bett'ring thy loss makes the bad causer worse:
   Revolving this will teach thee how to curse.
QUEEN ELIZABETH   My words are dull. O, quicken them
     with thine!
QUEEN MARGARET   Thy woes will make them sharp, and
     pierce like mine.   *Exit Margaret*
125 DUCHESS OF YORK   Why should calamity be full of
     words?
QUEEN ELIZABETH   Windy attorneys to their client's
     woes,
   Airy succeeders of intestine joys,
   Poor breathing orators of miseries!
   Let them have scope: though what they will impart
130   Help nothing else, yet do they ease the heart.
DUCHESS OF YORK   If so, then be not tongue-tied: go with
     me.
   And in the breath of bitter words let's smother

---

113 **mischance** misfortune   117 **Forbear** refrain, refuse   121 **Bett'ring** amplifying   **bad causer** person responsible for the evil   122 **Revolving** considering, reflecting on   123 **dull** lifeless, sluggish/blunt   **quicken** enliven/sharpen   126 **Windy . . . woes** (words are) empty, wind-blown representatives of the grief of the speakers   127 **intestine** internal (both in the sense of "experienced within" and in the sense of "digestive," the latter making words into farts)   129 **scope** range, room

My damnèd son, that thy two sweet sons smothered.   *Trumpet*

The trumpet sounds: be copious in exclaims.

Enter King Richard and his train

135 RICHARD   Who intercepts me in my expedition?

DUCHESS OF YORK   O, she that might have intercepted thee,

By strangling thee in her accursèd womb,

From all the slaughters, wretch, that thou hast done!

QUEEN ELIZABETH   Hid'st thou that forehead with a golden crown

140 Where't should be branded, if that right were right,

The slaughter of the prince that owed that crown,

And the dire death of my poor sons and brothers?

Tell me, thou villain slave, where are my children?

DUCHESS OF YORK   Thou toad, thou toad, where is thy brother Clarence?

145 And little Ned Plantagenet, his son?

QUEEN ELIZABETH   Where is the gentle Rivers, Vaughan, Grey?

DUCHESS OF YORK   Where is kind Hastings?

RICHARD   A flourish, trumpets! Strike alarum, drums!

Let not the heavens hear these tell-tale women

150 Rail on the lord's anointed. Strike, I say!

Flourish. Alarums

Either be patient and entreat me fair,

Or with the clamorous report of war

Thus will I drown your exclamations.

DUCHESS OF YORK   Art thou my son?

155 RICHARD   Ay, I thank God, my father, and yourself.

DUCHESS OF YORK   Then patiently hear my impatience.

---

134 exclaims outcries, exclamations   135 expedition military enterprise/haste   136 might
i.e. should   138 From i.e. to prevent   140 branded i.e. branded with   141 owed owned
143 villain wicked one/servant   148 flourish trumpet fanfare (usually signaling the arrival or
departure of a person in authority)   alarum call to arms   149 tell-tale prattling   150 Rail
rant   lord's anointed i.e. the king, supposedly chosen by God and anointed with holy oil at the
coronation to signify this   151 entreat me fair plead with me courteously   152 report loud
noise, specifically the explosion of a gun or cannon   156 impatience anger

RICHARD   Madam, I have a touch of your condition,
That cannot brook the accent of reproof.
DUCHESS OF YORK   O, let me speak!
160 RICHARD   Do then, but I'll not hear.
DUCHESS OF YORK   I will be mild and gentle in my words.
RICHARD   And brief, good mother, for I am in haste.
DUCHESS OF YORK   Art thou so hasty? I have stayed for
thee,
God knows, in torment and in agony.
165 RICHARD   And came I not at last to comfort you?
DUCHESS OF YORK   No, by the holy rood, thou know'st it
well,
Thou cam'st on earth to make the earth my hell.
A grievous burden was thy birth to me:
Tetchy and wayward was thy infancy:
170 Thy schooldays frightful, desp'rate, wild, and furious:
Thy prime of manhood daring, bold, and venturous:
Thy age confirmed, proud, subtle, sly and bloody,
More mild, but yet more harmful, kind in hatred.
What comfortable hour canst thou name,
175 That ever graced me with thy company?
RICHARD   Faith, none, but Humphrey Hour, that called your
grace
To breakfast once forth of my company.
If I be so disgracious in your eye,
Let me march on and not offend you, madam.
180 Strike up the drum.   *Drums*
DUCHESS OF YORK   I prithee hear me speak.
RICHARD   You speak too bitterly.

---

157 **condition** temperament   158 **brook . . . reproof** bear the language of rebuke
163 **stayed** waited   166 **rood** cross   169 **Tetchy** fretful   **wayward** willful, obstinate
170 **frightful** frightening   **desp'rate** reckless   171 **prime** early years   172 **age confirmed**
maturity   173 **kind in hatred** concealing hatred in kindness (**kind** may play on the sense of
"natural")   174 **comfortable** cheerful, comforting   176 **Humphrey Hour** unclear; possibly a
reference to "dining with Duke Humphrey," which meant going hungry, or perhaps an actual
person is meant   **grace** puns on **graced**   177 **forth** out

DUCHESS OF YORK   Hear me a word,
  For I shall never speak to thee again.
185 RICHARD   So.
  DUCHESS OF YORK   Either thou wilt die, by God's just
      ordinance
  Ere from this war thou turn a conqueror,
  Or I with grief and extreme age shall perish
  And never more behold thy face again.
190 Therefore take with thee my most grievous curse,
  Which in the day of battle tire thee more
  Than all the complete armour that thou wear'st!
  My prayers on the adverse party fight,
  And there the little souls of Edward's children
195 Whisper the spirits of thine enemies
  And promise them success and victory.
  Bloody thou art, bloody will be thy end:
  Shame serves thy life and doth thy death attend.   *Exit*
  QUEEN ELIZABETH   Though far more cause, yet much less
      spirit to curse
200 Abides in me: I say amen to her.
  RICHARD   Stay, madam, I must talk a word with you.
  QUEEN ELIZABETH   I have no more sons of the royal blood
  For thee to slaughter: for my daughters, Richard,
  They shall be praying nuns, not weeping queens,
205 And therefore level not to hit their lives.
  RICHARD   You have a daughter called Elizabeth,
  Virtuous and fair, royal and gracious.
  QUEEN ELIZABETH   And must she die for this? O, let her
      live,
  And I'll corrupt her manners, stain her beauty,
210 Slander myself as false to Edward's bed,
  Throw over her the veil of infamy:

---

186 **ordinance** law (plays on the sense of "artillery")   187 **turn** return   191 **tire** may it weigh
heavy on, exhaust   192 **complete** full, well-equipped   195 **Whisper** whisper to   198 **serves**
supplies/accompanies   **doth** i.e. will   205 **level** aim, set your target sights   209 **manners**
morals/courteous habits   210 **false** unfaithful   211 **veil** shroud (usually associated with
either modesty or mourning)

So she may live unscarred of bleeding slaughter,
I will confess she was not Edward's daughter.

RICHARD   Wrong not her birth, she is a royal princess.

215   QUEEN ELIZABETH   To save her life, I'll say she is not so.

RICHARD   Her life is safest only in her birth.

QUEEN ELIZABETH   And only in that safety died her
brothers.

RICHARD   Lo, at their birth good stars were opposite.

QUEEN ELIZABETH   No, to their lives ill friends were
contrary.

220   RICHARD   All unavoided is the doom of destiny.

QUEEN ELIZABETH   True, when avoided grace makes
destiny.
My babes were destined to a fairer death,
If grace had blessed thee with a fairer life.

RICHARD   You speak as if that I had slain my cousins.

225   QUEEN ELIZABETH   Cousins, indeed, and by their uncle
cozened
Of comfort, kingdom, kindred, freedom, life.
Whose hand soever lanched their tender hearts,
Thy head, all indirectly, gave direction.
No doubt the murd'rous knife was dull and blunt

230   Till it was whetted on thy stone-hard heart,
To revel in the entrails of my lambs.
But that still use of grief makes wild grief tame,
My tongue should to thy ears not name my boys
Till that my nails were anchored in thine eyes,

235   And I, in such a desp'rate bay of death,
Like a poor bark, of sails and tackling reft,
Rush all to pieces on thy rocky bosom.

---

212 So provided   of by   216 safest . . . birth only safeguarded by her high birth
218 opposite hostile, antagonistic   219 friends also "relatives"   contrary opposed
220 unavoided unavoidable   doom decree/destined judgment/condemnation
221 avoided grace an absence of God's grace (i.e. Richard)   222 fairer better/nobler/more
just   225 cozened cheated   227 Whose hand soever whoever's hand   lanched pierced
228 head brain/instigation/command   all indirectly through indirect means (plays on the
sense of "wrongly")   232 But . . . use did not the constant experience   235 bay cove,
inlet/point at which the cornered deer turns to face the hounds pursuing it   236 poor bark
shabby, ill-equipped ship   tackling rigging   reft deprived   237 Rush am dashed

RICHARD   Madam, so thrive I in my enterprise
And dangerous success of bloody wars,
240   As I intend more good to you and yours,
Than ever you and yours by me were harmed.

QUEEN ELIZABETH   What good is covered with the face of
heaven,
To be discovered, that can do me good?

RICHARD   Th'advancement of your children, gentle lady.

245   QUEEN ELIZABETH   Up to some scaffold, there to lose their
heads?

RICHARD   Unto the dignity and height of fortune,
The high imperial type of this earth's glory.

QUEEN ELIZABETH   Flatter my sorrow with report of it:
Tell me what state, what dignity, what honour,
250   Canst thou demise to any child of mine?

RICHARD   Even all I have; ay, and myself and all,
Will I withal endow a child of thine,
So in the Lethe of thy angry soul
Thou drown the sad remembrance of those wrongs
255   Which thou supposest I have done to thee.

QUEEN ELIZABETH   Be brief, lest that the process of thy
kindness
Last longer telling than thy kindness' date.

RICHARD   Then know, that from my soul I love thy
daughter.

QUEEN ELIZABETH   My daughter's mother thinks it with
her soul.

260   RICHARD   What do you think?

---

238 thrive I may I thrive   enterprise military undertaking   239 dangerous success risky
outcome   240 As only as far as   242 covered . . . heaven i.e. concealed by God
243 discovered revealed   244 Th'advancement the promotion, favoring (Elizabeth responds
to the literal sense)   245 scaffold raised platform on which executions took place
246 dignity honor, high rank   247 type symbol, emblem   248 Flatter increase, pander
to/alleviate, mollify   249 state high rank   250 demise convey, transfer (legal term)
251 Even exactly   252 endow bestow upon/give as a dowry   253 So if   Lethe in Greek
mythology, the river in the underworld that induced forgetfulness in any who drank from or
were immersed in it   254 remembrance memory   256 process story, narrative   257 telling
in the telling   date duration, end   259 thinks i.e. believes

QUEEN ELIZABETH   That thou dost love my daughter from
    thy soul.
    So from thy soul's love didst thou love her brothers,
    And from my heart's love I do thank thee for it.

RICHARD   Be not so hasty to confound my meaning:
265   I mean that with my soul I love thy daughter
    And do intend to make her Queen of England.

QUEEN ELIZABETH   Well then, who dost thou mean shall
    be her king?

RICHARD   Even he that makes her queen. Who else
    should be?

QUEEN ELIZABETH   What, thou?

270   RICHARD   Even so. How think you of it?

QUEEN ELIZABETH   How canst thou woo her?

RICHARD   That I would learn of you,
    As one being best acquainted with her humour.

QUEEN ELIZABETH   And wilt thou learn of me?

275   RICHARD   Madam, with all my heart.

QUEEN ELIZABETH   Send to her, by the man that slew her
    brothers,
    A pair of bleeding hearts: thereon engrave
    'Edward' and 'York', then haply will she weep:
    Therefore present to her — as sometime Margaret
280   Did to thy father, steeped in Rutland's blood —
    A handkerchief, which, say to her, did drain
    The purple sap from her sweet brother's body,
    And bid her wipe her weeping eyes withal.
    If this inducement move her not to love,
285   Send her a letter of thy noble deeds:
    Tell her thou mad'st away her uncle Clarence,
    Her uncle Rivers, ay, and, for her sake,
    Mad'st quick conveyance with her good aunt Anne.

---

261 from Elizabeth now shifts the sense to "away from, at variance with"   **264 confound** overturn, destroy   **270 How** what   **273 humour** temperament   **277 engrave** inscribe (plays on the sense of "place in the grave")   **278 haply** probably/perhaps   **279 sometime** once, formerly   **282 purple** blood-red   **283 withal** with it   **286 mad'st away** disposed of, killed   **288 conveyance** removal, dispatch (playing on the senses of "stealing" and "deceit, trickery")

RICHARD   You mock me, madam: this is not the way
290   To win your daughter.
QUEEN ELIZABETH   There is no other way,
Unless thou couldst put on some other shape,
And not be Richard that hath done all this.
RICHARD   Say that I did all this for love of her.
295   QUEEN ELIZABETH   Nay, then indeed she cannot choose
but hate thee,
Having bought love with such a bloody spoil.
RICHARD   Look what is done cannot be now amended:
Men shall deal unadvisedly sometimes,
Which after-hours give leisure to repent.
300   If I did take the kingdom from your sons,
To make amends, I'll give it to your daughter.
If I have killed the issue of your womb,
To quicken your increase, I will beget
Mine issue of your blood upon your daughter.
305   A grandam's name is little less in love
Than is the doting title of a mother;
They are as children but one step below,
Even of your mettle, of your very blood,
Of all one pain, save for a night of groans
310   Endured of her, for whom you bid like sorrow.
Your children were vexation to your youth,
But mine shall be a comfort to your age.
The loss you have is but a son being king,
And by that loss your daughter is made queen.
315   I cannot make you what amends I would:
Therefore accept such kindness as I can.
Dorset your son, that with a fearful soul

---

292 shape appearance/role/disguise   296 spoil booty gained from plunder   297 Look what
whatever   298 deal act, behave (plays on the sense of "kill")   299 after-hours later moments
302 issue offspring, children   303 quicken give life to   increase descendants, children
beget conceive   304 upon by   308 mettle substance, spirit, temperament   309 Of all one
causing the same amount of   310 of her by the younger Elizabeth (Queen Elizabeth's
daughter)   bid like sorrow endured similar pain   315 would would like to   316 can am
able (to offer)

Leads discontented steps in foreign soil,
This fair alliance quickly shall call home
320   To high promotions and great dignity.
The king that calls your beauteous daughter wife
Familiarly shall call thy Dorset brother.
Again shall you be mother to a king,
And all the ruins of distressful times
325   Repaired with double riches of content.
What? We have many goodly days to see.
The liquid drops of tears that you have shed
Shall come again, transformed to orient pearl,
Advantaging their love with interest
330   Of ten times double gain of happiness.
Go then, my mother, to thy daughter go:
Make bold her bashful years with your experience,
Prepare her ears to hear a wooer's tale,
Put in her tender heart th'aspiring flame
335   Of golden sovereignty, acquaint the princess
With the sweet silent hours of marriage joys.
And when this arm of mine hath chastisèd
The petty rebel, dull-brained Buckingham,
Bound with triumphant garlands will I come
340   And lead thy daughter to a conqueror's bed:
To whom I will retail my conquest won,
And she shall be sole victoress, Caesar's Caesar.
QUEEN ELIZABETH   What were I best to say? Her father's
brother
Would be her lord? Or shall I say her uncle?
345   Or he that slew her brothers and her uncles?
Under what title shall I woo for thee,
That God, the law, my honour and her love,
Can make seem pleasing to her tender years?

---

322 Familiarly as a family member   328 orient shining   329 Advantaging adding to the
value of   their love the love that caused the tears to be shed   331 mother mother-in-law
332 bold confident, prepared (with connotations of "sexually ready")   341 retail relate, re-tell
342 victoress female victor   Caesar's Caesar i.e. the conqueror of the victor   344 lord
husband

RICHARD   Infer fair England's peace by this alliance.

350   QUEEN ELIZABETH   Which she shall purchase with still
    lasting war.

RICHARD   Tell her the king, that may command, entreats.

QUEEN ELIZABETH   That at her hands which the king's
    king forbids.

RICHARD   Say she shall be a high and mighty queen.

QUEEN ELIZABETH   To vail the title, as her mother doth.

355   RICHARD   Say I will love her everlastingly.

QUEEN ELIZABETH   But how long shall that title 'ever'
    last?

RICHARD   Sweetly in force unto her fair life's end.

QUEEN ELIZABETH   But how long fairly shall her sweet life
    last?

RICHARD   As long as heaven and nature lengthens it.

360   QUEEN ELIZABETH   As long as hell and Richard likes of it.

RICHARD   Say I, her sovereign, am her subject low.

QUEEN ELIZABETH   But she, your subject, loathes such
    sovereignty.

RICHARD   Be eloquent in my behalf to her.

QUEEN ELIZABETH   An honest tale speeds best being
    plainly told.

365   RICHARD   Then plainly to her tell my loving tale.

QUEEN ELIZABETH   Plain and not honest is too harsh a
    style.

RICHARD   Your reasons are too shallow and too quick.

QUEEN ELIZABETH   O no, my reasons are too deep and
    dead:
    Too deep and dead, poor infants, in their graves.

370   RICHARD   Harp not on that string, madam: that is past.

---

349 Infer allege, give as a reason   350 purchase . . . war pay for with everlasting (personal)
strife   352 That i.e. a relationship (uncle/niece) considered by the Church as incestuous
king's king i.e. God   354 vail lower (in submission), yield   356 title claim (plays on the sense
of "queen's title")   357 in force in place, active (perhaps with sinister play on "enforce")
358 fairly justly/in safety   362 loathes puns on low   363 in on   364 speeds succeeds
plainly honestly/in simple terms, without adornment   367 quick hasty (Elizabeth plays on the
sense of "alive" when she responds with its opposite: dead)   368 too puns on "two"   deep
profound, learned (sense then shifts to "deep down, buried")

QUEEN ELIZABETH   Harp on it still shall I till heart-strings
break.

RICHARD   Now, by my George, my garter and my
crown—

QUEEN ELIZABETH   Profaned, dishonoured and the third
usurped.

RICHARD   I swear—

375 QUEEN ELIZABETH   By nothing, for this is no oath:
Thy George, profaned, hath lost his lordly honour;
Thy garter, blemished, pawned his knightly virtue;
Thy crown, usurped, disgraced his kingly glory.
If something thou wouldst swear to be believed,

380 Swear then by something that thou hast not
wronged.

RICHARD   Then, by myself—

QUEEN ELIZABETH   Thyself is self-misused.

RICHARD   Now, by the world—

QUEEN ELIZABETH   'Tis full of thy foul wrongs.

385 RICHARD   My father's death—

QUEEN ELIZABETH   Thy life hath it dishonoured.

RICHARD   Why then, by heaven—

QUEEN ELIZABETH   Heaven's wrong is most of all.
If thou didst fear to break an oath with him,

390 The unity the king my husband made
Thou hadst not broken, nor my brothers died.
If thou hadst feared to break an oath by him,
Th'imperial metal, circling now thy head,
Had graced the tender temples of my child,

395 And both the princes had been breathing here,
Which now, two tender bedfellows for dust,

---

371 **heart-strings** tendons or nerves supposed to brace the heart, hence intense feelings (puns on "harp strings")   372 **my George** the image of Saint George, patron saint of England, that formed part of the insignia of the Order of the Garter, the highest order of knighthood in England   **garter** band tied around the leg to keep up hosiery; Knights of the Garter wore a blue and gold one below the left knee   376 **his** its   382 **self-misused** disgraced, abused by yourself   389 **him** i.e. God   390 **unity** i.e. reconciliation between court factions in Act 2 Scene 1   391 **hadst** would have

Thy broken faith hath made the prey for worms.
What canst thou swear by now?

RICHARD   The time to come.

400 QUEEN ELIZABETH   That thou hast wrongèd in the time
o'erpast,
For I myself have many tears to wash
Hereafter time, for time past wronged by thee.
The children live whose fathers thou hast
slaughtered,
Ungoverned youth, to wail it with their age:
405 The parents live whose children thou hast butchered,
Old barren plants, to wail it with their age.
Swear not by time to come, for that thou hast
Misused ere used, by time's ill-used repast.

RICHARD   As I intend to prosper and repent,
410 So thrive I in my dangerous affairs
Of hostile arms. Myself myself confound.
Heaven and fortune bar me happy hours!
Day, yield me not thy light; nor, night, thy rest.
Be opposite all planets of good luck
415 To my proceeding if, with dear heart's love,
Immaculate devotion, holy thoughts,
I tender not thy beauteous princely daughter.
In her consists my happiness and thine:
Without her, follows to myself and thee,
420 Herself, the land and many a Christian soul,
Death, desolation, ruin and decay.
It cannot be avoided but by this:
It will not be avoided but by this.
Therefore, dear mother — I must call you so —
425 Be the attorney of my love to her:

---

400 o'erpast past   402 Hereafter time the future   404 Ungoverned parentless, without
a father's control   wail . . . age lament it in their maturity/throughout their lifetime
406 with along with   410 So thrive I to the same extent may I thrive   411 Myself myself
confound may I destroy myself   414 opposite hostile, adversarial   415 proceeding course of
action   417 tender not do not love, hold dear   princely royal   425 attorney representative,
pleader of a cause

Plead what I will be, not what I have been:
Not my deserts, but what I will deserve.
Urge the necessity and state of times,
And be not peevish found in great designs.

430 QUEEN ELIZABETH   Shall I be tempted of the devil thus?

RICHARD   Ay, if the devil tempt you to do good.

QUEEN ELIZABETH   Shall I forget myself to be myself?

RICHARD   Ay, if yourself's remembrance wrong yourself.

QUEEN ELIZABETH   Yet thou didst kill my children.

435 RICHARD   But in your daughter's womb I bury them,
Where in that nest of spicery they will breed
Selves of themselves, to your recomforture.

QUEEN ELIZABETH   Shall I go win my daughter to thy
will?

RICHARD   And be a happy mother by the deed.

440 QUEEN ELIZABETH   I go. Write to me very shortly,
And you shall understand from me her mind.

RICHARD   Bear her my true love's kiss, and so, farewell. *Kisses her*
Exit [Queen Elizabeth]

Relenting fool, and shallow, changing woman!—
How now, what news?

Enter Ratcliffe [with Catesby following]

445 RATCLIFFE   Most mighty sovereign, on the western coast
Rideth a puissant navy: to our shores
Throng many doubtful hollow-hearted friends,
Unarmed, and unresolved to beat them back.
'Tis thought that Richmond is their admiral,
450 And there they hull, expecting but the aid
Of Buckingham to welcome them ashore.

---

426 Plead offer as a plea in court   **427 my deserts** what I deserve   **428 times** affairs/the present time   **429 great designs** important affairs, the business of state (plays on the sense of "schemes aimed at attaining power")   **430 of** by   **432 forget . . . myself** forget my anguish and the wrongs done to me in order to be mother of a monarch   **433 if . . . yourself** if remembering yourself (i.e. collecting your wits/remembering your wrongs) compromises your future   **436 spicery** spices   **437 recomforture** new comfort   **441 mind** opinion, intention   **446 puissant** mighty, powerful   **447 doubtful** fearful/unreliable   **hollow-hearted** false, insincere   **449 their** i.e. the attacking navy's   **450 hull** float with sails furled

RICHARD   Some light-foot friend post to the Duke of
    Norfolk:
    Ratcliffe, thyself, or Catesby. Where is he?

CATESBY   Here, my good lord.

455 RICHARD   Catesby, fly to the duke.

CATESBY   I will, my lord, with all convenient haste.

RICHARD   Ratcliffe, come hither. Post to Salisbury.
    When thou com'st thither— Dull, unmindful villain, *To Catesby*
    Why stay'st thou here, and go'st not to the duke?

460 CATESBY   First, mighty liege, tell me your highness'
    pleasure,
    What from your grace I shall deliver to him.

RICHARD   O, true, good Catesby. Bid him levy straight
    The greatest strength and power that he can make,
    And meet me suddenly at Salisbury.

465 CATESBY   I go.   *Exit*

RATCLIFFE   What, may it please you, shall I do at
    Salisbury?

RICHARD   Why, what wouldst thou do there before I go?

RATCLIFFE   Your highness told me I should post before.

RICHARD   My mind is changed.—

Enter Lord Stanley [Earl of Derby]

470   Stanley, what news with you?

DERBY   None good, my liege, to please you with the
    hearing,
    Nor none so bad, but well may be reported.

RICHARD   Hoyday, a riddle: neither good nor bad.
    Why need'st thou run so many miles about,

475   When thou mayst tell thy tale the nearest way?
    Once more, what news?

DERBY   Richmond is on the seas.

---

452 light-foot swift-footed   post hurry   458 unmindful inattentive   463 strength and
power army   464 suddenly immediately   Salisbury town in Wiltshire, southwest England
472 well easily, readily   473 Hoyday exclamation of contemptuous impatience   475 nearest
most direct

RICHARD There let him sink, and be the seas on him!
White-livered runagate, what doth he there?

480 DERBY I know not, mighty sovereign, but by guess.

RICHARD Well, as you guess?

DERBY Stirred up by Dorset, Buckingham and Morton,
He makes for England, here to claim the crown.

RICHARD Is the chair empty? Is the sword unswayed?

485 Is the king dead? The empire unpossessed?
What heir of York is there alive but we?
And who is England's king but great York's heir?
Then tell me, what makes he upon the seas?

DERBY Unless for that, my liege, I cannot guess.

490 RICHARD Unless for that he comes to be your liege,
You cannot guess wherefore the Welshman comes.
Thou wilt revolt, and fly to him, I fear.

DERBY No, my good lord: therefore mistrust me not.

RICHARD Where is thy power, then, to beat him back?

495 Where be thy tenants and thy followers?
Are they not now upon the western shore,
Safe-conducting the rebels from their ships?

DERBY No, my good lord, my friends are in the north.

RICHARD Cold friends to me: what do they in the north,

500 When they should serve their sovereign in the west?

DERBY They have not been commanded, mighty king.
Pleaseth your majesty to give me leave,
I'll muster up my friends and meet your grace
Where and what time your majesty shall please.

505 RICHARD Ay, thou wouldst be gone to join with
Richmond.
But I'll not trust thee.

---

479 **White-livered runagate** cowardly renegade, runaway   484 **chair** throne   **sword** official
sword of office   **unswayed** not wielded   485 **empire** kingdom   **unpossessed** not
inherited/not ruled   488 **makes he** is he doing   489 **that** i.e. the crown   490 **for that**
because   491 **the Welshman** i.e. Richmond, grandson of the Welsh Owen Tudor and
Katherine of Valois (widow of Henry V)   494 **power** army   495 **tenants** who would have
been required to undertake military service for their lord   499 **Cold** unfriendly, distant (plays
on the fact that the north of England often undergoes cold weather)   502 **Pleaseth** if it please

DERBY   Most mighty sovereign,
　　　You have no cause to hold my friendship doubtful:
　　　I never was nor never will be false.
510 RICHARD   Go then and muster men, but, leave behind
　　　Your son, George Stanley. Look your heart be firm,
　　　Or else his head's assurance is but frail.
DERBY   So deal with him as I prove true to you.

Exit Stanley [Earl of Derby]

Enter a Messenger

MESSENGER   My gracious sovereign, now in Devonshire,
515 As I by friends am well advertisèd,
　　　Sir Edward Courtney and the haughty prelate,
　　　Bishop of Exeter, his elder brother,
　　　With many more confederates, are in arms.

Enter another Messenger

SECOND MESSENGER   In Kent, my liege, the Guildfords
　　　are in arms,
520 And every hour more competitors
　　　Flock to the rebels, and their power grows strong.

Enter another Messenger

THIRD MESSENGER   My lord, the army of great
　　　Buckingham—
RICHARD   Out on ye, owls! Nothing but songs of death?

He striketh him

　　　There, take thou that, till thou bring better news.
525 THIRD MESSENGER   The news I have to tell your majesty
　　　Is that by sudden floods and fall of waters
　　　Buckingham's army is dispersed and scattered,
　　　And he himself wandered away alone,
　　　No man knows whither.
530 RICHARD   I cry thee mercy:
　　　There is my purse to cure that blow of thine.   *Gives money*

---

508 hold consider, deem   **511 Look** make sure   **512 assurance** safety   **515 advertisèd**
informed   **520 competitors** associates, allies   **523 owls** thought to be birds of ill omen,
whose cry portended death   **526 fall of waters** i.e. heavy rain, storms   **530 cry thee mercy**
beg your pardon

Hath any well-advisèd friend proclaimed
Reward to him that brings the traitor in?
THIRD MESSENGER   Such proclamation hath been made,
    my lord.

Enter another Messenger

535 FOURTH MESSENGER   Sir Thomas Lovell and Lord
    Marquis Dorset,
'Tis said, my liege, in Yorkshire are in arms.
But this good comfort bring I to your highness:
The Breton navy is dispersed by tempest.
Richmond, in Dorsetshire, sent out a boat
540 Unto the shore, to ask those on the banks
If they were his assistants, yea or no,
Who answered him they came from Buckingham
Upon his party: he, mistrusting them,
Hoised sail and made his course again for Brittany.
545 RICHARD   March on, march on, since we are up in arms.
If not to fight with foreign enemies,
Yet to beat down these rebels here at home.

Enter Catesby

CATESBY   My liege, the Duke of Buckingham is taken:
That is the best news. That the Earl of Richmond
550 Is with a mighty power landed at Milford
Is colder news, but yet they must be told.
RICHARD   Away towards Salisbury! While we reason
    here,
A royal battle might be won and lost.
Someone take order Buckingham be brought
555 To Salisbury. The rest march on with me.

                        Flourish.   Exeunt

---

532 well-advisèd prudent   541 assistants supporters   543 his party Richmond's faction
544 Hoised hoisted   548 taken captured   550 Milford Milford Haven, on the coast of
southwest Wales   551 colder less welcome   552 reason talk

[Act 4 Scene 5]

Enter [Stanley, Earl of] Derby and Sir Christopher

DERBY   Sir Christopher, tell Richmond this from me:
That in the sty of the most deadly boar
My son George Stanley is franked up in hold.
If I revolt, off goes young George's head:
5   The fear of that holds off my present aid.
So get thee gone: commend me to thy lord.
Withal say that the queen hath heartily consented
He should espouse Elizabeth her daughter.
But tell me, where is princely Richmond now?
10   CHRISTOPHER   At Pembroke, or at Ha'rfordwest, in
        Wales.
DERBY   What men of name resort to him?
CHRISTOPHER   Sir Walter Herbert, a renownèd soldier,
Sir Gilbert Talbot, Sir William Stanley,
Oxford, redoubted Pembroke, Sir James Blunt,
15   And Rice ap Thomas with a valiant crew,
And many other of great name and worth:
And towards London do they bend their power,
If by the way they be not fought withal.
DERBY   Well, hie thee to thy lord: I kiss his hand,
20   My letter will resolve him of my mind. Farewell.

Exeunt

4.5 Location: *unspecified; possibly Stanley's home in the north of England, to which
Richard sent him to muster troops, or his London residence*   2 sty pen   boar i.e.
Richard   3 franked penned   hold custody   8 espouse marry   10 Pembroke town in
southwest Wales, just south of Milford Haven   Ha'rfordwest Haverfordwest, a town north of
Milford Haven   11 name rank/reputation   resort gather   14 redoubted revered/feared
Pembroke Earl of Pembroke (Richmond's uncle)   15 Rice i.e. Rhys   17 bend direct   18 by
on   20 resolve . . . mind explain my intentions

Act 5 Scene 1

Enter Buckingham with [Guards bearing] halberds [and the Sheriff],
led to execution

BUCKINGHAM Will not King Richard let me speak with
him?

SHERIFF   No, my good lord: therefore be patient.

BUCKINGHAM Hastings, and Edward's children, Grey and
Rivers,
Holy King Henry, and thy fair son Edward,

5   Vaughan, and all that have miscarrièd
By underhand corrupted foul injustice,
If that your moody discontented souls
Do through the clouds behold this present hour,
Even for revenge mock my destruction!—

10   This is All Souls' day, fellow, is it not?

SHERIFF   It is.

BUCKINGHAM Why, then All Souls' day is my body's
doomsday.
This is the day which, in King Edward's time,
I wished might fall on me, when I was found

15   False to his children and his wife's allies:
This is the day wherein I wished to fall
By the false faith of him whom most I trusted:
This, this All Souls' day to my fearful soul
Is the determined respite of my wrongs.

20   That high all-seer which I dallied with
Hath turned my feignèd prayer on my head
And given in earnest what I begged in jest:

5.1 **Location: Salisbury**   5 miscarrièd come to harm, died   7 moody angry   10 All Souls'
day November 2, the day in the Church calendar devoted to prayer for the souls of the dead
13 This . . . allies Buckingham refers to his speech in Act 2 Scene 1, in which, following the
formal reconciliation of court factions, he wished to be punished with treacherous friends if he
was ever disloyal to Elizabeth and her allies   19 determined respite of ordained end to the
postponement in punishing   20 all-seer i.e. God   dallied with trifled with, mocked
21 feignèd insincere, pretend   22 in jest in pretense

Thus doth he force the swords of wicked men
To turn their own points in their masters' bosoms.
25   Thus Margaret's curse falls heavy on my neck:
'When he', quoth she, 'shall split thy heart with
    sorrow,
Remember Margaret was a prophetess.'
Come lead me, officers, to the block of shame.
Wrong hath but wrong, and blame the due of blame.

Exeunt Buckingham with Officers

Act 5 Scene 2   *running scene 19*

*Enter Richmond, Oxford, Blunt, Herbert and others, with Drum and
Colours*

RICHMOND   Fellows in arms, and my most loving friends
Bruised underneath the yoke of tyranny,
Thus far into the bowels of the land
Have we marched on without impediment;
5   And here receive we from our father Stanley
Lines of fair comfort and encouragement.
The wretched, bloody, and usurping boar —
That spoiled your summer fields and fruitful vines,
Swills your warm blood like wash, and makes his
    trough
10   In your embowelled bosoms — this foul swine
Is now even in the centre of this isle,
Near to the town of Leicester, as we learn.
From Tamworth thither is but one day's march.
In God's name, cheerly on, courageous friends,
15   To reap the harvest of perpetual peace
By this one bloody trial of sharp war.

---

28 **block** execution block   **5.2 Location: Tamworth, in the East Midlands**   3 **bowels**
center, inmost part   5 **father** stepfather   8 **spoiled** stripped, despoiled   9 **Swills** gulps
wash pig food   10 **embowelled** disemboweled   12 **Leicester** chief town of Leicestershire,
east of Tamworth   14 **cheerly** cheerfully, hopefully   16 **sharp** harsh, merciless

OXFORD   Every man's conscience is a thousand men,
To fight against this guilty homicide.

HERBERT   I doubt not but his friends will turn to us.

20 BLUNT   He hath no friends but what are friends for fear,
Which in his dearest need will fly from him.

RICHMOND   All for our vantage. Then, in God's name, march.
True hope is swift, and flies with swallow's wings:
Kings it makes gods and meaner creatures kings.

Exeunt

[Act 5 Scene 3]   *running scene 20*

Enter King Richard in arms, with Norfolk, Ratcliffe and the Earl of Surrey [with Soldiers, who pitch Richard's tent]

RICHARD   Here pitch our tent, even here in Bosworth Field.
My lord of Surrey, why look you so sad?

SURREY   My heart is ten times lighter than my looks.

RICHARD   My lord of Norfolk—

5 NORFOLK   Here, most gracious liege.

RICHARD   Norfolk, we must have knocks, ha? Must we not?

NORFOLK   We must both give and take, my loving lord.

RICHARD   Up with my tent! Here will I lie tonight,
But where tomorrow? Well, all's one for that.

10 Who hath descried the number of the traitors?

NORFOLK   Six or seven thousand is their utmost power.

RICHARD   Why, our battalia trebles that account:
Besides, the king's name is a tower of strength,
Which they upon the adverse faction want.

15 Up with the tent! Come, noble gentlemen,

---

18 homicide murderer   22 vantage advantage   24 meaner humbler   **5.3 Location:**
Bosworth Field, to the east of Leicester   2 sad solemn, grave   6 knocks hard blows
9 all's . . . that it doesn't matter, it makes no difference   10 descried discovered, seen
12 battalia army   account number   14 want lack

Let us survey the vantage of the ground.
Call for some men of sound direction:
Let's lack no discipline, make no delay,
For, lords, tomorrow is a busy day.

Exeunt [into the tent]

Enter Richmond, Sir William Brandon, Oxford, [Blunt] and Dorset
[with Soldiers, who pitch Richmond's tent]

20   RICHMOND   The weary sun hath made a golden set,
And by the bright tract of his fiery car,
Gives token of a goodly day tomorrow.
Sir William Brandon, you shall bear my standard.
Give me some ink and paper in my tent:
25   I'll draw the form and model of our battle,
Limit each leader to his several charge,
And part in just proportion our small power.
My lord of Oxford, you, Sir William Brandon,
And you, Sir Walter Herbert, stay with me.
30   The Earl of Pembroke keeps his regiment;
Good Captain Blunt, bear my goodnight to him,
And by the second hour in the morning
Desire the earl to see me in my tent.
Yet one thing more, good captain, do for me:
35   Where is Lord Stanley quartered, do you know?
BLUNT   Unless I have mista'en his colours much —
Which well I am assured I have not done —
His regiment lies half a mile at least
South from the mighty power of the king.
40   RICHMOND   If without peril it be possible,
Sweet Blunt, make some good means to speak with
    him,
And give him from me this most needful note.

---

16 **vantage . . . ground** best position for military action   17 **sound direction** good tactical
judgment   21 **tract** traces, streaks   **car** chariot (which in classical mythology was driven by
the sun god)   23 **standard** flag, military banner   25 **form and model** arrangement and
ground-plan   26 **Limit** appoint, designate   **several** separate, respective   **charge** duty
27 **part . . . proportion** distribute evenly   30 **keeps** stays with   35 **quartered** encamped
36 **colours** identifying battle flags   42 **needful** urgent

BLUNT   Upon my life, my lord, I'll undertake it.
And so, God give you quiet rest tonight.   [*Exit*]

45 RICHMOND   Good night, good Captain Blunt. Come gentlemen,
Let us consult upon tomorrow's business;
Into my tent: the dew is raw and cold.

They withdraw into the tent

Enter Richard, Ratcliffe, Norfolk and Catesby [and other Soldiers]

RICHARD   What is't o'clock?

CATESBY   It's supper-time, my lord: it's nine o'clock.

50 RICHARD   I will not sup tonight.
Give me some ink and paper.
What, is my beaver easier than it was?
And all my armour laid into my tent?

CATESBY   It is, my liege, and all things are in readiness.

55 RICHARD   Good Norfolk, hie thee to thy charge:
Use careful watch, choose trusty sentinels.

NORFOLK   I go, my lord.

RICHARD   Stir with the lark tomorrow, gentle Norfolk.

NORFOLK   I warrant you, my lord.   *Exit*

60 RICHARD   Ratcliffe!

RATCLIFFE   My lord?

RICHARD   Send out a pursuivant at arms
To Stanley's regiment: bid him bring his power
Before sun-rising, lest his son George fall

65 Into the blind cave of eternal night.—
Fill me a bowl of wine. Give me a watch.   *To other Soldiers*
Saddle white Surrey for the field tomorrow.
Look that my staves be sound, and not too heavy.   *Exit some*
Ratcliffe!   *Soldiers*

70 RATCLIFFE   My lord?

52 **beaver** helmet's visor   **easier** looser, moving more efficiently   53 **into** in   55 **hie** hasten
charge duty/post   59 **warrant** assure, guarantee   62 **pursuivant at arms** officer attendant
on a herald, i.e. messenger   66 **watch** watch light, a slow-burning candle or one marked at
regular divisions to measure the passing of time/guard, watchman   67 **Surrey** the name of a
horse   68 **staves** staffs used as weapons   **sound** in good condition

RICHARD	Saw'st the melancholy Lord Northumberland?
RATCLIFFE	Thomas the Earl of Surrey and himself,

Much about cockshut time, from troop to troop
Went through the army, cheering up the soldiers. *Enter a Soldier*

75 RICHARD   So, I am satisfied.— Give me a bowl of wine:—
I have not that alacrity of spirit,
Nor cheer of mind, that I was wont to have.—
Set it down.— Is ink and paper ready?

RATCLIFFE   It is, my lord.

80 RICHARD   Bid my guard watch. Leave me.
Ratcliffe, about the mid of night come to my tent
And help to arm me. Leave me, I say.

Exeunt Ratcliffe [and Soldiers]

Richard withdraws to his tent, writes, and then sleeps

Enter Derby to Richmond in his tent

DERBY   Fortune and victory sit on thy helm!

RICHMOND   All comfort that the dark night can afford

85 Be to thy person, noble father-in-law!
Tell me, how fares our noble mother?

DERBY   I, by attorney, bless thee from thy mother
Who prays continually for Richmond's good.
So much for that. The silent hours steal on,

90 And flaky darkness breaks within the east.
In brief — for so the season bids us be —
Prepare thy battle early in the morning,
And put thy fortune to th'arbitrement
Of bloody strokes and mortal-staring war.

95 I, as I may — that which I would I cannot —
With best advantage will deceive the time,

---

73 **cockshut time** dusk, twilight (when poultry are cooped up)   74 **cheering up** encouraging, rallying   76 **alacrity** readiness, sharpness   77 **wont** used, accustomed   78 **it** presumably the wine   82 **arm me** put on my armor   83 **helm** helmet   85 **father-in-law** stepfather
87 **attorney** proxy   90 **flaky** streaked with light   91 **season** time of day   93 **th'arbitrement** the decision, final judgment   94 **mortal-staring** deathly-faced, with fatal gaze   95 **that . . . would** what I would like to do (i.e. fight openly on your side)   96 **With . . . time** with every opportunity I get, I will be strategically duplicitous (toward Richard)

And aid thee in this doubtful shock of arms.
But on thy side I may not be too forward
Lest, being seen, thy brother, tender George,
100   Be executed in his father's sight.
Farewell. The leisure and the fearful time
Cuts off the ceremonious vows of love
And ample interchange of sweet discourse
Which so long sundered friends should dwell upon:
105   God give us leisure for these rites of love!
Once more, adieu. Be valiant, and speed well!

RICHMOND   Good lords, conduct him to his regiment:
I'll strive with troubled noise to take a nap,
Lest leaden slumber peise me down tomorrow,
110   When I should mount with wings of victory.
Once more, good night, kind lords and gentlemen.

Exeunt. Richmond remains

O thou, whose captain I account myself,   *Kneels*
Look on my forces with a gracious eye:
Put in their hands thy bruising irons of wrath,
115   That they may crush down with a heavy fall
Th'usurping helmets of our adversaries!
Make us thy ministers of chastisement,
That we may praise thee in thy victory!
To thee I do commend my watchful soul,
120   Ere I let fall the windows of mine eyes:
Sleeping and waking, O, defend me still!   *Sleeps*

Enter the Ghost of Prince Edward, son to Henry VI

GHOST OF PRINCE EDWARD   Let me sit heavy on thy soul
    tomorrow!   *To Richard*
Think how thou stab'st me in my prime of youth

---

97 **doubtful shock** clash of forces, the outcome of which is uncertain/frightening military
encounter   98 **forward** eager   99 **brother** stepbrother   **tender** young   101 **leisure** time
available   103 **ample interchange** full exchange   **sweet discourse** pleasant conversation
104 **sundered** separated   108 **with** against   109 **peise** weigh   112 **account** consider
113 **gracious** filled with divine grace/favorable   114 **irons** swords   119 **watchful** wakeful
Prince Edward son of Margaret and Henry VI

At Tewkesbury: despair therefore, and die!—
125   Be cheerful, Richmond, for the wrongèd souls

To Richmond

Of butchered princes fight in thy behalf.
King Henry's issue, Richmond, comforts thee.   *[Exit?]*

The Ghosts either exit individually or remain onstage

Enter the Ghost of Henry the Sixth

GHOST OF KING HENRY VI   When I was mortal, my   *To Richard*
    anointed body
By thee was punchèd full of holes;
130   Think on the Tower and me: despair and die!
Harry the Sixth bids thee despair and die!—
Virtuous and holy, be thou conqueror!   *To Richmond*
Harry, that prophesied thou shouldst be king,
Doth comfort thee in sleep: live and flourish!   *[Exit?]*

Enter the Ghost of Clarence

135   GHOST OF CLARENCE   Let me sit heavy in thy soul   *To Richard*
    tomorrow!
I, that was washed to death with fulsome wine,
Poor Clarence, by thy guile betrayed to death!
Tomorrow in the battle think on me,
And fall thy edgeless sword: despair and die!—
140   Thou offspring of the House of Lancaster,

To Richmond

The wrongèd heirs of York do pray for thee.
Good angels guard thy battle! Live and flourish!

[Exit?]

Enter the Ghosts of Rivers, Grey and Vaughan

GHOST OF RIVERS   Let me sit heavy in thy soul tomorrow,   *To Richard*
Rivers that died at Pomfret: despair and die!

---

124 despair experience spiritual hopelessness (thought to precede suicide)   **127 issue** child,
offspring   **128 anointed** marked with holy oil, the sign of monarchy   **129 punchèd**
punctured, pierced   **130 Tower** of London, where Henry was murdered (see *3 Henry VI*, Act 5
Scene 6)   **136 washed** i.e. drowned (in a butt of malmsey, a strong sweet wine)   **fulsome**
nauseating/an abundant quantity of   **139 fall** drop, let fall   **edgeless** blunt, useless
142 battle army

145 GHOST OF GREY   Think upon Grey, and let thy soul   *To Richard*
    despair!

GHOST OF VAUGHAN   Think upon Vaughan, and, with   *To Richard*
    guilty fear,

    Let fall thy lance: despair and die!   *To Richmond*

ALL   Awake, and think our wrongs in Richard's bosom

    Will conquer him! Awake, and win the day!

        [Exeunt Ghosts?]

Enter the Ghost of Lord Hastings

150 GHOST OF HASTINGS   Bloody and guilty, guiltily awake   *To Richard*

    And in a bloody battle end thy days!

    Think on Lord Hastings: despair and die!

    Quiet untroubled soul, awake, awake!   *To Richmond*

    Arm, fight, and conquer, for fair England's sake!   *[Exit?]*

Enter the Ghosts of the two young Princes

155 GHOSTS OF PRINCES   Dream on thy cousins smothered   *To Richard*
    in the Tower:

    Let us be laid within thy bosom, Richard,

    And weigh thee down to ruin, shame, and death!

    Thy nephews' souls bid thee despair and die!—

        To Richmond

    Sleep, Richmond, sleep in peace and wake in joy:

160   Good angels guard thee from the boar's annoy!

    Live and beget a happy race of kings!

    Edward's unhappy sons do bid thee flourish.   *[Exit Ghosts?]*

Enter the Ghost of Anne, his wife   *To Richard*

GHOST OF ANNE   Richard, thy wife, that wretched Anne
    thy wife,

    That never slept a quiet hour with thee,

165   Now fills thy sleep with perturbations.

    Tomorrow in the battle think on me,

    And fall thy edgeless sword: despair and die!—

    Thou quiet soul, sleep thou a quiet sleep: *To Richmond*

156 laid buried   **160 annoy** injury, harm   **164 quiet** peaceful

Dream of success and happy victory!
170 Thy adversary's wife doth pray for thee.   [*Exit?*]

Enter the Ghost of Buckingham   *To Richard*

GHOST OF BUCKINGHAM   The first was I that helped thee to the
    crown:
The last was I that felt thy tyranny.
O, in the battle think on Buckingham,
And die in terror of thy guiltiness!
175 Dream on, dream on, of bloody deeds and death:
Fainting, despair; despairing, yield thy breath!—
I died for hope ere I could lend thee aid;   *To Richmond*
But cheer thy heart, and be thou not dismayed:
God and good angels fight on Richmond's side,
180 And Richard fall in height of all his pride.   [*Exit?*]

If the Ghosts have not exited individually, they all vanish at this point

Richard starts out of his dream

RICHARD   Give me another horse! Bind up my wounds!
Have mercy, Jesu! — Soft, I did but dream.
O coward conscience, how dost thou afflict me!
The lights burn blue. It is not dead midnight.
185 Cold fearful drops stand on my trembling flesh.
What? Do I fear myself? There's none else by.
Richard loves Richard: that is, I am I.
Is there a murderer here? No. Yes, I am.
Then fly. What, from myself? Great reason why:
190 Lest I revenge. What? Myself upon myself?
Alack, I love myself. Wherefore? For any good
That I myself have done unto myself?
O no! Alas, I rather hate myself
For hateful deeds committed by myself!
195 I am a villain: yet I lie, I am not.
Fool, of thyself speak well: fool, do not flatter.
My conscience hath a thousand several tongues,

176 **Fainting** staggering, losing consciousness/losing heart   **yield** give up   180 **Richard** may
Richard   182 **Soft** wait   184 **lights burn blue** thought to be a sign of the presence of ghosts
185 **drops** i.e. of sweat   191 **Wherefore?** Why?   197 **several** different, separate

And every tongue brings in a several tale,
And every tale condemns me for a villain.
200 Perjury in the high'st degree,
Murder, stern murder, in the direst degree,
All several sins, all used in each degree,
Throng all to th'bar, crying all, 'Guilty! Guilty!'
I shall despair. There is no creature loves me;
205 And if I die, no soul shall pity me.
Nay, wherefore should they, since that I myself
Find in myself no pity to myself?
Methought the souls of all that I had murdered
Came to my tent, and every one did threat
210 Tomorrow's vengeance on the head of Richard.

Enter Ratcliffe

RATCLIFFE   My lord?
RICHARD   Who's there?
RATCLIFFE   Ratcliffe, my lord, 'tis I. The early village cock
Hath twice done salutation to the morn.
215 Your friends are up and buckle on their armour.
RICHARD   O Ratcliffe, I fear, I fear—
RATCLIFFE   Nay, good my lord, be not afraid of shadows.
RICHARD   By the apostle Paul, shadows tonight
Have struck more terror to the soul of Richard
220 Than can the substance of ten thousand soldiers
Armèd in proof, and led by shallow Richmond.
'Tis not yet near day. Come, go with me:
Under our tents I'll play the eavesdropper,
To hear if any mean to shrink from me.

Exeunt Richard and Ratcliffe

Enter the Lords to Richmond, sitting in his tent

225 LORDS   Good morrow, Richmond!

---

198 brings in introduces (as evidence)   **202 used . . . degree** committed at every degree of
severity   **203 th'bar** i.e. of the court   **204 creature** person/minion created through favor,
i.e. not a genuine supporter   **209 threat** threaten   **217 shadows** something insubstantial
(Richard shifts the sense to "ghosts")   **221 proof** impenetrable armor   **224 shrink from** i.e.
desert

RICHMOND   Cry mercy, lords and watchful gentlemen,
That you have ta'en a tardy sluggard here.

LORDS   How have you slept, my lord?

RICHMOND   The sweetest sleep, and fairest-boding dreams
230   That ever entered in a drowsy head,
Have I since your departure had, my lords.
Methought their souls, whose bodies Richard
   murdered,
Came to my tent and cried on victory:
I promise you my heart is very jocund
235   In the remembrance of so fair a dream.
How far into the morning is it, lords?

LORDS   Upon the stroke of four.

RICHMOND   Why, then 'tis time to arm and give
   direction.—   *His oration to his Soldiers*
More than I have said, loving countrymen,
240   The leisure and enforcement of the time
Forbids to dwell upon. Yet remember this:
God and our good cause fight upon our side,
The prayers of holy saints and wrongèd souls,
Like high-reared bulwarks, stand before our faces,
245   Richard except, those whom we fight against
Had rather have us win than him they follow:
For what is he they follow? Truly, gentlemen,
A bloody tyrant and a homicide:
One raised in blood, and one in blood established;
250   One that made means to come by what he hath,
And slaughtered those that were the means to help
   him:
A base foul stone, made precious by the foil

---

226 **Cry mercy** forgive me   **watchful** alert/protective, guarding   227 **ta'en** caught
233 **cried on** invoked, called out to   234 **jocund** lively, joyful   239 **said** already said, said
before   240 **leisure** time available   **enforcement** constraints   244 **bulwarks** fortifications
245 **except** excepted   249 **raised** promoted (to the throne)   **established** confirmed in power
250 **made means** contrived, grasped opportunities, used any resource   252 **stone** jewel
foil setting for a jewel (designed to highlight the jewel's beauty)

Of England's chair, where he is falsely set:
One that hath ever been God's enemy.
255 Then if you fight against God's enemy,
God will in justice ward you as his soldiers:
If you do swear to put a tyrant down,
You sleep in peace, the tyrant being slain:
If you do fight against your country's foes,
260 Your country's fat shall pay your pains the hire:
If you do fight in safeguard of your wives,
Your wives shall welcome home the conquerors:
If you do free your children from the sword,
Your children's children quits it in your age.
265 Then, in the name of God and all these rights,
Advance your standards, draw your willing swords.
For me, the ransom of my bold attempt
Shall be this cold corpse on the earth's cold face:
But if I thrive, the gain of my attempt
270 The least of you shall share his part thereof.
Sound drums and trumpets boldly and cheerfully.
God and Saint George, Richmond and victory!   [*Exeunt*]

*Enter King Richard, Ratcliffe and Catesby [with Attendants and
Soldiers]*

RICHARD   What said Northumberland as touching
     Richmond?
RATCLIFFE   That he was never trainèd up in arms.
275 RICHARD   He said the truth: and what said Surrey then?
RATCLIFFE   He smiled and said, 'The better for our
     purpose.'
RICHARD   He was in the right, and so indeed it is.

Clock strikes

253 chair throne   falsely wrongfully, treacherously/artificially   256 ward protect   260 fat
wealth, prosperous growth   hire recompense   264 quits requites, repays   age old age
266 Advance your standards raise your battle flags   267 the . . . face i.e. if I fail the only
ransom to be paid for me shall be my death (noblemen captured in war were often released on
payment of a ransom)   269 thrive succeed/live   272 Saint George patron saint of England
273 touching regarding

Tell the clock there. Give me a calendar.
Who saw the sun today?

280 RATCLIFFE   Not I, my lord.

RICHARD   Then he disdains to shine, for by the book
He should have braved the east an hour ago
A black day will it be to somebody. Ratcliffe!

RATCLIFFE   My lord?

285 RICHARD   The sun will not be seen today:
The sky doth frown and lour upon our army.
I would these dewy tears were from the ground.
Not shine today? Why, what is that to me
More than to Richmond? For the selfsame heaven

290 That frowns on me looks sadly upon him.

Enter Norfolk

NORFOLK   Arm, arm, my lord: the foe vaunts in the field.

RICHARD   Come, bustle, bustle. Caparison my horse.   *He arms*
Call up Lord Stanley, bid him bring his power.
I will lead forth my soldiers to the plain,

295 And thus my battle shall be orderèd:
My foreward shall be drawn in length,
Consisting equally of horse and foot:
Our archers shall be placèd in the midst;
John Duke of Norfolk, Thomas Earl of Surrey,

300 Shall have the leading of the foot and horse.
They thus directed, we will follow
In the main battle, whose puissance on either side
Shall be well wingèd with our chiefest horse.
This, and Saint George to boot! What think'st thou,
    Norfolk?

---

278 **Tell** count (the chimes of)   **calendar** almanac, containing astrological predictions that
dealt with meteorology   281 **book** almanac   282 **braved the east** i.e. risen   **braved** made
splendid/challenged   283 **black** dark, gloomy/evil, disastrous   286 **lour** glower, threaten
darkly   287 **from** not on   290 **sadly** solemnly   291 **vaunts** flaunts itself proudly
292 **Caparison** harness, equip   296 **foreward** vanguard, front line of troops   **drawn**
extended   297 **horse and foot** cavalry and infantry, horsemen and foot soldiers
301 **directed** positioned, deployed   302 **puissance** power   303 **wingèd** flanked   **chiefest
horse** best cavalry   304 **to boot** (to support us) as well

305 NORFOLK   A good direction, warlike sovereign.
        This found I on my tent this morning: *Shows a paper*
        'Jockey of Norfolk, be not so bold,   *Reads*
        For Dickon thy master is bought and sold.'
     RICHARD   A thing devisèd by the enemy.
310   Go, gentleman, every man to his charge
        Let not our babbling dreams affright our souls:
        For conscience is a word that cowards use,
        Devised at first to keep the strong in awe.
        Our strong arms be our conscience, swords our law.
315   March on, join bravely, let us to't pell-mell:
        If not to heaven, then hand in hand to hell.—
        What shall I say more than I have inferred?   *His oration to his army*
        Remember whom you are to cope withal:
        A sort of vagabonds, rascals and runaways,
320   A scum of Bretons and base lackey peasants,
        Whom their o'er-cloyèd country vomits forth
        To desperate adventures and assured destruction.
        You sleeping safe, they bring you to unrest:
        You having lands, and blest with beauteous wives,
325   They would restrain the one, distain the other.
        And who doth lead them but a paltry fellow,
        Long kept in Bretagne at our mother's cost?
        A milksop, one that never in his life
        Felt so much cold as over-shoes in snow?
330   Let's whip these stragglers o'er the seas again,
        Lash hence these overweening rags of France,

307 Jockey contraction of "John-kin," a nickname for "John" (Norfolk's first name)
308 Dickon diminutive of Dick, i.e. Richard   **bought and sold** betrayed for a bribe   **315 join**
join battle   **pell-mell** with headlong haste/at close quarters, with hand-to-hand combat
317 inferred stated   **318 cope** fight, grapple   **319 sort** gang   **321 o'er-cloyèd** overfull and
sickened   **325 restrain** deprive you of   **distain** defile, soil, rape   **326 fellow** with lower-class
connotations   **327 Bretagne** Brittany   **mother's** an error (for "brother's") that appears in
the second edition of Shakespeare's major source, Holinshed's *Chronicles*; just conceivably
"mother" might refer to "mother England"   **328 milksop** weak, cowardly person/infant still
on a milk diet   **329 over-shoes in snow** when snow is above the level of one's shoes
330 whip these stragglers i.e. as vagabonds were whipped out of the parish by a local official
331 Lash hence whip away from here   **overweening** ambitious, overreaching   **rags**
vagrants/old scraps

These famished beggars, weary of their lives,
Who, but for dreaming on this fond exploit,
For want of means, poor rats, had hanged
    themselves.
335   If we be conquered, let men conquer us,
And not these bastard Bretons, whom our fathers
Have in their own land beaten, bobbed and thumped,
And on record, left them the heirs of shame.
Shall these enjoy our lands? Lie with our wives?
340   Ravish our daughters?   *Drum afar off*
                    Hark! I hear their drum.
Fight, gentlemen of England! Fight boldly, yeomen!
Draw, archers, draw your arrows to the head!
Spur your proud horses hard, and ride in blood:
Amaze the welkin with your broken staves!
    Enter a Messenger
345   What says Lord Stanley? Will he bring his power?
MESSENGER   My lord, he doth deny to come.
RICHARD   Off with his son George's head!
NORFOLK   My lord, the enemy is past the marsh
After the battle let George Stanley die.
350   RICHARD   A thousand hearts are great within my bosom.
Advance our standards, set upon our foes.
Our ancient word of courage, fair Saint George,
Inspire us with the spleen of fiery dragons!
Upon them! Victory sits on our helms.   [*Exeunt*]
    Alarum, excursions. Enter Catesby

---

333 **but** were it not for   **fond exploit** foolish military undertaking   334 **want** lack   337 **land**
with connotations of "sexual territory," i.e. wives and daughters   **bobbed and thumped**
beaten, pounded/had sex with, raped (their women)   338 **on record** as is officially recorded
the . . . shame in disgrace/illegitimate children   339 **Lie** have sex with   340 **Ravish** rape
341 **yeomen** property-owning men below the level of gentlemen   343 **proud** splendid/rearing
blood i.e. the blood drawn from spurring the horses so hard   344 **Amaze** terrify, alarm,
bewilder   **welkin** sky   **broken** i.e. shattered from energetic use   346 **deny** refuse   348 **past**
the marsh i.e. advancing   350 **great** full of emotion   352 **word of courage** i.e. battle cry
353 **spleen** fury   **dragons** Saint George was famed for the legendary killing of a dragon
Alarum, excursions trumpet call to arms and bouts of fighting across the stage

355 CATESBY   Rescue, my lord of Norfolk, rescue, rescue!
The king enacts more wonders than a man,
Daring an opposite to every danger:
His horse is slain, and all on foot he fights,
Seeking for Richmond in the throat of death.
360 Rescue, fair lord, or else the day is lost!

Alarums. Enter Richard

RICHARD   A horse! A horse! My kingdom for a horse!
CATESBY   Withdraw, my lord: I'll help you to a horse.
RICHARD   Slave, I have set my life upon a cast,
And I will stand the hazard of the die.
365 I think there be six Richmonds in the field:
Five have I slain today instead of him.
A horse! A horse! My kingdom for a horse!   [*Exeunt*]

Alarum. Enter Richard and Richmond: they fight. Richard is slain.
Retreat and flourish. Enter Richmond, Derby bearing the crown, with
divers other Lords

RICHMOND   God and your arms be praised, victorious
friends!
The day is ours, the bloody dog is dead.
370 DERBY   Courageous Richmond, well hast thou acquit
thee.
Lo, here, these long-usurpèd royalties
From the dead temples of this bloody wretch
Have I plucked off, to grace thy brows withal:
Wear it and make much of it.
375 RICHMOND   Great God of heaven, say 'Amen' to all!
But, tell me, is young George Stanley living?
DERBY   He is, my lord, and safe in Leicester town,
Whither, if you please, we may withdraw us.
RICHMOND   What men of name are slain on either side?

---

356 a man is humanly possible   357 Daring an opposite defying an enemy   363 set . . . cast
gambled my life on the throw of a die   364 stand await, endure   hazard chance   die
singular of "dice" (with connotations of death)   365 six Richmonds probably refers to the
military precaution of disguising other soldiers as their commander   370 acquit thee
acquitted yourself   371 royalties emblems of sovereignty, i.e. the crown   379 name rank

380 DERBY   John Duke of Norfolk, Walter Lord Ferris,
    Sir Robert Brackenbury, and Sir William Brandon.

RICHMOND   Inter their bodies as become their births:
    Proclaim a pardon to the soldiers fled
    That in submission will return to us:
385   And then, as we have ta'en the sacrament,
    We will unite the white rose and the red.
    Smile heaven upon this fair conjunction,
    That long have frowned upon their enmity!
    What traitor hears me and says not 'Amen'?
390   England hath long been mad, and scarred herself;
    The brother blindly shed the brother's blood,
    The father rashly slaughtered his own son,
    The son, compelled, been butcher to the sire:
    All this divided York and Lancaster,
395   Divided in their dire division.
    O, now let Richmond and Elizabeth,
    The true succeeders of each royal house,
    By God's fair ordinance conjoin together.
    And let thy heirs — God, if thy will be so —
400   Enrich the time to come with smooth-faced
        peace,
    With smiling plenty and fair prosperous days!
    Abate the edge of traitors, gracious Lord,
    That would reduce these bloody days again,
    And make poor England weep in streams of blood;
405   Let them not live to taste this land's increase
    That would with treason wound this fair land's peace.
    Now civil wounds are stopped, peace lives again:
    That she may long live here, God say 'Amen'!   *Exeunt*

---

382 become their births befits their social standing   **385 ta'en the sacrament** confirmed an oath by taking Holy Communion   **386 unite . . . red** i.e. unite the Houses of Lancaster (symbolized by a red rose) and York (a white rose) by marrying Elizabeth, daughter of Edward IV   **387 conjunction** union (literally, proximity of planets)   **393 sire** father **397 succeeders** inheritors, heirs   **398 ordinance** decree   **402 Abate** blunt   **edge** sword edge   **403 reduce** bring back   **405 increase** growth, harvest, prosperity   **407 stopped** staunched, stopped from bleeding/no longer inflicted

TEXTUAL NOTES

Q = First Quarto text of 1597
F = First Folio text of 1623
F2 = a correction introduced in the Second Folio text of 1632
Ed = a correction introduced by a later editor
SD = stage direction
SH = speech heading (i.e. speaker's name)

List of parts = Ed

1.1.1 SH RICHARD = Ed. *Not in* F   **77 was . . . his** = Q. F = was, for her
1.2.210 SH RICHARD = Q. F *assigns line to Lady Anne*
1.3.6 If . . . me? *accidentally printed twice in* F   **17 come the lords** = Q. F =
  comes the Lord   **158 of** *spelled* off *in* F   **305 on** = Q. F = an   **310 SH**
  QUEEN ELIZABETH = Q. F = *Mar.*   **343 SH FIRST MURDERER** = Ed. F
  = *Vil. (for Villain)*
2.1.108 at = Q. F = and
2.2.1 SH BOY = Q. F = *Edw.*   **3 you** = Q. *Not in* F   **47 I** = Q. *Not in* F   **83 weep**
  = Q. F = weepes   **84–5 and . . . they** = Q. F = so do not they *(i.e. one line*
  omitted due to eyeskip)   **87 Pour** *spelled* Power *in* F   **121 Ludlow** = Q. F =
  London   **146 God's** = Q. F = God   **153 Ludlow** = Q. F = London
3.1.124 as = Q. F = as, as,
3.4.26 cue *spelled* Q *in* F
3.5.104 Penker = Ed. F = *Pevker*
4.1.16 SH BRACKENBURY = Ed. F = *Lieu.*
Act 4 Scene 4 = Ed. F = *Scena Tertia*   **36 seniory** = Q. F = signeurie
  44 holp'st *spelled* hop'st *in* F   **289 this is not** = Q, F2. F = this not
  370 Harp . . . past *mistakenly printed after the following line in* F   **442 SD**
  Exit [Queen Elizabeth] = Ed. F = *Exit (directly after her last speech)*
  457 Ratcliffe = Ed. F = *Catesby*   **519 SH SECOND** = Ed. *Not in* F   **522 SH**
  THIRD = Ed. *Not in* F   **535 SH FOURTH** = Ed. *Not in* F   **538 Breton**
  spelled Brittaine *in* F   **544 Brittany** *spelled* Brittaine *in* F
Act 4 Scene 5 = Ed. F = *Scena Quarta*   **10 Ha'rfordwest** = Ed. F = Hertford
  West
5.2.11 centre = Q. F = Centry
5.3.29 you = F2. F = your   **122 SH GHOST OF PRINCE EDWARD** = Ed. F =
  Gh   **128 SH GHOST OF KING HENRY VI** = Ed. F = *Ghost*   **135 SH**
  GHOST OF CLARENCE = Ed. F = *Ghost*   **143 SH GHOST OF RIVERS** =
  Ed. F = *Riu*   **145 SH GHOST OF GREY** = Ed. F = *Grey.*   **146 SH GHOST**

OF VAUGHAN = Ed. F = *Vaugh.* **150 SH GHOST OF HASTINGS** = Ed. F = *Gho.* **155 SH GHOSTS OF PRINCES** = Ed. F = *Ghosts.* **158 souls bid** = Q. F = soule bids **163 SH GHOST OF ANNE** = Ed. F = *Ghost* **171 SH GHOST OF BUCKINGHAM** = Ed. F = *Ghost* **225 SH LORDS** = Q. F = *Richm.* **317 SD** *his . . . army* = Q. *Not in* F **341 Fight** = Q. F = Right **354 helms** = Q. F = helpes

QUARTO PASSAGES THAT DO NOT APPEAR IN THE FOLIO

Lines are numbered continuously, for ease of reference.

Following 4.2.103:

BUCKINGHAM My lord!

RICHARD   How chance the prophet could not at that time
Have told me, I being by, that I should kill him?

BUCKINGHAM My lord, your promise for the earldom,—

5 RICHARD   Richmond! When last I was at Exeter,
The mayor in courtesy showed me the castle,
And called it Rougemont: at which name I started,
Because a bard of Ireland told me once
I should not live long after I saw Richmond.

10 BUCKINGHAM My lord!

RICHARD   Ay, what's o'clock?

BUCKINGHAM I am thus bold to put your grace in mind
Of what you promised me.

RICHARD   Well, but what's o'clock?

15 BUCKINGHAM Upon the stroke of ten.

RICHARD   Well, let it strike.

BUCKINGHAM Why let it strike?

RICHARD   Because that, like a Jack, thou keep'st the stroke
Betwixt thy begging and my meditation.

20   I am not in the giving vein today.

Following 5.3.212:

RICHARD   O Ratcliffe, I have dreamed a fearful dream!
What thinkest thou, will our friends prove all true?

RATCLIFFE   No doubt, my lord.

---

2 prophet i.e. Henry VI   **3 by** nearby   **him** Henry VI/Richmond   **5 Exeter** town in the
county of Devon, southwest England   **7 Rougemont** puns on **Richmond**   **8 bard** (prophetic)
poet   **18 Jack** small figure of a man that struck the clock bell every hour (plays on the sense
of "knave, base fellow")   **keep'st the stroke** observe the hour by striking the bell, i.e.
regularly interrupt   **19 meditation** thoughts, reflection   **22 true** loyal

SCENE-BY-SCENE ANALYSIS

ACT 1 SCENE 1

Lines 1–41: The play opens with a soliloquy by Richard, revealing his skillful use of language. He outlines recent history, emphasizing that the action of this play is part of a wider series of events. The civil war between the royal Houses of York and Lancaster has ended, and Yorkist Edward IV is king, creating a "glorious summer" of peace in contrast to the previous "winter" of "discontent." Richard's speech moves away from matters of state toward himself, creating links and tensions between political and personal. Richard describes how men who were soldiers are now lovers. He claims that his own physical deformities prevent him from courting, describing himself bitterly as "Deformed" and "unfinished." His apparent preoccupation with his looks establishes the play's interest in appearance and identity (genuine and feigned). He declares that since he "cannot prove a lover" he will "prove a villain" and outlines his plans against his brothers, the king and the Duke of Clarence. He has set abroad rumors of a prophecy, "which says that 'G' / Of Edward's heirs the murderer shall be," the first in a series of references to prophecies, dreams, and omens. Richard sees Clarence being led in, guarded, and cuts short his soliloquy, urging his thoughts to "Dive" down to his "soul," emphasizing his ability to conceal his true self and the disparity between appearance and reality.

Lines 42–147: Richard asks why Clarence is being taken to the Tower. Clarence reveals that it is because his name "is George," showing that Richard's false prophecy has had effect on Edward, who "hearkens after prophesies and dreams" (although, ironically, being Duke of Gloucester, Richard himself is also "G"). Richard feigns sympathy and suggests that Clarence's downfall is the result of the influence of the queen. Various political undercurrents are revealed: we also learn that the Lord Chamberlain, Hastings, has been freed from the Tower, apparently due to the influence of the king's mistress, Jane Shore. Lord Brackenbury claims that he has been charged with ensuring that "no man shall have private conference" with Clarence, but Richard argues that they are discussing "no treason" and assures Clarence that he will speak to the king. Clarence is led away as Hastings arrives, vowing revenge on the "kites and buzzards" who have had him arrested, establishing the animal imagery that recurs through the play. Hastings reports that the king is "sickly, weak and melancholy." Richard feigns sadness, saying that he will follow Hastings to see the king.

Lines 148–165: Richard fears that Edward will die before Clarence has been executed. He plans to see that Clarence is "packed with post-horse up to heaven" by stirring up Edward's hatred. Once Clarence and Edward are dead, he will "bustle in." He reveals his plan to marry Lady Anne Neville. Although the specific reasons for this remain a "secret close intent," it is clearly a political move. Despite acknowledging that he killed both Anne's husband and Henry VI (her father-in-law), Richard seems confident that he will achieve this, suggesting a confidence with the opposite sex that his earlier speech denied and illustrating the complexities of his characterization.

ACT 1 SCENE 2

Lines 1–233: The guarded coffin of Henry VI is brought on, attended by Anne. She laments the fall of the House of Lancaster and the death of Henry, and curses Richard. She wishes him a worse fate than "spiders" and "toads," reinforcing the animal imagery introduced in the previous scene. She instructs the men carrying Henry's coffin to carry him to Chertsey Monastery. Richard enters and commands the men to put the coffin down. Anne compares his entrance to that of a "fiend" conjured up by a "black magician," introducing a series of images associating Richard with hell. She uncovers Henry's body and invites everyone look at "dead Henry's wounds," calling on God to revenge his death. Richard appeals to be allowed to explain. He describes Anne as an angel and "divine perfection," which aims at flattery but also contrasts with the hellish images she uses for him, establishing them as opposing representatives of good and evil. The balance of imagery is reflected in the stichomythic structure of their argument. Initially, Anne seems to be a worthy opponent in what Richard calls their "keen encounter of . . . wits." Richard's mastery over language and ability to manipulate become evident, however, as he overcomes Anne's anger. He claims that he killed Anne's husband because he loves her. He praises her beauty and offers her his sword, saying that if her "vengeful heart cannot forgive" she must kill him. She cannot, and, despite fearing that both Richard's tongue and heart are false, she softens. He places a ring on her finger, claiming his heart is hers, and begs to be allowed to take Henry's body to Chertsey so that he may "wet his grave" with "repentant tears." Pleased that he has "become so penitent," she agrees.

Lines 234–272: Richard instructs the men to take Henry to Whitefriars, not Chertsey. Any vicarious belief the audience may have had in his sincerity is destroyed as he marvels at his ability to manipulate Anne (and, perhaps, us) and comments that he has her, but "will not keep her long." He appears surprised that Anne finds him "a marv'llous proper man," despite his physical appearance, and resolves to employ "a score or two of tailors / To study fashions to adorn my body." The clothing imagery reinforces the obsession with appearance and identity, as do repeated references to looking glasses.

ACT 1 SCENE 3

Lines 1–109: Lord Rivers and Lord Grey try to reassure Queen Elizabeth, who worries about what will "betide" her after Edward's death. They remind her that her son, Prince Edward, will be her "comforter," but she is concerned that his youth means that he will be under the protection of Richard. Derby and Buckingham report that the king wishes to make peace between Richard and the queen's brothers, and between the queen's brothers and Hastings, and has summoned them all. Richard arrives with Hastings and Dorset, complaining that people have been telling the king "dissentious rumours" about him. He argues, ironically, that he "cannot flatter and look fair" and asks the assembled company to tell him how he has "injured" them and caused them to trouble the king "with lewd complaints." The queen retorts that it is his own behavior that has caused the king to send for him. Richard accuses the queen of using her power to achieve status and positions in court for her family, and complains that his brother Clarence is imprisoned by Elizabeth's "means." She denies this and their argument escalates, with Elizabeth declaring that she has "Small joy" in being queen and being constantly "bated, scorned and stormed at." Queen Margaret, the widow of Henry VI, enters unnoticed.

Lines 110–324: Elizabeth and Richard argue as Margaret watches, making comments aside. Her presence as an "audience" reinforces our sense of Richard as an actor. Margaret's observations show her hatred of Richard and Elizabeth: she wishes Elizabeth that even her "Small joy" be lessened and observes that Richard is a "cacodemon" (evil spirit) whose kingdom is hell, reinforcing Anne's previous imagery. She steps forward and accuses them of being "wrangling pirates" who argue over what has been "pilled" from her. The following exchange, which centers on past struggles for the kingdom, reminds us that the events of the play are part of wider history, and of the violent nature of the struggle for power. Margaret invokes a series of prophetic curses, as Richard calls her "witch" and "withered hag." Margaret hopes that Elizabeth's son, Edward, will "Die in his youth" by "untimely violence," as her own son did, and that Elizabeth will "Die neither mother, wife, nor England's queen." Elizabeth remains silent during Margaret's outburst, but Richard argues. Margaret warns that Richard will soon suspect his friends "for traitors" and "take deep traitors" for his "dearest friends." She abuses Richard's appearance, invoking the images of animals and hell that have previously been associated with him. Her comparison of Richard to a "bottled spider" with a "deadly web" shows her awareness of his manipulative nature. Buckingham urges Margaret to "have done" and she warns him against Richard and his "venom tooth" before leaving, saying that they will remember her words and think of her as a "prophetess." Richard assumes an air of forgiveness and says that Margaret "hath had too much wrong" and that he repents of any part he has had in this. He adds that he hopes God will pardon those who have wronged Clarence. Rivers comments that this is "virtuous and . . . Christian-like." Catesby summons them to the king's presence.

Lines 325–357: Richard stays and considers how he has convinced Derby, Hastings, and Buckingham that the queen and her family are plotting against himself and Clarence. He is pleased with the effectiveness of his "piece of scripture," saying that he uses "old ends stol'n forth of holy writ" to "clothe" his villainy, so that he can "seem a saint" when in reality he "play[s] the devil." Once again we see opposing images of heaven and hell, and of clothing, suggesting Richard's ability to disguise his true self. Two murderers enter and Richard gives them a warrant to be admitted to Clarence. Richard warns them to be "sudden in the execution" and not to let Clarence plead with them, as he is "well-spoken," showing the play's concern with the power of language.

ACT 1 SCENE 4

Lines 1–97: Clarence describes a dream to his keeper in vivid and poetic language, demonstrating that Richard was right: he is "well-spoken." Clarence recounts how, in his dream, he had escaped and was sailing to Burgundy with Richard. As they stood on deck, looking back at England, Richard stumbled and knocked Clarence overboard. He describes the sights and sounds as he drowned, including "gold," "pearls," and "jewels" all "scattered in the bottom of the sea" "in dead men's skulls," a reminder of the link between death and the desire for wealth and power. He goes on to describe nightmarish visions of the afterlife and acknowledges his own guilt for past deeds before asking the keeper to sit by him "awhile" as he goes to sleep. As Clarence sleeps, Brackenbury, the Lieutenant of the Tower, arrives. He watches Clarence and considers how all men are the same, regardless of rank. The Murderers bring Brackenbury the warrant, ordering him to leave them. Brackenbury does so, observing that he will not "reason what is meant hereby, / Because I will be guiltless from the meaning," lines symptomatic of a recurrent exploration of guilt and innocence.

Lines 98–280: In a darkly humorous exchange, the Murderers contemplate what they are about to do, weighing spiritual consequences against monetary reward. Clarence wakes and stalls them with powerful speeches, but they insist that they have been commanded to kill him by the king. Clarence asks them to go to Richard, but they reveal that Richard actually sent them. Clarence refuses to believe this, describing how Richard loves him and how he "hugged [him] in his arms, and swore, with sobs" to gain his "delivery," a testament to Richard's acting skills and ambiguity in language. Clarence shows his own powers of persuasion as the Second Murderer decides that he cannot go through with the deed. The First Murderer, however, stabs Clarence and takes his body to be drowned in a butt of malmsey wine. He returns and threatens to tell Richard how "slack" his companion was, but the Second Murderer says he can tell Richard and take the entire fee, as he repents.

ACT 2 SCENE 1

The king expresses satisfaction that, although he is very ill, he has achieved peace among the quarreling factions and so his soul "shall part to heaven" in peace. Hastings and Rivers shake hands and Edward warns that they must mean it or God will "Confound" their "hidden falsehood," emphasizing the recurring deceptions of the play but also suggesting a justice beyond the human court. Richard arrives and praises Edward for his "blessèd labor" and begs to be reconciled in "friendly peace" with everyone. The queen asks her husband to pardon Clarence, but Richard accuses her of mocking him, saying, "Who knows not that the gentle duke is dead?" Edward, shocked, claims that he reversed the order to execute Clarence. Richard explains that the "countermand" was not delivered in time. Derby enters and kneels before Edward, asking that Edward will spare the life of his servant. Edward grows angry, bitter that he can "give pardon to a slave," but could not do so for his own brother. He blames the assembled company for not pleading hard enough on

Clarence's behalf and has to be helped away. Richard takes the opportunity to provoke dissent, observing to the remaining courtiers that "the guilty kindred of the queen" had obviously urged Edward to execute Clarence.

ACT 2 SCENE 2

Lines 1–33: Clarence's children question the Duchess of York about the death of their father. Despite her denials, Clarence's son tells her that "good uncle Gloucester" has told them that King Edward was responsible for their father's death, "provoked to it by the queen." He describes how Richard wept as he told him the news and asked the boy "to rely on him." The duchess observes that Richard hides his "deep vice" "with a virtuous visor," another image of clothing and concealment. Once more, it is a woman who appears to have insight into Richard's true character: so far only Anne, Elizabeth, and the duchess have directly expressed their distrust.

Lines 34–100: The queen arrives, clearly distressed, and announces that King Edward has died. The duchess sympathizes: she too has lost a husband. Sustaining the association between images of mirrors and the theme of identity, she adds that until now she had comfort in two of her sons, "two mirrors" of their father's "princely semblance." Now, however, she claims that she only has "but one false glass," Richard. Clarence's children declare that they cannot share in their aunt's grief, as she "wept not" for their father, another example of events of the past reinforcing divisions in the present. Both of the women and the children then exclaim in grief over their losses. In contrast to these personal emotions, Rivers and Dorset focus on the political circumstances, urging Elizabeth to send for the young Prince Edward and "Let him be crowned."

Lines 101–153: Richard arrives, offering comfort to the queen and asking his mother's blessing, although his brief aside reminds us of the disparity between his words and true feelings/intentions. Buckingham smoothly suggests that Prince Edward be brought to London, accompanied "with some little train" in case "the new-healed wound of malice should break out." Rivers and Hastings agree and

Richard asks his mother and Elizabeth to go and give their "censures in the business." He remains behind with Buckingham and they plot to "part the queen's proud kindred from the prince."

ACT 2 SCENE 3

In a contrast to the court-based action so far, and demonstrating the important link between king and kingdom, three citizens discuss the current circumstances. While one remains optimistic, the others express their fears about a "land that's governed by a child." They show distrust of Richard and worry what the struggles between Richard and the queen's relatives will do to the kingdom.

ACT 2 SCENE 4

The archbishop, the queen, the duchess, and young York wait for the prince's arrival. The intimate and domestic discussion between mother and grandmother concerning the comparative heights of Edward and York contrasts with the political arguments that have dominated so far. York reports that his "uncle Gloucester" said that "Small herbs have grace, great weeds do grow apace," an image that evokes the destructive nature of Richard's speedy rise to power. The family exchange is gently humorous, although once again the duchess expresses doubt over Richard's character, until a messenger brings the news that Rivers, Grey, and Vaughan have been imprisoned on the command of Richard and Buckingham. Elizabeth sees that Richard has begun the "ruin" of her family, comparing him to a hunting "tiger," and foresees "as in a map, the end of all." She decides to take York into sanctuary, and the duchess offers to go with them. The archbishop gives them the king's seal of authority that he carries and takes them to safety.

ACT 3 SCENE 1

Lines 1–94: Prince Edward enters London, accompanied by Richard, Buckingham, and the Lord Cardinal. Edward asks why none of his "uncles" on his mother's side are there to greet him and asks where his mother and brother are. As he does so, Hastings arrives with the news that the queen and York have "taken sanctuary" and that Elizabeth prevented York from coming to greet his brother. Buckingham, annoyed, sends the Lord Cardinal to "persuade" Elizabeth to send York to Prince Edward, and orders Hastings that if she will not give in to "pluck him perforce" from his mother's arms. When the Cardinal objects, Buckingham cleverly argues that York is too young to "have the wit" to claim sanctuary and therefore to take him is to "break no privilege nor charter." It is interesting that here, as in the rest of this scene, it is Buckingham, not Richard, who is making decisions and giving orders, demonstrating his increasing power. The Cardinal and Hastings depart and the prince asks where he is to stay until his coronation. Richard suggests the royal residence at the Tower, but Edward is not keen. We see that Edward has a similar control over language to Richard's and that he is not fooled by his uncle's clever arguments.

Lines 95–201: York is brought in and the brothers show that they are a match for Richard verbally, but they are still powerless to prevent him, as "Lord Protector," from sending them to stay in the Tower. When the brothers have gone, Richard, Buckingham, and Catesby discuss their plans to place Richard on the throne. Buckingham argues that they will find it difficult to convince Hastings and sends Catesby to "summon him tomorrow to the Tower" under the pretext of discussing the coronation, so that they can test his loyalty. Richard adds that Catesby should tell Hastings that the queen's relatives are to be executed the next day, as this will please him. Buckingham asks Richard what they will do if Hastings will not join their conspiracy and Richard answers simply "Chop off his head." He promises Buckingham "the earldom of Hereford" once he is king.

ACT 3 SCENE 2

Lines 1–34: Hastings is woken in the early hours by a messenger from the Earl of Derby. He reports that Derby has had a prophetic dream in which a boar (Richard's heraldic emblem) "razèd off his helm." Derby is worried about the "two councils" that Richard

intends to hold, a technique clearly intended to create political division. He asks if Hastings will join him in escaping north to "shun the
danger that his soul divines." Demonstrating his own lack of percep-
tion, Hastings replies that there is nothing to fear from the "separated council."

Lines 35–123: Catesby arrives and Hastings asks for news of the
"tott'ring state," evoking the country's turmoil. Catesby comments
that he thinks the world will not "stand upright" again until Richard
is king. Shocked, Hastings asks if this is Richard's intention and
learns that it is, and that Richard hopes for his backing. Catesby adds
that Hastings' enemies, "the kindred of the queen," "must die at
Pomfret." Apparently oblivious to the danger he is placing himself
in, Hastings declares that he is glad of this, but that he will not help
Richard to the throne. Derby arrives in person and Hastings jokingly
asks where his "boar-spear" is. Derby insists that the "several councils" bode ill, but Hastings is unmoved. As Derby and Catesby head to
the Tower, Hastings jokes with a Pursuivant and shows his pleasure
that his enemies are to be executed. Buckingham arrives to escort
Hastings to the Tower.

ACT 3 SCENE 3

Ratcliffe escorts Rivers, Grey, and Vaughan to their executions. They
proclaim their loyalty to the prince and remember Margaret's earlier
curses upon them. Rivers reminds them that she also cursed Richard
and Buckingham.

ACT 3 SCENE 4

Lines 1–57: The council assembles. Hastings announces that they
are there to "determine of the coronation," asking, "when is the
royal day?" The bishop suggests the next day, and Buckingham asks
if anyone knows Richard's mind on the subject. The bishop suggests
that Buckingham should, but Buckingham's response is ambiguous.
He suggests that Hastings might know, and, although Hastings
denies this, he offers to speak on Richard's behalf. Richard arrives

and Buckingham informs him that Hastings was about to pronounce his "part" on the coronation, implying that Hastings aspires to Richard's power, and creating an awareness of theater and performance, also emphasized by the word "cue." Richard seems cheerful and asks the bishop to send for a bowl of strawberries. Richard draws Buckingham aside and reports that Catesby "hath sounded Hastings" and found that he "will lose his head" rather than help depose Prince Edward. They withdraw. Hastings comments on Richard's good humor and ironically suggests that Richard can never "hide his love or hate."

Lines 58–106: Richard returns in a changed mood. He angrily claims that people are conspiring his death "with devilish plots / Of damnèd witchcraft" and have placed "hellish charms" on his body. Hastings suggests that the penalty for such an action must be death. Richard shows them the withered arm he has had since birth, claiming that he has been bewitched by Elizabeth, "that monstrous witch" and "that harlot, strumpet Shore." Hastings is uncertain, and Richard immediately accuses him of treachery and conspiracy with Mrs. Shore and orders his execution. Too late, Hastings realizes his blindness and recounts the omens that he has ignored, including Margaret's curses. He makes his own prophecy that England is about to enter "the fearful'st time," before being led away.

ACT 3 SCENE 5

Richard and Buckingham are dressed in damaged armor, a deliberate choice of "costume" for the events they are about to stage. This theatrical self-awareness is emphasized by Richard asking if Buckingham can pretend to be "distraught and mad with terror" and Buckingham's assurance that he can "counterfeit the deep tragedian." Catesby arrives as arranged, bringing the Mayor. Richard and Buckingham feign confusion and appear to be defending the Tower. Lovell and Ratcliffe bring in Hastings' head and Richard sets about convincing the Mayor that Hastings was a traitor. Buckingham helps, reporting that Hastings, in league with "Mistress Shore," had plotted to kill Richard. He expresses regret that Lovell and Ratcliffe have already carried out the execution, as he would have liked the Mayor to hear Hastings' confession so as to reassure the citizens that his execution was necessary. It becomes clear that this episode has been to further Richard's cause with the English people and to prevent "the censures of the carping world." After the Mayor has left, Richard sends Buckingham to talk to the citizens of London, slurring the reputation of the old king and suggesting that his children are illegitimate. Buckingham assures him that he will "play the orator." Richard goes to make secret arrangements "To draw the brats of Clarence out of sight."

ACT 3 SCENE 6

The opinion of England's subjects is represented by a scrivener, who comments that the execution of Hastings is a "palpable device" by Richard.

ACT 3 SCENE 7

Lines 1–93: Buckingham reports on his speech, in which he undermined the reputation of King Edward and his children and praised Richard, rallying the crowds to shout "God save Richard, England's royal king!" In response to this, however, the people "spake not a word" and their silence provides a powerful contrast to the abundance of language so far. Richard is perplexed and angry. Buckingham tells him that the Mayor is coming, advising him to "get a prayer-book" and "stand between two churchmen." Richard leaves and the Mayor arrives, as does Catesby. Catesby pretends that Richard refuses to see any of them as he is "Divinely bent to meditation" and Buckingham sends him back to ask again. He observes to the Mayor that Richard is "virtuous," unlike "lewd" Edward, and pretends to be concerned that Richard will not accept the crown, commenting on how difficult it is to draw "holy and devout religious men" from their "zealous contemplation."

Lines 94–245: Richard appears with two clergymen. Buckingham apologizes for interrupting his devotion and begs that he will listen to their requests. He urges Richard to accept the crown. Initially Richard refuses, allowing Buckingham to repeat all of the persuasive arguments for him and against Edward and his children. The Mayor tells Richard that his citizens "entreat" him to accept, but Richard still feigns reluctance. Finally, he piously accepts the "burden" of kingship.

ACT 4 SCENE 1

Elizabeth, Dorset, and the duchess meet Anne, now Richard's wife, with a little girl (probably Clarence's daughter). They are all going to the Tower to visit "the gentle princes," but Brackenbury refuses them entry on the orders of "the king." Confused, they question him and he corrects his phrasing to "the Lord Protector." Elizabeth asserts her right as a mother to see her children and Anne supports her, saying that she will "bear the blame," but Brackenbury refuses. Derby arrives, bringing the news that Richard is to be crowned and that Anne is to become queen. She is dismayed at these "Despiteful tidings!" Elizabeth instructs her son Dorset to "cross the seas, / And live with Richmond" (the Lancastrian heir). The duchess curses her own womb for bringing forth Richard, a "cockatrice." Derby urges Anne to go with him, but she would rather die than become queen. As Elizabeth sympathizes, Anne regrets her weakness in believing Richard's "honey words" and expresses her belief that he means to kill her. As they part, Elizabeth encourages everyone to "look back" at the Tower, and asks that the "ancient stones" will pity her "tender babes."

ACT 4 SCENE 2

King Richard ascends his throne with the assistance of Buckingham, a visual metaphor of events so far. Establishing the scene's quick shifts between public and private and demonstrating the increasingly thin margin between Richard's personal and public personae, he and Buckingham speak aside from the rest of the court. Richard fears his kingship is not safe while Prince Edward lives. Announcing that he will "be plain," in direct contrast to his usual linguistic style, he asks Buckingham to kill the princes, but Buckingham asks for "some pause" to think. Buckingham leaves. Aside, Catesby observes that Richard is angry; Richard clearly feels that Buckingham is no longer trustworthy. He calls his page and asks quietly if he knows of anyone whom "corrupting gold / Will tempt unto a close exploit of death." The page suggests a man called Tyrrell. Richard sends the page to fetch him and resolves to himself that Buckingham will "No more" be "neighbor to [his] counsels." Derby brings the news that Dorset has fled to join Richmond. Drawing Catesby aside, Richard sends him to put about the rumor that Anne is ill "and like to die." He contemplates his next plan: to marry Elizabeth's daughter and secure his kingship, which "stands on brittle glass." The page brings Tyrrell, who agrees to kill the princes. Buckingham returns and claims the "earldom of Hereford," as promised, but Richard ignores him and continues discussing Richmond with Derby. This division between the two men marks a turning point in the play: Richard becomes increasingly isolated by his desire to retain power and has lost an ally through distrust, recalling Margaret's curse of Act 1 Scene 3. Realizing that he is out of favor, and therefore in danger, Buckingham flees to Wales.

ACT 4 SCENE 3

Tyrrell reveals that the "bloody act is done." He is shaken, and describes the remorse of the men he hired to do the killing, "fleshed villains, bloody dogs," who nonetheless "Melted with tenderness" and wept when they reported to him. He gives a moving description of the princes, "girdling one another / Within their alabaster innocent arms." Richard arrives and questions Tyrrell: did Tyrrell see the princes' bodies? Did he see them buried? Richard's inhumanity is heightened by the contrast with Tyrrell and the hired men, who, despite their harsh natures, still felt remorse for their actions. Tyrrell leaves and Richard contemplates the latest developments in his plans: Clarence's son is imprisoned, his daughter is "meanly matched" in marriage, and Anne is dead. He leaves to "woo" the young Princess Elizabeth. Ratcliffe brings news that "Morton is fled to Richmond" and that Buckingham is increasing his armies.

Richard resolves to act: in direct contrast to his earlier reliance on language, he declares that "fearful commenting / Is leaden servitor to dull delay" and prepares to do battle.

ACT 4 SCENE 4

Lines 1–134: Margaret has remained concealed in England, watching the "waning" of her enemies. She hears the duchess and Queen Elizabeth approaching, and again withdraws to watch. As the two women mourn the princes, she comments with satisfaction on their grief, seeing it as revenge for her own losses. She comes forward and points out that her curses have come true: Elizabeth is "a most distressed widow," has lost her sons, and is "queen of sad mischance." She starts to leave, but Elizabeth begs her to teach her to curse her enemies. Margaret says that the way to do this is to "Compare dead happiness with living woe" and her grief and therefore her words will pierce like Margaret's. Margaret leaves and Elizabeth and the duchess vow to smother Richard "in the breath of bitter words."

Lines 135–444: Richard arrives and the two women launch a bitter attack on him, directly accusing him of killing the princes and Clarence. Reinforcing the attention to disguise, Elizabeth suggests that his "golden crown" conceals a "branded" forehead, a reference to Cain that also emphasizes the accusations of fratricide. Richard calls for trumpets and drums to drown out "these tell-tale women," saying that he will only listen if they speak courteously. The duchess asserts her right as his mother to speak to Richard, and accuses him of making the earth her "hell." She curses him, hoping that he will die shamed in battle, and leaves. Elizabeth is about to follow, but Richard detains her. She bitterly comments that she has "no more sons" for Richard to "slaughter," but he is only interested in her "royal and gracious" daughter. He explains that he wishes to make her his queen and asks how to win her. Queen Elizabeth bitterly suggests that he send her the bleeding hearts of her brothers. Richard attempts to persuade her in a speech that shows his old command over language, but his charming imagery is juxtaposed by the repellent idea of what he is suggesting, which he is either choosing to ignore or genuinely cannot see. Elizabeth points this out, asking if she should say to her daughter that "her father's brother / Would be her lord?" Echoing the argument with Anne in Act 1 Scene 2, Elizabeth verbally matches Richard, defeating his every move, but he persists until she apparently gives in, although her final words to Richard are ambiguous. However, he chooses to see her as defeated and describes her as a "Relenting fool."

Lines 445–555: Ratcliffe and Catesby report that Richmond's navy is approaching the coast, with the intention of joining Buckingham and his army. Richard orders Catesby to go to the Duke of Norfolk, and grows angry when he does not leave. Catesby explains that he has not been given any message for Norfolk, the first sign of genuine weakness in Richard. Derby brings confirmation that Richmond intends "to claim the crown." Angry, Richard questions Derby's loyalty and, despite Derby's assurances, holds his son George hostage until he has mustered his forces to join Richard in battle. A series of messengers bring bad news, until Richard strikes one man before he can even speak, suggesting his increasing loss of self-control. The man reports that Buckingham's army has been dispersed by floods and that Buckingham is missing. The confusion continues as it is reported first that Richmond is returning to France, and then that he has landed at Milford, but Buckingham has been taken prisoner by Richard's forces. Richard heads for Salisbury to do battle.

ACT 4 SCENE 5

Derby sends word to Richmond of his support, but explains that Richard is holding his son hostage. He also reveals that Queen Elizabeth has consented to Richmond marrying her daughter.

ACT 5 SCENE 1

Buckingham, under guard, asks to speak to Richard, but is refused. He knows that it is his "doomsday," and recalls the words of Margaret's prophecy.

ACT 5 SCENE 2

Richmond's army marches toward Leicester.

ACT 5 SCENE 3

The action shifts quickly between events and the opposing camps, building pace and tension.

Lines 1–19: Richard and followers pitch his tent in Bosworth Field. The mood is somber, but Richard is cheered by news that the "traitors" number only "six or seven thousand," a third the size of his own army. They go to survey the battleground.

Lines 20–47: Richmond and followers pitch his tent on the opposite side of the battlefield, a visual representation of their conflict. Richmond is optimistic, seeing the "golden" sunset as a good omen for the following day. The solar imagery returns us to the opening lines of the play and associated ideas of "summer" replacing a "winter of discontent." Richmond draws up his battle plans and sends Blunt with a "needful note" to Derby.

Lines 48–82: Richard also sends a message to Derby, instructing him to "bring his power / Before sun-rising" or his son will die. He then commands that his horse, "white Surrey," is saddled for the next day, but complains that he lacks "cheer of mind." He writes, then sleeps.

Lines 83–121: Derby secretly visits Richmond to assure him of his loyalty, but tells him that he "may not be too forward" because Richard has his son. He leaves, and Richmond prays before sleeping.

Lines 122–224: As both men sleep, a series of Ghosts appears on stage, all victims of Richard. In turn, they approach Richard and curse him for his role in their deaths, repeating that he will "despair and die." Each Ghost also addresses Richmond, blessing him and wishing him victory. When the last Ghost, that of Buckingham, has spoken, Richard awakes suddenly, crying out: "Give me another horse! Bind up my wounds!" His self-doubt is evident in marked contrast to his earlier confidence and his confusion is clear as he asserts "I am I," then argues "I am not."

Lines 225–272: Richmond wakes from "the sweetest sleep." He reports his "fairest-boding" dream and then addresses his soldiers. His patriotic speech reminds them that "God" and their "good cause" are on their side. He condemns Richard's tyranny.

Lines 273–354: Richard, observing that the sun "disdains to shine," issues orders that Derby and his men are to be summoned. He addresses his troops, focusing on the weaknesses of the enemy and describing Richmond as "a paltry fellow." A messenger informs Richard that Derby has defected, but he has no time to kill his son: the battle has begun.

Lines 355–408: Catesby reports that Richard is fighting on foot, having lost his horse, and is determined to kill Richmond. Richard enters, calling for a horse, but will not withdraw when Catesby asks him to, focusing only on Richmond and sustaining his single-minded desire to retain power until the last. Richmond appears. They fight, and Richard is killed. Richmond declares that "the bloody dog is dead" and claims the throne. He announces his intention to marry Princess Elizabeth, thus uniting "divided York and Lancaster." As Henry VII, he will restore peace to the long-fractured kingdom.

RICHARD III IN PERFORMANCE: THE RSC AND BEYOND

The best way to understand a Shakespeare play is to see it or ideally to participate in it. By examining a range of productions, we may gain a sense of the extraordinary variety of approaches and interpretations that are possible—a variety that gives Shakespeare his unique capacity to be reinvented and made "our contemporary" four centuries after his death.

We begin with a brief overview of the play's theatrical and cinematic life, offering historical perspectives on how it has been performed. We then analyze in more detail a series of productions staged over the last half-century by the Royal Shakespeare Company. The sense of dialogue between productions that can only occur when a company is dedicated to the revival and investigation of the Shakespeare canon over a long period, together with the uniquely comprehensive archival resource of promptbooks, program notes, reviews, and interviews held on behalf of the RSC at the Shakespeare Birthplace Trust in Stratford-upon-Avon, allows an "RSC stage history" to become a crucible in which the chemistry of the play can be explored.

Finally, we hear the voices of an array of practitioners via interviews with a distinguished actor who has played Richard, the director of a highly successful production, and a designer of a complete cycle of Shakespeare's history plays. After the interviews, there is a brief essay by Richard Eyre on the experience of directing the play and touring it in Eastern Europe.

FOUR CENTURIES OF *RICHARD III*: AN OVERVIEW

To judge by the number of contemporary references to the play and reprints of the 1597 Quarto, *Richard III* was an immediate popular success from its first performances in the early 1590s—it did much to make the names of both Shakespeare as playwright and Richard Burbage as leading actor. In his commonplace book, *Palladis Tamia* (1598), Francis Meres cites it as an example of Shakespeare's excellence as a writer of tragedies. The success of Burbage's performance is evidenced in a well-known anecdote recorded in the diary of a law student, John Manningham:

> Upon a time when Burbage played Richard III there was a citizen grew so far in liking with him, that before she went from the play she appointed him to come that night unto her by the name of Richard III. Shakespeare overhearing their conclusion went before, was entertained, and at his game ere Burbage came. Then message being brought that Richard III was at the door, Shakespeare caused return to be made that William the Conqueror was before Richard III.[1]

Apart from the light cast upon the relationship between Shakespeare and Burbage, the story, if true, attests to the success of Richard's seductive onstage persona.

A performance at court was recorded in November 1633 after the birth of Queen Henrietta Maria's son, the Duke of York (later James II), suggesting that the play remained in the repertoire of the King's Men until the closure of the theaters when the country collapsed into civil war in 1642.

After the reopening of the theaters with the Restoration of the monarchy in 1660, *Richard III* was assigned to Thomas Killigrew's company and revived briefly with a new prologue. Thomas Betterton, the best-known actor in the period, played Richard, not in Shakespeare's play, but in an adaptation by John Caryll, *The English Princess* (1666). This was based on events leading up to the Wars of the Roses and Lady Elizabeth's choice of Richmond over Richard. When Shakespeare's play was revived, Betterton played King Edward IV and Richard was played by Samuel Sandford, who specialized in villains. It was with Sandford in mind that Colley Cibber wrote his own immensely successful adaptation, first performed at Drury Lane in 1699.

Cibber's play is little more than half the length of Shakespeare's, with Richard's part even more dominant: the number of his soliloquies is increased whereas the roles of characters such as Buckingham are cut. Hastings, Clarence, Edward, and Margaret are eliminated altogether. There is a concomitant simplification of other characters: Derby (Stanley) and the queen are less ambiguous and Henry Richmond is idealized and given lines from Shakespeare's *Henry V*. Supposing the audience to have a less intimate knowledge of English history and the identity of the various characters than the original Shakespearean playgoers, Cibber invents scenes with Henry VI at the beginning to clarify the politics and history and to demonstrate Richard's past evil-doings. Cibber stages the murder of the princes, although this short scene is unique to the edition of 1700 and it is generally believed that it was cut in performance. In the printed version Shakespeare's lines are in italics while Cibber's are in Roman type. In his introduction Cibber relates how he was obliged to cut the first act in performance on the grounds that the plight of King Henry VI might remind people of the banished James II. The overall effect of Cibber's revisions is twofold: to simplify the plot to make the play more easily understood and to enhance the role of Richard. Cibber's play dominated the stage until 1821 and was, as the critic Stanley Wells points out, "for a couple of centuries probably the most popular play on the English stage."[2] Innovations such as the inclusion of Richard's self-revelatory soliloquy from *3 Henry VI* and the adapted line "Off with his head! So much for Buckingham" continued to be used even in the Laurence Olivier film version of 1955.

Sandford withdrew and Cibber, more comedian than villain, took the part of Richard himself, giving a performance which was almost universally derided. The eighteenth-century theater historian Thomas Davies records how finally "the public grew out of patience and fairly hissed him off the stage."[3] It was David Garrick making his acting debut as Richard in the "illegitimate" theater in Goodman's Fields in 1741 who made the role his own. Garrick's performance and "naturalistic" acting style drew instant acclaim. Recognizing the significance of his performance, fellow actor James Quin commented "if the young fellow was right, he and the rest of the players had all been wrong."[4] In his biography of Garrick, Davies describes the effect of his first performance:

> Mr. Garrick's easy and familiar, yet forcible style in speaking and acting, at first threw the critics into some hesitation concerning the novelty as well as propriety of his manner. They had been long accustomed to an elevation of the voice, with a sudden mechanical depression of its tones, calculated to excite admiration, and to intrap applause. To the just modulation of the words, and concurring expression of the features from the genuine workings of nature, they had been strangers, at least for some time. But after he had gone through a variety of scenes, in which he gave evident proofs of consummate art, and perfect knowledge of character, their doubts were turned into surprise and astonishment, from which they relieved themselves by loud and reiterated applause.[5]

John Philip Kemble played the part but it hardly suited his scholarly, dignified persona, whereas the eccentric George Frederick Cooke at Covent Garden at the beginning of the nineteenth century won considerable acclaim. In her study of the play in performance, Julie Hankey says that "Cooke's Richard was neither subtle and protean like Garrick's, nor lofty like Kemble's; it seems to have been joyfully, gloatingly horrible."[6] The Romantics admired the individualism, if not the villainy of Richard. Of Edmund Kean's performance, William Hazlitt said: "If Mr. Kean does not completely succeed in concentrating all the lines of the character, as drawn by Shakespear [*sic*], he gives an animation, vigor, and relief to the part which we have never seen surpassed. He is more refined than Cooke; more bold, varied and original than Kemble in the same character."[7] Junius Brutus Booth modeled his performance on Kean's and achieved some success, despite the efforts of Kean's supporters to drown him out. Booth later emigrated to America and became a successful actor-manager there. His performance as Richard was noted for its physicality, especially in the concluding battle scenes, as were those of his American successor in the role, Edwin Forrest. The Cibber text was still being used in these performances, though the play was billed as Shakespeare's.

In England, meanwhile, William Charles Macready attempted to restore Shakespeare's text:

> Though he used Cibber's adaptation, this was a Richard more Shakespearian than most, and his own briefly performed adaptation of Shakespeare, while not successful, demonstrated his aims. His Richard was intellectually supple, witty, proud, and commanding. He was less bitter than Kean, full of an organizing energy, with a passionate enjoyment of his vengeance. The performance was thus witty and controlled, with much evidence of suppressed power.[8]

Henry Irving was praised for finally eliminating Cibber in his production at the Lyceum in 1877. He managed to restore even more of Shakespeare's text in a subsequent revival of 1896. Gone with Cibber's text, though, was his fundamental conception of the role and Irving was blamed for this change of approach. As a reviewer explained in the *Athenaeum*:

> All that is conventional in tragedy is gone, leaving us musing whether after all we were wise in demanding its removal . . . We have no "sawing of the air with your hand thus" [*Hamlet*, 3.2.4–5], and we have no search for the flea in the actor's bosom, as was irreverently described a favourite gesture of Charles Kean, Macready, and Phelps. We have, on the contrary, a polished presentment of Court manners, in which nothing offends and is as nearly as possible real. Where, however, is tragedy? It is gone. Richard III is not now a tragic role. It is what is conventionally called "a character part." Very fine is some of the acting, and the character of Richard is charged with a ferocity that is impressive and we dare say original. We are, however, never scorched or electrified. We are gratified, tickled, amused.[9]

The old-style melodrama was still in evidence, for example in John Barrymore's 1920 performance at the Plymouth Theater in New York, a production which incorporated even more of *3 Henry VI* than Cibber had done. The show lasted until one o'clock in the morning, but still had a rapturous reception. Tyrone Guthrie at the Old Vic in London in 1937 offered, by contrast, an ironic modern production. As the London *Times* reviewer explained:

> Mr. Emlyn Williams might have attempted the difficult return to full-blooded stage tradition and sought to carry conviction by storm. Instead he wisely took oblique means to the same end. By giving Richard a humorous relish of his own excesses he did what he could to prevent the audience from smiling at them in the wrong way . . . if we were amused, so in his own devilish way was the royal murderer. The actor had cleverly outflanked our criticism of a demoded tragic villain, and at the same time had contrived to make of him an arresting theatrical figure—a figure of stealthy, cat-like cunning, with more perhaps of the poisoner than the soldier in his composition but formidably, relentlessly dominant and consistently exciting.[10]

The Second World War changed attitudes to the play and saw the start of productions which related more or less obliquely to fascism. Donald Wolfit confessed that his study of Richard in the 1942 production at the Strand Theater had been influenced by Hitler.[11] The most famous postwar Richard, indeed the most famous Richard of all time thanks to his later film version, was Laurence Olivier. His acclaimed performance reconciled different facets of Richard, as the critic J. C. Trewin recognized:

> A Richard must make his theatrical effects boldly; at the same time he must expose the man's brain. It is the marriage of intellect and dramatic force, of bravura and cold reason, which so distinguishes Mr. Laurence Olivier's study at the New Theatre.[12]

Kenneth Tynan analyzed Olivier's performance in detail:

> From a sombre and uninventive production this brooding, withdrawn player leapt into life, using the circumambient

gloom as his springboard. Olivier's Richard eats into the memory like acid into metal, but the total impression is one of lightness and deftness. The whole thing is taken at a baffling speed when one recalls how perfectly, even finically, it is articulated: it is Olivier's trick to treat each speech as a kind of plastic vocal mass, and not as a series of sentences whose import must be precisely communicated to the audience: the method is impressionistic. He will seize on one or two phrases in each paragraph which, properly inserted, will unlock its whole meaning: the rest he discards, with exquisite idleness. To do this successfully he needs other people on the stage with him: to be ignored, stared past, or pushed aside during the lower reaches, and gripped and buttonholed when the wave rises to its crested climax. For this reason Olivier tends to fail in soliloquy—except when, as in the opening speech of Richard, it is directed straight at the audience, who then become his temporary foils . . . Olivier the actor needs reactors: just as electricity, *in vacuo*, is unseen, unfelt, and powerless.[13]

Actors since the 1950s have inevitably felt the burden of Olivier's performance as they have sought to offer their own representations of the role. Despite this a number of actors have succeeded in thoughtful, original, and exciting productions of the play; for example, Antony Sher in Bill Alexander's 1984 production, Simon Russell Beale in that of Sam Mendes, and Ian McKellen for Richard Eyre at the National Theatre in London in 1992.

The play was edited to form part of Peter Hall and John Barton's radical analysis of power politics, *The Wars of the Roses*, for the RSC in 1963, a production that received great acclaim and that was shown (in much abridged form) on television.

David Wheeler's production at the Cort Theater, New York, starring Al Pacino in 1979, received mixed reviews; Pacino's quest for the essence of the character was further developed in his idiosyncratic film *Looking for Richard* (1996), in which he explores the text and the rehearsal process in a series of workshops while attempting to relate the plot to the world around him. The Rustaveli Company of Soviet Georgia created a highly politicized production in 1979–80.

Directed by Robert Sturua, it received rave reviews, especially for physical inventiveness of a kind that also characterized a production by the Odeon Theatre of Bucharest that toured internationally in 1994, making particularly strong use of masks suggestive of Richard's animal crest, the boar. In 2003 Barry Kyle directed the play at the Globe Theatre with an all-female cast. Kathyrn Hunter's engagingly "ironic and humorously amoral Richard"[14] was generally admired, as was Linda Bassett's powerful Queen Margaret.

The most notable films have been Laurence Olivier's (1955) and Ian McKellen's (1995). Olivier's was set in the Middle Ages and is theatrical in its use of long shots, which give it a static feel. The diction, especially Olivier's famously clipped tones, now seems dated. For the McKellen film, which was developed out of Richard Eyre's stage production for the National Theatre in London, director Richard Loncraine updated the period and set, relating the play to the 1936 British abdication crisis and the rise of Oswald Mosley's British Union of Fascists. Both movies open spectacularly and employ what film critics call the "forbidden look": in soliloquy, Olivier and McKellen stare straight into the camera, engaging the audience in a similar manner to the stage actor speaking directly into the auditorium.

AT THE RSC

Richard: A Discovery of Evil

In the last fifty years *Richard III* in performance has come to symbolize evils particularly relevant to our times. When performed as part of a history play cycle involving the three parts of *Henry VI*, the play and the character's significance become part of a wider examination of sociopolitical concerns. When performed in isolation, the character of Richard becomes dominant, and the play usually delves into psychological territory encompassing modern beliefs on the nature of evil in man. In creating the early RSC landmark production *The Wars of the Roses* in 1963, directors Peter Hall and John Barton edited and rewrote the three parts of *Henry VI* so they could be played in conjunction with *Richard III* as a trilogy. *Richard III* was subsequently performed as part of a sequence involving the *Henry VI* plays in 1988, 2001, and 2006–08.

The Wars of the Roses, strongly influenced by the politically charged, "alienating," "epic theater" of Bertolt Brecht and the work of the Berliner Ensemble, took the play away from an acting tradition which had revolved around the star actor/director. It was a conscious repudiation of the "Olivier tradition," which, in the words of theater historian Hugh Richmond, "was largely marked by an extremely naïve moral structure supposedly excusing a delight in the portrait of melodramatic evil incarnate." "We can," Richmond continues, "find a far greater range of sociological interests in Hall's production than any before it."[15]

Peter Hall's examination of the tragedy of kingship in the program note pointed to the dilemma of whether a ruler can remain moral when the instincts which placed him in a position of power are essentially selfish and amoral, animalistic:

> Man in action is basically an animal . . . To hunt better, men unite into packs. Then the man who kills the beast becomes the king, and must kill his rivals to remain king . . . The tension between man the animal in action, murdering to protect, or lying to save, and the moral man trying to rule by a developed human ethic is what makes history tragic. I believe this is still the dilemma of power.[16]

Short in stature and boyish in appearance, Ian Holm cut a remarkably different figure from the likes of Olivier and Christopher Plummer, who played the part for the RSC in 1961. Critics seemed to miss the point of this new-look Richard, commenting on how his physicality diminished his domination of the play. This deliberate choice on the part of the director emphasized that Richard was only one in a long line of pretenders to the throne. What the designer referred to as the "great steel cage of war" portrayed the battle between the Yorkists and the Lancastrians as a disintegration of the country from feudal to fascist, its protagonists crushed or shaped by the processes of history, and the warring ethos of their families: "Richard, once on the throne [rules] by police-state methods. The barons supporting him are dressed in the black helmets and jackboots of bully-boy Fascists and tramping in unison to his every command."[17]

Connecting *Richard III* with the major experience of evil in political form during the twentieth century—the rise of Fascism in Germany, resulting in the election of Hitler and the horrors which followed, demonstrated how the play could be taken away from medieval melodrama and conferred with contemporary relevance. It also pointed to a more nihilistic vision of the play, reminding the audience while they were watching that, although this tyrant was stopped, many more were to follow who were far worse.

In 1974 Barry Kyle's production at The Other Place studio theater took place in "an asylum with all the characters dressed in costumes vaguely reminiscent of concentration camps."[18] Ian Richardson, who played Richard, was fascinated by what he called

The schizophrenia . . . in the very last soliloquy, the nightmare one where he seems to be two people talking to each other. The one is some horrid, monstrous spectre, the other what is left of the good soul of Richard, if anything is left at all. Any examination of that soliloquy will show that Richard's mind has completely gone, in much the same way as some of the monsters of our own lifetime—Stalin, Hitler, Idi Amin all spring to mind. This is total schizophrenia born out of megalomania.[19]

In order to make the psychology behind his Richard something recognizable, Henry Goodman (2003) found a parallel for Richard's deranged mind with modern fictional serial killers, such as Hannibal Lecter. Similarly, actor Antony Sher described how he looked at the behavior of recent real-life serial killers in order to get a handle on Richard's completely amoral behavior. Dennis Nilsen was a British serial killer who lived in London; during a murderous spree which started in 1978 and lasted five years, he killed more than a dozen men in his home and disposed of the bodies in his garden, attic, and other rooms about his house. Reading up on the case in preparation to play Richard, Sher became fascinated by the banal normality of elements of the psychopath's character sitting alongside the perversity.

Richard's "unnatural" tendencies are linked in the text with animal imagery. In Elizabethan times man was held to be the highest of creatures and exhibiting animalistic behavior was seen as a fall from grace, a sin against the order of the universe, which rendered the sinner somehow subhuman. In Shakespeare, characters who upset the natural order of things, whether turning against their family members or against the state, are often referred to as predatory or poisonous animals. Richard is referred to as a "poisonous bunch-backed toad," a "bottled spider." In productions of *Richard III* these beliefs about "unnatural" behavior are embodied in Richard's deformity, physically demonstrating his twisted nature and his closeness to the animal world. In 1970 Norman Rodway repulsed many a critic by his resemblance to swine: "He lumbers onstage at Stratford, blinking at the sun: his great pig-head appears to have been crew-cut, and some animal's skin is slung over his hump."[20] Antony Sher (1984) paid more attention to the spiderlike qualities of Richard as he wove his web of deception around the court: "The central image of his Richard he built on the 'bottled spider,' the assumption being that here was a creature too venomous to be set free."[21]

The most dominant characteristic of the Sher portrayal was his use of crutches to give Richard an extraordinary mobility: "huge black arachnid-legs which flew him across the stage in giant leaps, and which he used as extension limbs to fight off attackers, beat lackeys and, in one famous moment, lift Lady Anne's skirt and probe between her legs."[22] Dressed entirely in black throughout most of the production he appeared for the opening soliloquy like a black spider emerging through the finely wrought gothic screen which covered the stage, from the tombs of the dead, which lay behind in darkness. The *Sunday Times* critic described the effect:

The opening lines are spoken quietly, almost didactically; but with "But I, that am not framed for sportive tricks" [1.1.14], Sher advances menacingly on the audience, his body swinging like a missile on the adeptly manipulated callipers that support it, his hump displayed with a kind of inverted pride . . . we are

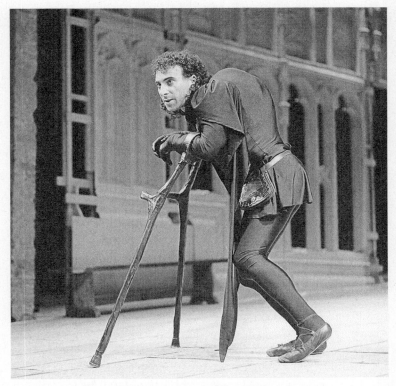

2. Bottled spider with calipers—Antony Sher, 1984.

spellbound by a sense of fiendish energy and huge physical
strength.[23]

Simon Russell Beale (1992) admitted: "I haven't the physical dex-
terity to play him as a spider, as Tony Sher did. I'm the 'bunch-
backed toad.'"[24] This was another performance much admired by
the critics:

He supremely shows physical self-hatred rebounding into
social revenge . . . Shrouded in ankle-length cloaks hiding

who knows what deformities, small flat head rocking with reptilian cunning on a roll of neck fat, he outdoes even Queen Margaret's catalogue of bestial comparisons.[25]

We are first aware of him not as a body, however, but as an undefined threat, a sinister creaking noise as he paces about shrouded in darkness.[26]

A stick is heard tapping across the stage, the lights go up, and there he is with his scrubbed skull, pink jowls and vast hump: a depraved blend of Mr. Punch and A. A. Milne's Piglet, gloating over the havoc he will wreak.[27]

Many actors have found Richard's deformity a pitiable circumstance, motivating his decision to "prove a villain" and take the path of evil. Like Iago, he despises the beauty in other people's lives that makes him seem ugly by comparison. Unlike Iago, he is outwardly marked and this sets him apart: "I am myself alone." Deformity lay at the center of Alan Howard's performance in 1980. This is how various newspaper critics described the performance:

Howard's Gloucester is not an unfathomable monster; still less a scourge of God visited upon a sacrilegious land. He is a cripple getting even with those who have the use of their legs . . . Besides the surgical boot, Mr. Howard is encumbered with a chain round the left thigh which he has to tug to get the leg moving.[28]

His dangling right arm seems to contain a built-in dagger ever ready to point at people's throats.[29]

Where all recent Richards have limped and scuttled efficiently round the stage, this one is uncomfortable, liable to stumble, often in pain . . . while Buckingham talks to the citizens, he practices a straight walk with slow agonized concentration, a performance he repeats at his coronation. . . . As this Richard's preoccupation with his grotesque body grows, so does his suspicious isolation from those around him. When Buckingham lightly says that he would play the orator "as if the fee were for myself," he eyes him with real suspicion . . . This is no Mr. Punch, but the bitter self-hating Richard of an earlier tradition.[30]

David Troughton, who played Richard in the manner of a sinister clown in Steven Pimlott's 1995 production, was helped in his performance by relating Richard's deformity to a genuine medical condition:

According to history, Richard had come into the world feet first, a breach birth . . . As Richard was dragged out by his feet, one of his hips might have been displaced causing extreme discomfort all his life. As he grew up, because of the pain of walking, a severe limp would develop, forcing his spine to grow crooked, giving the appearance of one shoulder being higher than the other . . . His arm could also have been deformed at birth or through an illness such as polio. In pain all his life? What an insight into a character. Here was one very simple explanation for Richard's malevolence.[31]

In modern productions Richard is also often associated with childishness, exhibiting the selfish amorality of a young child who only sees his own needs. This might be the arrested development of a man of war in a domestic, social world. Anton Lesser (1988) described how in the first half of the play Richard "is entirely concerned with getting":

"I want that, I want that" and then "I've got it, I've got it . . . Oh, I'm bored now." So I decided to rush to the throne with a scream of possessive delight and leap into it . . . they all go and just leave him sitting there on his own in a throne that is miles too big for him, his legs dangling down like a little child's, quite unable to reach the floor. The pathos of that image is important at this pivotal point in the play, the wild excitement of leaping into that seat followed in a second or two by the loneliness and stillness of the little figure dwarfed by it.[32]

In Sean Holmes' 2003 production childhood became an essential theme and part of the scenic design, even extending to the throne, which looked like an outsized high chair:

> [A] rocking-horse became connected with the young Duke of York, Richard's namesake . . . it provided a link with Richard's own childhood . . . on a horse, even a rocking horse, he is freed of his deformity and becomes big and grown-up and cured of his illness . . . at the end, the rocking horse would reappear when . . . the ghosts were revealed, young York now riding it with terrible energy, and Richard's cry "My kingdom for a horse" taking on a disturbing sense of the need to escape again into childhood innocence.[33]

The production also featured inclusion of an unscripted character, "a page, a young boy in his own image . . . a frequent, silent presence near Richard, his only companion."[34]

In 1970 Norman Rodway's performance verged on that of the naughty adolescent. When sealing Hastings' fate at the council meeting, he "fairly shrieks with delight as he jumps away from Hastings, leaving him holding what's supposed to be a withered arm."[35] As reviewer D. A. N. Jones put it:

> We are in a haunted nursery, with a toy-box full of sharp swords and real skulls . . . Richard, himself puerile, likes playing with children; he has a dressing-up box, with wigs and rusty armor, which he uses when stage-managing his coups. There's a fascinating sequence, while he is awaiting news from the Lord Mayor, when he simply fidgets and makes faces, like a bored and repulsive toddler.[36]

The other side of Richard is the side he shows to the audience, the actor, the comedian, the arch-manipulator. By use of humor Richard gets the audience on his side, so that, in the first half of the play, when he commits some hideous act, the audience cannot help but laugh with him. This humor is of the blackest kind, also making the audience complicit, a fact that, if the production is done well, they should later

3. Richard the showman—Henry Goodman, 2003.

regret. This black comedy, "pushing the extremes of horror and
farce,"[37] is very modern and in tune with contemporary tastes, the
technique having been adopted by many directors of horror films.*

Many productions have emphasized Richard the self-conscious
actor. In 2003 Henry Goodman emerged through a traditional red
curtain for his soliloquy and was picked out by a spotlight. Goodman's intention was to

> make absolutely clear . . . that Richard has to dress up for this
> new summer of opportunity . . . And it sickens him . . . In per-

---

* In *Man Bites Dog* (Belgium, 1992, dir. Rémy Belvaux) and *The Last Horror Movie* (UK, 2003,
dir. Julian Richards), the serial killer, like Richard, talks to the audience directly about his
actions, plots, and feelings (or lack of them) about what he does, often comically. These films,
including others such as *Funny Games* (Austria, 1997, dir. Michael Haneke), act as an
indictment against media violence and the viewers' ability to watch violent acts without
appropriate emotion. Ultimately, they shock the audience back into a sense of their own
humanity. As with *Richard III* there is a breaking point between the audience and the
protagonist where laughter dies and creeping horror takes hold, not least because of their
earlier complicity through humor.

formance, I became so debonair and deft as the opening character, audiences thought I was playing an actor who strips off his clothes and plays Richard—but that is never what I intended.[38]

Observer critic Susannah Clapp described the effect:

Cock-eyed, hobble-legged, leering with scorn, Henry Goodman gives us Richard III as angry showman. As he nuzzles into Queen Anne's breast, he rolls a knowing eye at the audience . . . From the beginning, Sean Holmes's Edwardian production underlines the idea of Richard as the manic trickster . . . He delivers the winter of discontent speech as a rapid music-hall turn, garishly snickering and capering.[39]

The horror of the violence onstage is often relieved by moments of nervous laughter. On the line about dogs barking at him, Goodman's Richard "limps into the wings and stabs some poor yelping cur to death."[40] The beheading of Hastings has provided ample opportunity for "horrid laughter." In 1995 David Troughton explained how:

During the mock siege of London, Hastings's severed head . . . covered in a white, blooded cloth, is brought on by Ratcliffe, invariably causing a laugh of revulsion from the audience as it is hurled into the air, landing on stage with a heavy thud. This is perfectly in keeping with the humorous charade that Richard is perpetrating, and indeed, I heighten the moment by stabbing my knife through it, then presenting the skewered head to the Mayor of London. More laughter follows. The blade, however, gets stuck and only comes free with a struggle . . . which heightens the audience's gleeful horror.[41]

In 2003, Hastings' head was accidentally trodden and tripped over by Richard. Likewise, in Bill Alexander's 1984 production the head of Hastings was thrown from one character to another like a rugby ball, testing the Mayor's loyalty to Richard when he is obliged to join in the game:

When the head was tossed about, the audience froze; but sec-
onds later they were thawed by laughter . . . He was, flat-out, a
man obsessed with power, a man who wanted to attain the
throne as quickly as possible, and a man who wanted to have
fun along the way . . . and he demands that we engage in it
with him.[42]

Simon Russell Beale (1992) was so repulsive in appearance that
when he came onto the stage, the sound of barking dogs heralded his
entrance. The historian David Starkey, doubling as a theater
reviewer, gave a good account:

He is wearing Doc Martens, dark pegtop trousers, a long
scruffy coat and an open-necked shirt. . . . This is Richard the
alternative comedian . . . The head is shaven; the eyes pop; the
lips stretch hungrily; the body distends like an air-cushion
with a spring inside . . . The effect is grotesque and horribly
funny; pure slapstick, when Richard squashes a dish of strawberries on his forehead to simulate a wound to persuade the
Lord Mayor of the reality of the plot against him.[43]

The idea of Richard as "jester" or comedian was built into the costume design of the 1992 production, with David Troughton don-
ning an "Elizabethan-looking doublet together with very odd short
culottes," giving Richard "a mischievous 'Mr. Punch' feel . . . not
only was he a joker, he was an evil joker, bent on mass destruction for
his own ends which made him very dangerous indeed—the funny
man in red whom no-one suspects . . . smiling as he stabs his victims
in the back."[44]

Cursing Women

Richard's lack of understanding with regard to women proves his
downfall. Actor Henry Goodman noted that "there is a real misog-
yny about Richard as he fantasizes about love but is incapable of giving or receiving it. In his deformity he reasons . . . that love is
something he will never receive because of the world's love of
beauty."[45]

The cursing of Richard by his mother is often performed as the moment which undoes him, shakes him out of his bravura, unsettles him and seals his fate. For David Troughton's Richard, the twisted relationship between mother and son was central to the character. His hatred of the world was derived from the Duchess of York's complete absence of love for him. For his meeting with his mother in the fourth act he placed himself, with great awkwardness, on the ground, his head in her lap. Wanting her blessing he received only her curse. Director Steven Pimlott identified it as "a peculiarly terrible scene, a mother cursing her child in a way that is unique in Shakespeare." Open-mouthed with horror (Troughton was influenced by Edvard Munch's famous painting *The Scream*), Richard "hurled himself away from her and toward the crown which he had placed on the ground."[46]

Anton Lesser described the devastating effect the mother's curse had on his Richard:

> She needs to express the horror at what she has given birth to . . . to make it terminal. "I shall never speak to thee again." . . . In our production Richard's response was punctuated by his rhythmically wounding himself in the hand with his dagger. The idea I wanted to express was that he feels he must hurt, must mutilate himself because if he doesn't he will kill his mother in his rage at what, in his eyes, she has been responsible for.[47]

The curse on Alan Howard's Richard (1980) created a mental disturbance from which he never recovered: "His mother's curse leaves him so shattered that he plays the next scene with Elizabeth in earnest, as though he might really find in her a new mother. From then on he is on the edge of madness."[48]

The duchess' lack of motherly love has an impact on how Richard relates to other women in the play. The "wooing" scene of Lady Anne reveals much but, often heavily cut in performance, is a particularly difficult scene to make convincing. Actor Anton Lesser explains:

> Richard must not be seen by Anne to be "acting." The more she is confused about how genuine his feelings are, the more

unbalancing it will be for her . . . Richard bases his strategy
on attack: everything she accuses him of he accepts, with the
proviso that everything he has done he has done for her. He
makes her, quite specifically, an "accessory" . . . producing a
sense of guilt . . . she is forced into the belief that it was her
body, her physicality, all that she as a devout Christian is trying to rise above, which provoked his behaviour. The idea we
were aiming for was that guilt about her own sexuality, rather
than any particular attraction toward his, is what governs her
behaviour here.[49]

Lisa Stevenson, who played Lady Anne in 2003, found a truth to the
scene through this guilt, and through the belief in the centrality of
cursing to the structure of the play:

A lot of women suffer from guilt when they're grieving . . . So
when Richard comes along and tells Anne that it is her fault
that her husband and father-in-law died, she was so vulnerable
that on some weird level she believed it. I think that's why she
doesn't kill him . . . I had an idea for the play that the sickness
might be pregnancy-related . . . when she returns as a ghost,
she says "thy wife, that wretched Anne . . . That never slept a
quiet hour with thee." I think Richard has been raping her and
I think that it's been horrific . . . Her prophecy about Richard's
marriage comes true: "If ever he have wife, let her be made /
. . . miserable." And she says "If ever he have child, abortive
be it / Prodigious and untimely brought to life." I had an idea
that I was going to know that I was pregnant and the baby
(Richard's baby) was going to have died in my womb, but still
be there, which would lead to terrible blood poisoning.[50]

In other productions Lady Anne has been portrayed as slightly more
resistant and knowing than the text suggests. Although Aislin
McGuckin (2000) put up "a particularly dignified resistance to his
wooing," she seemed "grimly aware that in doing so she has signed
her own death warrant."[51] Annabel Apsion as Lady Anne in 1992
"calls his bluff to the extent of actually nicking his proffered breast

with his sword. For a split second, Richard is disoriented by the drawn blood, but then his cold, appraising eyes flick back to Anne, keenly monitoring how this upset may work to his advantage."[52]

However, there have also been productions where Lady Anne's desperate state has made her a more willing conquest. Of Terry Hands' 1980 production one critic wrote:

> "Did you not kill this King?" "I grant ye." I have never heard this cheeky exchange without it raising a laugh until last night when it was lost in the high-speed passionate crescendo between [Alan] Howard and Sinead Cusack, which is played toward her capitulation with the drive of an orgasm.[53]

> Lady Anne (Sinead Cusack) . . . throws off her black gown at the moment of her submission to reveal a warm red dress beneath.[54]

For his production in 1970 Hands' direction suggested that

> her attraction is a kind of kinkiness . . . One moment she is self-righteously whacking him over the back with a large cross, in a naïve attempt to exorcise him; the next, she is giggling and dabbling lips with him, notwithstanding the corpse of her husband nearby. The hand-maiden of the Lord is abruptly revealed as the Devil's concubine.[55]

In 1984 and 2001 Queen Elizabeth became the prime target of Richard's misogynistic rage. The *Times Literary Supplement* reviewer of Michael Boyd's production (2001) commented:

> His wooing of her—as mother-in-law, rather than as wife . . . seems almost more of a showdown than the one soon to ensue on Bosworth Field . . . At first traumatized into shaking incoherence by her husband's death, she discovers reserves of strength and eloquence that make her, theatrically, Richard's most potent antagonist. As a tall, intelligent, determined woman of non-royal birth, she embodies all that Richard finds most threatening.[56]

In 1984 the tussle between the two of them was played as more physical than verbal. The critic Chris Hassel wrote in the *Shakespeare Quarterly* that

> [Antony] Sher is brutal with Elizabeth from the start. He forces her face to him with his sceptre. He pulls her around by the bodice to make her face him again on the throne. Once he throws her to the ground. But she is not without her own weapons against this intimidation. She has those withering words of irony . . . also . . . a venomous kiss for Richard at the end, from which he recoils as from an adder's sting.[57]

Like a primeval spirit conjured by both grief past and grief to come, Margaret emerges as the embodiment of female revenge. Her curses on the court prophesy the play's events and, almost too late, the distressed wives and mothers desire knowledge of her powers in order to stop Richard. Margaret's evocation of ancient tribalism is often emphasized in modern productions by representations of witchcraft. In 2001, Fiona Bell, who also played Queen Margaret in the three parts of *Henry VI*, carried the bones of her dead son around with her in a sack, taking them out and arranging them as a human skeleton when conjuring her curses on the court. Penny Downie, who played Margaret in 1988, explained how

> one could see her as this ageless figure of moral nemesis, who brings on to the stage the entire Wars of the Roses and who has herself been purified by suffering to play this final moral role . . . People have to hear the curse if it is to work . . . Like an aborigine pointing the bone—you have to believe you are going to die if you are going to die. And the fact is that they all do believe in these curses, none more so than Richard.[58]

In 1992, Cherry Morris as Margaret "intoned from a chalk circle,"[59] and appeared at the death of each of Richard's victims:

> The almost ritual manner in which all of Margaret's prophetic curses are fulfilled is brought out by the simple but powerful

way [Sam] Mendes has her stand aloft each time in one of the doors of the back-screen and reintone the curse over the last speeches of Richard's various victims.[60]

At the battle of Bosworth Field, when Richard was on the point of victory, the appearance of Margaret "mesmerises him and seals his doom."[61]

Providence and the Supernatural

It is interesting that Shakespeare doesn't write "The Battle," as he does in other History plays. He writes 12 or 14 pages on the night before the Battle of Bosworth and about a page on the battle. Which means that, in a way, Richard's battle is lost the night before it has begun.[62]

Traditional religious imagery of good and evil often permeates modern productions, making powerful statements on the nature of providence. For Adrian Noble's 1988 production Anton Lesser described how:

The goblet in which Ratcliffe brought the wine . . . has something of symbolic potency for Richard in his dream, so that the cup of wine becomes the communion cup, the blood of Christ . . . here is a symbol of retribution, deliverance, sin, forgiveness, ceremony, final judgement . . . when he snaps back into consciousness, and realizes it was all a dream, the power of all those curses hits him: "I shall despair"—and die. The impact of that was increased, we felt, by having Richard also hear what is said to Richmond . . . During [the soliloquy that follows the dream] he continues verbally the action of stabbing himself, which in our production, had followed his mother's curse. He pins himself like a butterfly to a board . . . he cannot escape the truth . . . It is as though a veil has been taken away from Richard; he has been in a state of deep illusion, not just through the dream but through his life, and the curtain has now been drawn back and he looks in the mirror and sees every line on his own face—like the picture of Dorian Gray.[63]

David Troughton described something similar in his 1995 rendition of the role:

> Alone at last, Richard attempts a final reconciliation with the audience and God. I take both the bread and the wine and set up a simple altar on the rubble-strewn stage, using my cross-handled dagger as a primitive crucifix. But instead of finding a restored friendship and possible redemption in this act of the Last Sacrament, on drinking the blood of Christ I conjure up a manifestation of the audience's hatred; the ghosts of all Richard's past victims who sit beside him at a large oblong table, surrounding the beatific Richmond, praying for Richard's defeat and the future King Henry's success. The image of Jesus and his disciples looms large but this time it is Richard, the devil, and not Richmond, the Son of God, who has certainly had his Last Supper.[64]

This approach has continuity with William Hogarth's famous painting of David Garrick at the same moment, in which the crucifix is prominent.

The Ghosts are also effective representatives of the force of providence. In 1984 they emerged from behind four large tombs which dominated the gothic set:

> Each ghost holds a single candle. Smoke swirls around their feet . . . Some, of course, have been buried there since Tewkesbury. Each prophesies with the stillness of truth; each remains on stage as the others appear. Occasionally all echo key words of prayer and prophecy, like participants in a supernatural ritual.[65]

Michael Boyd in 2001, and again when his production was revived and adapted in 2006–08, populated his stage with the ghosts of the dead, "emphasising the mad futility of the endless cycle of revenge killings, which only ends with the arrival of the future Henry VII at the end of Richard III."[66] The Shakespearean scholar Barbara Hodgdon provides an excellent account:

At Richard III's coronation . . . the huge upstage doors opened, revealing a procession of ghostly victims . . . Among them . . . was Margaret, leading her dead son, and then Henry VI, robed in white, entered to prostrate himself on the floor, hands outstretched as though crucified. Last of all was York, and it was he who proclaimed "God save King Richard, of that name the third!" echoed by the others . . . the line between the dead and the living began to blur: apparitions all, caught momentarily in the "bottled spider's" web . . . [Following the battle and Richard's demise] . . . With Richard's body lying alone on stage, all drew back: standing in the exits and aisles, they watched him rise . . . and prepare to leave. But as he turned upstage to go, the doors of the fortress opened: there stood Henry VI, all in white. For an instant, the two faced one another, double faces of kingship: Richard, symptomatic of the tyranny of the individual . . . Henry, his complete opposite . . . Richard's mantra—"I am myself alone"—seemed to apply equally to them both.[67]

The Ghosts almost always appear in the final battle in order to oversee the working out of the curse, and sometimes to actively assist in Richard's execution. In 1980, Terry Hands "pull[ed] out all the stops at the end with the ghosts of all Richard's victims lining up at Bosworth and crowding round him in clusters while Richmond puts the sword in . . . it certainly gives you the sense that England has been purged of evil."[68] In 1998:

Instead of visiting Richard in a dream in his tent on the eve of Bosworth, the ghosts of his casualties wait to intervene and distract him with counsels of despair in his climactic sword fight with Jo Stone-Fewing's squeaky-clean Richmond. The spectres of the young princes jump with demonic playfulness on Richard's shoulder and pop up between his legs. The transpositions give graphic emphasis to the idea that it is the recognition of what he has done, rather than Richmond that defeats him.[69]

Terry Hands' first (1970) production omitted the final battle, and instead Richard was "encircled by ghosts of his murdered victims, who perform a dance of death"[70] and then lead him off stage.

In 1995 the Ghosts of Richard's victims had occupied a specific area of the stage during the production. At the end of the play the battle again was omitted and Richard was not murdered but, aware of the inevitability of his death, put down his sword and made his way to the Ghosts' area, watched by them from above. After Richmond's final speech he gave him a slow ironic handclap.

ACTOR, DIRECTOR, AND DESIGNER: SIMON RUSSELL BEALE (RICHARD, 1992), BILL ALEXANDER (DIRECTOR, 1984), AND TOM PIPER (DESIGNER, 2006)

The Actor: Simon Russell Beale, born in 1961, studied at Cambridge University. He came to prominence as a Shakespearean actor with the RSC in the early 1990s, when he played Thersites in *Troilus and Cressida*, Ariel in *The Tempest*, and Richard III in the production discussed here, which toured the country in an intimate, mobile auditorium set up in sports halls in towns that generally lacked access to professional theater. All three productions were directed by Sam Mendes, with whom Beale has continued to work in Shakespearean and other classical roles, including Iago at London's National Theatre and Malvolio at Mendes' Donmar Warehouse. Also a notable Hamlet at the National, he is especially admired for the intelligence of his verse-speaking.

The Director: Bill Alexander, born in 1948, trained as a theater director at the Bristol Old Vic. He joined the RSC as an assistant director in 1977 and then became a resident director in 1980. His reputation was strongly established through three productions starring Sir Antony Sher: *Tartuffe* and a play about its author Molière, and then the *Richard III* of 1984, which he talks about here. The experience of being in this famous production, which transferred to London's Barbican Theatre in 1985 and then toured internationally the following year, was recorded by Sher in his book *The Year of the King*.

From 1992 to 2000, Bill Alexander was artistic director of the Birmingham Repertory Theatre.

The Designer: Tom Piper was appointed Royal Shakespeare Company associate designer in 2003. He graduated from Trinity College, Cambridge, before training at the Slade School of Art. He has designed productions from pantomime to opera, staged in every kind of theater including the Royal National Theatre, Abbey Theatre Dublin, Lyric Hammersmith Studio, and the Royal Albert Hall. His sets are characterized by striking uncluttered designs which allow imaginative use of the stage space. Materials tend to be stylish but undecorated: wood, metal, plain colored cloth. He designed RSC artistic director Michael Boyd's tetralogy of the three parts of *Henry VI* and *Richard III* in both their small-scale versions in the intimate Swan Theatre (2000) and their larger-scale reincarnation in the Stratford Courtyard Theatre and the London Roundhouse (2006–08).

In terms of Shakespeare's vision of the Wars of the Roses and the eventual resolution at Bosworth Field, with Henry Richmond becoming king and inaugurating the Tudor dynasty, the world of the play is very medieval, very fifteenth century. At the same time, the rise and fall of a tyrant is a perennial historical theme, and there have been very successful productions set in, say, 1930s Germany or the Baghdad of Saddam Hussein. What sort of a setting did you and your designer choose, and why?

Alexander: We chose a medieval setting. Our starting point was the relationship between this early play of Shakespeare's and the great cycles of mystery and miracle plays that were fading memories during the writer's youth. Richard seemed to me a direct descendant of the Vice figure in these plays—wicked yet beguiling; fascinating, seductive, and deadly. At least this is his starting point, but his tragedy is to develop a conscience, or at least a terrifying sense of self-consciousness that also forms a bridge from the ritualistic, allegorical past to the emergent psychologically realistic present that Shakespeare was helping to create. The set was modeled on the interior of the chapter house in Worcester Cathedral, linking the play to

4. Tom Piper's set design for Michael Boyd's history cycle at Stratford-upon-Avon: a bare platform with a cylindrical metallic tower behind. Entrances could be made through the clanging doors or down ladders and ropes. Ghosts and overhearers could appear in the recess above the doors.

the roots of medieval religious drama. The central character's mental progress from mythical mask of evil to vulnerable self-awareness for me shaped the play. Analogies with figures such as Hitler or Saddam seemed pointlessly superficial, nor did I want to lose the significance of the *actual* historical moment—late medieval to early modern and *its* relevance to now.

Piper: The designer works with the director through discussions, sketches, and models to create the world of the play—an environment in which the actors can tell the story dressed in clothes that reflect their nature, wealth, and status within that world. That world may alter over time as characters and their situations change. With a Shakespeare play especially, where so much of the sense of location is given by the language, the design needs only to be suggestive and does not have to slavishly create a real location. As *Richard III* moves swiftly from street to tower to court to battle, the set design needs to be a springboard for the imagination of the audience, to transport them instantly from place to place. The director then works with the actors through rehearsal to discover the meaning of the text, and how best to tell the story in the created world.

I tend to believe that there are broadly three periods in which you can set a play: the period it is set in, the time it was written, or now. Any other time setting risks adding another layer of interpretation; for example, seeing the play set in 1930s Germany has all the layers of our twenty-first-century interpretation of that time and place imposed on a play written in the sixteenth century.

Our production was in effect *Henry VI Part 4*, as it played on the back of the earlier trilogy and, for practical changeover reasons between one play and the next, had to be played in the same basic environment. Those *Henry VI* plays were definitely medieval in feel, with clothes influenced by medieval references. But at the end of *Henry VI Part 3* King Edward calls for an end to bloodshed—the dawning of a glorious summer is promised and the past will be left behind. So for *Richard III* we decided to break with the past and create a contemporary world influenced by, but not directly copying, Eastern European political situations.

Where did you start with Richard, from a physical/stylistic point of view? With prosthetics? With changing attitudes to bodily difference (we no longer regard physical disability as a sign of divine disapproval . . .)? Or perhaps with the play's imagery: he's variously described as a spider, boar, wolf, and "poisonous bunch-backed toad"?

Alexander: In the first week of rehearsal Tony Sher (who played Richard) and I were taken to the Wardrobe Department to find that all previous humps had been lined up for our inspection, and we were invited to choose between Ian Holm's hump, Alan Howard's hump, Norman Rodway's hump, etc. etc. We politely said we'd like our own hump. In fact there were three humps used in performance; one worn for the majority of scenes; one under the armor for the battle with a specially designed slit for Richmond's sword as he ritualistically plunged it deep into Richard's back as he knelt praying; and a third hump (very detailed and realistic, and very expensive!) as he and Lady Anne knelt, backs to the audience, during their wedding, stripped naked to the waist as was the custom. I inserted the wedding ceremony, which is not in the play, asking our composer Guy Woolfenden to write a dramatic piece of wedding music closely modeled on *Carmina Burana*. He never stopped worrying about being sued by Carl Orff!

Beale: Unusually for me I was very keen to get a visual image for him early on. I'm not usually concerned that early on about how I look, but in this case I did want to get an image of him. I suppose that's the nature of the part because you've got to face the question of his disability. I didn't actually use so much of the spider, boar, wolf, toad imagery as the nature of his job. I had this idea that he should look like a retired American footballer. A soldier who had gone to seed. It was his job before that was important for me—that he should look massive and muscled, old muscle. I had a body suit with a hump put in, as a lot of Richards do, and gradually realized that it was looking like a toad. We just happened to slip into one of the images for him, which was quite interesting. And it was picked up on by people that I looked like a toad. But it came from his work as a soldier rather than anything from the imagery of the play. I knew that we were going to do a broadsword fight—although it wasn't a period production in the design sense, they fought with broadswords at the end—so I wanted the heavy look of someone who was used to wielding a broadsword, with huge shoulders. The hump just became a continuation of those muscles on his back.

Piper: The starting point really had to be with the actor (Jonathan Slinger) and how he wanted to approach the part, rather than imposing any ideas of how he might be disabled. Jonathan was keen to explore a journey in the character through his route from third son of York to eventual king. There is a brilliant monologue in *Henry VI Part 3*, where Richard first talks to the audience directly, in which he accepts his disabilities, which up to that point he has been keen to cover up, and starts almost to celebrate his deformity. We began by assuming that the young Richard would not have had any special clothes made, but at the same time would try to be quite dandyish and youthful, thrilled by the violence around him. He sported a wolfish fur coat over a basic black robe, which did come from the bottled spider line, and a wig to cover a large birthmark over his temple. At the end of the monologue he ripped off the wig, exposing the vivid stain: "I am myself alone." I did some research into spinal deformities and we created a hump that would be appropriate. It is dangerous to actually build up a foot to create a limp, so the limping and the withered arm are created through Jonathan's movement. In *Richard III* he was in a contemporary black suit and polo neck (a reference to [Russian president] Putin), with a leg brace strapped over his trousers.

And psychologically? "Since I cannot prove a lover . . . I am determinèd to prove a villain" sounds like a "compensation" theory of character, doesn't it? In defense of my client, m'lud, he may be a serial killer but you see he was a misfit as a child . . . that sort of thing?—or emphatically not?

Beale: That was inevitably part of the psychological makeup, although I suspect that compensation behavior, which is what I probably did alight on, was as much to do with his relationship with his parents. I remember being very keen that in Richard's mind his father was an adored figure, a hero figure. We ignored the *Henry VI* plays, but I just had the image of him as having had a relationship with a strong and powerful father who didn't acknowledge his disabilities, but treated him as an equal with his other sons. That is in contrast of course with his mother. The scene when she lambasts him was about her revealing, consciously or unconsciously, what she has always felt about him, and what he, consciously or unconsciously, perhaps unconsciously, knew that she thought about him. It was a question of him realizing that she has always regarded him as some sort of diseased, malformed creature, as opposed to his brothers, and his father never thought that. That was what was going through my mind. He was hurt by it, but it wasn't unexpected. It just confirmed what he'd always thought about his mother. So I think it was as much to do with the mother and the father as with him compensating for being deformed, although that is obviously an element of it. It's a bit of simple bravado at the beginning. "I can do this, you just watch me." I

remember during another production the director Roger Michell saying something to me that I always use now, which is to cast the audience in a role for the soliloquy. For instance Iago couldn't give a shit
about what the audience thinks, and that's their role. Hamlet wants
friends, somebody to help him. Richard is the leader of the gang. It's
like he's saying, "You wait till you see me do this. I'm going to do
something so unexpected, like woo Lady Anne, and I will do it, I promise." I think that's part of the compensation theory too.

**The sheer quantity of "backstory" is a problem for the audience of
this play, isn't it? Did you have particular ways of dealing with that?
There's a venerable tradition, going back to Colley Cibber in the
eighteenth century, of importing large chunks from *Henry VI Part 3*.**

Alexander: I think *Richard III* stands alone well as a story even
when detached from the three parts of *Henry VI*. There would perhaps be an argument for cutting large chunks, or indeed all, of the
Queen Margaret scenes, as the play does need cutting anyway, but
even in those the vividness of the psychological conflict carries its
own explanatory narrative. He changed a lot as a writer between
Henry VI and *Richard III* and it has a completely different feel from
the earlier plays. It stands alone without great knowledge of the
backstory. *Henry VI* 1, 2, and 3 are Chronicle plays, almost pageant-
like in their parade of incident. *Richard III*, on the other hand, is on
the way to becoming a full-blown psychodrama of the type finally
perfected with *Macbeth* a decade later. It doesn't really feel like the
fourth part of a tetralogy. But it is a strange hybrid in some ways with
some scenes that verge on the ritualistic.

Piper: The set was the same but the characters were now in a stylized
modern dress. For those actors who were playing the same character
as they had in *Henry VI Part 3*, I tried to create a look that reflected
their period costumes in silhouette and color, yet were contemporary
in feel. So, for example, Edward and Elizabeth end *Henry VI Part 3* in
white coronation robes, and in *Richard III* they were both dressed in
long cream coats. Some characters, like Margaret, we deliberately
left in a broken-down version of their period look from *Henry VI*. As
we had the same actress playing both the young, sexy Margaret in

Henry VI Part 1 and the old Margaret in *Richard III*, it was a way of suggesting that she had aged, without applying prosthetics—she became a more stylized, mythic character. The great advantage of doing the tetralogy of plays together is that the backstory is so much clearer, and the audience have seen how Richard's personality has been forged in the brutality of the Wars of the Roses. Margaret's cycles of curses, and Richard's hatred of her, have a greater resonance when you have seen her stab his father York in the back.

What was the journey that you went on with regard to Richard's relationship with Buckingham? That's crucial, isn't it?

Alexander: Yes, it certainly is a central relationship. Our starting point was to make the audience believe it would last. Or *could* last. We have to believe in Richard's capacity to generate a sense of security in someone who thinks of themselves as a friend. Most of his immediate male colleagues seem to regard him as loyal, honest, funny, and friendly. Most of them seem to actually like him as he is so effective at portraying himself as one of the blokes. A good egg. Only the women suspect him. Only the women ever refer to his deformity. From the assumption that Buckingham was an ambitious politician we wanted to go one stage further and have him regard Richard as not only trustworthy but innocent, and therefore potentially *gullible*. We imagined that it was at the back of Buckingham's mind that he may be able to double-cross Richard in the future.

Beale: In our production Buckingham was smooth, educated; a class political act with a class political brain. In a way he was the brains behind the operation. One of my favorite moments in the play was the scene when the princes return to London. I was waiting there with balloons for them, and the Prince of Wales says of the Tower, "Did Julius Caesar build that place, my lord?" Buckingham answers, but in our version "my lord" went to me. Richard gave a face to suggest "I don't know and I care less." Buckingham had to step in and reply. In other words, Richard's political instinct was to do with a deep-seated psychological need to prove himself, but with no real political sophistication behind it. It was just brute desire. Whereas Buckingham was much more subtle. He has the idea of

5. Simon Russell Beale (*right*) as a sinisterly jovial Richard with balloons for the princes.

pretending to be religious, he's the PR man, he can spin. Of course what is so fantastic about it is that in the end brute force wins.

When I was crowned, I was very keen that Richard should want to make it a fabulous occasion. Originally I wore very obvious make-up, because I'd read that George VI had to wear makeup and that these were very staged events. The makeup was cut eventually, but Richard was dressed in a glorious, very long blue cloak and as he went toward the throne he got tangled in the cloak and fell. The sheer biting humiliation of that sent him into a fury. The person he reached for was Buckingham, and quite precisely, because he had to rely on Buckingham to help him up, that meant that he had to go. That was the immediate psychological reaction to having been humiliated in front of everybody—that he would have to get rid of the man who helped him. That was a mini-version of the bigger version, which is that he had to be got rid of anyway as he'd served his purpose and become too dangerous. There is a part of Buckingham's psychology which is that help is humiliation in the political sphere.

And the development of Richard's language, especially in soliloquy? Is there a huge change as the play unfolds, beginning from the astonishing confidence of the opening monologue and culminating in the fragmentation of the nightmare before the battle?

Alexander: Absolutely. The language reflects the change from theatrical and impish self-confidence to terrified self-awareness. It also reflects a change in his relationship with the audience, from confiding in a huge crowd of assumed admirers to a deserted man, bereft of an audience, with no one to talk to but himself; trying to find the feedback that once sustained him but finding only his own echo.

Beale: He doesn't soliloquize after his crowning, except for that last battle scene. He starts with this fantastic bravado, this fantastic relationship with the audience, and as soon as he's crowned and especially, and this in my mind is the turning point for Richard, after the murder of the children, from then on he simply does not. He has a line after the Elizabeth scene, which is almost muttered to himself. I think it is always fascinating with Shakespeare *when* people stop soliloquizing. Hamlet stops after the boat. He doesn't need his friends in the audience anymore. He's gone to a different place. Iago stops simply because things get too busy. He can barely speak to us in the first place because he is spinning a whole load of lies that he doesn't believe either. Richard stops because the crown is not what he expected it to be and he doesn't know how to cope with that. And then you have the death of the children. He can kill grown-ups in this play. Most grown-ups seem prepared to kill any other grown-up, they all seem to be on that level of ruthlessness, but you don't kill children. Even the Murderer says this is beyond the pale. I had this

6. Jonathan Slinger as Richard in Michael Boyd's production.

package brought on, which I'd based on [the soap opera] *Coronation Street* actually. When Stan Ogden died, Hilda Ogden got his glasses and his remaining bits and bobs, the last bit of him if you like, in a brown paper packet delivered to her house and she opened it over the credits with no music. It was a fantastically moving performance. I wanted to do something like that. In our production Richard received a brown paper packet with the boys' pajamas in it and he smelled the pajamas, which smelled of talc and children. That I think is the moment when he switches off. He has no desire or need to communicate anymore to people outside the play. And so consequently that last soliloquy at Bosworth is fiendishly difficult and also comes at slightly the wrong time. I can understand why people cut it because that late on is the last moment you want a soliloquy. It's a completely different beast.

Richard loves playacting, doesn't he? As in the scene with the prayer-book. Presumably that dramatic self-consciousness is one of the keys to his charisma in the theater?

Alexander: Richard loves acting because he has fully absorbed the idea that one may smile and smile and be a villain. It seems amusing and hilarious to him how easy it is to dupe people, to experience up close their vanity leading directly to their gullibility. This dramatic self-consciousness makes him charismatic to audiences because he realizes they are more entertained by audacious, immoral, and downright wicked behavior than they would be by someone spouting pieties and lecturing them on goodness or the art of sanctity. I wanted Tony to think of the audience as one thousand selves, or an audience of Richard fans, near clones needing only that particular soliloquy to be perfect clones: not talking to himself but to a mass of near-selves close to the perfect him. But it withers to horrifying loneliness with "I am I" and "When I die no man will pity me." Charisma is nothing without love.

Beale: Less so than the question implies. He wasn't a very good play-actor in the religious scene in my version. I think he can don a persona, as he does with Anne, but I don't think the Richard that I played was particularly conscious of playacting. He just adapted himself to the situation that he was in and the objective that he needed to achieve. I think he believes things from the moment he has said them. I don't remember playacting being particularly important. He liked his relationship with the audience. He liked being able to achieve something in public view, which I suppose is playacting in a way. He liked the audience to see how the cogs were moving.

The initial setup of the wooing of Lady Anne seems unpromising: Richard has stabbed her first husband (Edward Prince of Wales)

to death in *Henry VI Part 3* and now he's courting her over the corpse of her father-in-law (Henry VI), whom he's also killed. And yet he wins her over. Did your rehearsal process reveal the secret of his success?

Alexander: He makes her believe he loves her and, despite everything, she's moved by that. He makes her believe he's a good man and misunderstood. Besides, these are dangerous times and she needs a powerful protector.

Beale: No! I don't think I ever cracked that one. I know Annabelle Apsion, who played Lady Anne, felt uncomfortable a lot of the time, both when I played it and when Ciaran Hinds took over from me after I slipped a disc in my back. I don't know what the secret of it is. It was always the scene that was the most difficult for me. It doesn't play to my particular strengths. If I were a sexier actor perhaps it would, but I couldn't really use that part of the man's armory in my dealings with her. I also think there is some mystery there, that I'm sure a lot of Richards have unlocked, but that I found very hard indeed. I was in Milton Keynes [a commuter town in the English Midlands] and somebody suggested playing it extremely slowly, against all the technical rules, which perhaps we should have tried. But I can't pretend I ever got that one.

The women eventually play a big part in bringing Richard down: there's a definite shift in the power structure when his mother (the Duchess of York) and sister-in-law (Queen Elizabeth) gang up on him in the fourth act. Did that feel like a turning point to you?

Alexander: The trinity of women, Anne, Margaret, and Elizabeth, are a very, very potent presence in the play, so you have no choice but to make them a strong focus in any production. The fact that they *all* initially see through him in a way the men apparently don't offers him an intriguing challenge the men don't present. He defeats Margaret simply by giving voice to what all the men feel. He turns Anne by the brilliance of his acting and survives the encounter with Elizabeth through pure determination, although you can feel the strain that he has put himself under gradually taking effect.

Beale: The most important scene in the whole play was for me the one with Elizabeth. I had this feeling that it is Richard at his most genuine and desperate, and that is why it doesn't work for him. This is a man who is tired, he's older, kingship isn't as much fun as he thought it would be. He's on the road, halfway through the campaign, and he meets a woman who is the key to stability and he genuinely wants it. And when he says about marrying her daughter, "It cannot be avoided but by this; / It will not be avoided but by this," it is absolutely a genuine statement. There is no other answer that he can see out of the mess that they have got themselves into. What she does is something that he's never thought about, which is to talk about grief. And to say, "Do you realize that there are parents up and down this country who are weeping for their dead children, and children who are weeping for their dead parents? And that it is you who have done that." I don't think Richard has ever thought about the personal consequences of killing somebody, it has never occurred to him. He has a moment after killing the children, realizing that he has stepped over a line, but I don't think he stops to consider how their mother feels. I think he genuinely finds it disturbing that he is responsible for mass misery, because I don't think it had ever occurred to him before. He just wanted the crown because he felt he needed and deserved it, but I don't think he realizes that in doing so he has made a whole country miserable. And in our version, as I think in most productions, he doesn't win the argument with Elizabeth at all, but he has that funny little line at the end of it: "Relenting fool, and shallow, changing woman!" He tries to fool himself into believing that he's been dealing with a stupid and weak woman, rather than the full-length soliloquy "Was ever woman in this humour wooed?" which is somebody who has succeeded and is at the top of his deceptive powers. This is the genuine Richard laying his heart on the line, what little heart he has at any rate, and is faced with something that is implacably stronger than that, which is a mother's grief. I think it is the absolute turning point for Richard. He essentially dies. I don't think he's amoral. Iago I think is amoral, a very small and mean man, without a sense of beauty or love or life. But I think Richard does have a sense of these things. He is a moral man, brought up with moral codes, but they have been distorted beyond recognition. Otherwise he couldn't wake up before Bosworth. Otherwise he wouldn't stop eating. At the end of scenes there's quite a lot about food, people arranging to meet after dinner, "I saw good strawberries in your garden there." And then just before Bosworth he no longer wants to eat or drink, and I think the people around him think "Oh my God!" when he's lost his appetite. I mentioned this to a Shakespeare scholar when I did it and they told me there had just been a production in Lyon entirely based on that!

How did you approach the technical problem of the scene with the Ghosts the night before the battle? It seems to require some theatrical equivalent of a cinematic split-screen effect—that maybe worked especially well on the wide, shallow stage of the Elizabethan Rose. How did you make it work in your space?

Alexander: The fact that the whole of the action was set in a cathedral made it fairly obvious that by parking Richard and his tent stage-right and Richmond and his tent stage-left simultaneously, we were in the setting of a medieval Mystery Play with heaven on one side and hell's mouth on the other. In fact, in a way, it was the culminating image of the whole scenic concept.

Piper: We were working in a thrust stage so it made it very easy to divide the space with Richmond asleep downstage and Richard midstage. The Ghosts entered in a steady stream from double doors in the upstage tower, which dominated the space. Thus they encountered Richard first and then went on to Richmond, before exiting through the audience.

And for all the blood, the murders, the choreographed onstage fighting: I suppose there's a basic choice between "stylization" (slow motion battles, red silk for blood) and "realism" (the clash of metal, lashings of mud and Kensington Gore): where did you aim to find yourselves on that spectrum?

Piper: We were fairly realistic, and as it was contemporary we used guns, including a very brutal shot to the head in Pomfret. The mumming to the Mayor was a mock terrorist attack and Hastings' head

was delivered in a clear plastic bag. The fights, however, were styl-
ized, especially the final section in Bosworth, which involved all the
Ghosts as abstract combatants. The final encounter between Rich-
mond and Richard took place on a swiveling set of metal steps with
Richard trapped at the top, firing rapidly to try and hit the whirling
Richmond as he spun them around.

**Most of Shakespeare's history plays are ensemble pieces, but
Richard is a huge solo part—he speaks a third of the entire play
and has more than three times as many lines as anybody else.
The role was clearly written to showcase the rising star of
Richard Burbage. For a director, there must be an unusually difficult task of balancing the work that must be done with Richard
and with the rest of the cast. Are there enough rewards for the
other actors?**

Alexander: Yes. Buckingham, Anne, Clarence, and Margaret are all
good parts, but it's a very valid point; the play is unbalanced in that
sense. It's one of the reasons it needs careful cutting. Tony was
always saying that Shakespeare learns later in his career how to give
the central actors decent rests with large sections of the action in
which they don't appear. Lear, Macbeth, Othello, Antony, Cleopatra,
Coriolanus, etc., all have a significant amount of time offstage. The
physical demands on the actor playing Richard are huge, and if one
sees it as a star vehicle then you certainly need a star who is a mod-
est soul and a company person. A vain and self-centered actor would
be death to company spirit—rather as Richard is death to those who
try to support him.

Which murder did your Richard enjoy the most? And the least?

Beale: I've answered that about the least with the princes. I don't think
he ever enjoys a murder to be honest. I think he thinks killing Clarence
is quite funny. He never does the deed himself anyway, and it's a more
functional thing, getting rid of people who are in the way. I think he
quite enjoys terrifying Hastings. I think he enjoys the terror in people's
faces, but as for the killing, I think that's entirely functional.

Would you say it was physically the most demanding part you've ever played? Quite apart from the hunchback, the limp or whatever, he speaks one-third of the play, three times as much as anyone else, and doesn't really get that extended fourth act feet-up-in-the-dressing-room-before-the-big-climax that even Hamlet and Lear are allowed. And then to go so quickly from the nightmare speech to the battle itself . . . how did you survive?!

Beale: Well, I didn't survive. It was physically exhausting, but I don't know whether it is any more exhausting than Hamlet, or indeed Iago, which probably takes as much as Richard. I remember Sam [Mendes, the director] saying to me beforehand, "You must be careful, it's a ball breaker." Although I had prosthetics on my back and a raised shoe, inevitably I fed my body into the prosthetic. I did a run at The Other Place and then a twelve-week tour and I came to London and on the very first night I slipped my disc so badly I couldn't move, and then had to have an operation. It was quite a serious injury and I was out for about three months. Funnily enough one of the best performances I think I gave of it was a week after I'd slipped the disc and I refused to admit that I was that badly injured, although I literally couldn't walk! I had to stay on all fours in the wings and then pull myself up and get onto the stage and I did one performance, which was almost completely stationary, with people moved around me, and we didn't do the fight obviously, I just fell over! But I was so angry that I think in a way it was one of the best performances that I gave of it.

RICHARD AND TYRANNY: REFLECTIONS BY RICHARD EYRE

Sir Richard Eyre was artistic director of Britain's National Theatre from 1987 to 1997, where his Shakespearean productions included *Hamlet* with Daniel Day-Lewis and *King Lear* with Ian Holm. His 1990 production of *Richard III*, with Ian McKellen in the title role, toured the world and its transposition of the play to a world suggestive of 1930s Fascism inspired the McKellen film version of 1996. Eyre reflects here on the play's enduring political power.

I came to know tyranny at first hand through visiting Romania. Over a period of nearly thirty years I watched their dictator, Ceauşescu, graduate from being a malign clown to a psychotic ogre. His *folies de grandeur* consisted of razing villages to the ground in order to rehouse peasants in tower blocks, sweeping aside boulevards because the streets from his residence to his office were insufficiently straight, building miles of preposterously baroque apartment blocks which echoed in concrete the lines of Securitate men standing beneath them, and led the eye toward a gigantic palace which made Stalin's taste in architecture look restrained. They ran out of marble to clad the walls and the floors, and had to invent a process to make a synthetic substitute out of marble dust; and there was never enough gold for all the door handles of the hundreds of rooms, or the taps of the scores of bathrooms. It was a palace of Oz, built for a demented wizard, costing the lives of hundreds of building workers who, numbed by cold, fell from the flimsy scaffolding and were brushed away like rubble, to be laid out in a room reserved solely for the coffins of the expendable workforce. There was a photograph of Ceauşescu that showed only one ear, and there's a Romanian saying that to have one ear is to be mad. So another ear was painstakingly painted on the official photograph. Such are the ways of great men.

The language of demagoguery in modern times has a remarkable consistency: Ceauşescu, Stalin, Mao Tse-tung and Bokassa shared a predilection for large banners, demonstrations and military choreography, and the same architectural virus; totalitarianism consistently distorts proportion by eliminating human scale. Mass becomes the only consideration in architecture, armies, and death. The rise of a dictator and the accompanying political thuggery are the main topics of Shakespeare's *Richard III*, which could be said to be a handbook for tyrants—and for their victims. I directed the play with Ian McKellen as Richard in 1990 for the National Theatre and took it to its spiritual home in Bucharest early in 1991.

We have to keep rediscovering ways of doing Shakespeare's plays. They don't have absolute meanings. There is no fixed, frozen way of doing them. Nobody can mine a Shakespeare play and discover a "solution." And to pretend that there are fixed canons of style, fashion, and taste is to ignore history. When there is talk of "classical acting," what is often meant is an acting style that instead of revealing the truth of a text for the present day, reveals the bombast of yesterday.

How do we present the plays in a way that is true to their own terms, and at the same time bring them alive for a contemporary audience? It's very much easier to achieve this in a small space, and it's no coincidence that most successful Shakespeare productions of recent years have been done in theaters seating a couple of hundred people at most, where the potency of the language isn't dissipated by the exigencies of voice projection, and the problems of presentation—finding a physical world for the play—become negligible. It's hard at one end of the spectrum to avoid latching on to a visual conceit which tidies up the landscape of a Shakespeare play, and, at the other end of the spectrum, to avoid imposing unity through a rigorously enforced discipline of verse-speaking. Verse-speaking should be like jazz: never on the beat, but before, after, or across it.

The life of the plays is in the language, not alongside it, or underneath it. Feelings and thoughts are released at the moment of speech. An Elizabethan audience would have responded to the pulse, the rhythms, the shapes, sounds, and above all meanings, within the consistent ten-syllable, five-stress lines of blank verse. They were an audience who listened. To a large extent we've lost that priority; nowadays we see before we hear. Verse drama places demands on the audience, but a greater demand still on the actors, habituated by naturalistic speech, and to private, introspective, emotional displays. "You should be able to feel the language," says the poet and dramatist Tony Harrison. "To taste it, to conscript the whole body as well as the mind and the mouth to savour it."

For a director, working with a designer can often be the most satisfying and enjoyable part of a production. You advance slowly, day by day, in a kind of amiable dialectic, helped by sketches, anecdotes, photographs, and reference books. The play starts as a tone—of voice, or color, and a shape as formless as the shadow of a sheet on a washing line; through reading and discussion and illustration, it acquires a clear and palpable shape. When I started working on *Richard III* with Ian McKellen and the designer, Bob Crowley, I had no definite plan about the setting. We never sought to establish literal equivalents between medieval and modern tyrants. We worked simply, day by day, reading the play aloud to each other, and refusing to jump to conclusions.

Some actors start with trying to establish the details of how the character will look, some with how they will think or feel. It was said of Olivier that he started with the shoes; with Ian McKellen it's the face and the voice. I have a postcard he sent me when we were working on *Richard III*—a droll cartoon of a severe face, recognizable as his own, with sharply receding hair, an arrow pointing to a patch of alopecia; at the throat is a military collar, above the shoulder the tip of a small hump. He is a systematic, fastidious, and exacting actor; each word is picked up and examined for its possible meanings, which are weighed, assessed, discarded, or incorporated. In rehearsals he is infinitely self-aware, often cripplingly so. His waking, and perhaps sleeping, dreams are of how he will appear onstage—his position, his spatial relationships with the other actors. But in performance that inhibition drops away like a cripple's crutches and he is pure performer. All the detail that has been so exhaustively documented becomes a part of an animate whole. In sport, in a great performance, there must always be an element of risk, of danger. The same must be true of the theater. I wouldn't say there is not a good or even effective actor without this characteristic, but there is certainly no celebrated one.

As Ian, Bob, and I talked, a story emerged: Richard's occupation's gone. He's a successful soldier who, in the face of great odds, has welded a life together in which he has a purpose, an identity as a military man. His opening speech describes his depression at the conclusion of war, his bitterness at the effeminacy of peace. He's a man raging with unconsummated energy, needing a world to "bustle" in. This hunger to fill the vacuum left by battle is the driving force of the play. It has a deep resonance for me. When I made *Tumbledown*, a film about the Falklands War, I saw this sense of unfulfilled appetite at first hand in people who had fought in the war and were unable to come to terms with peace. The experience of battle is a profound distillation of fear, danger, and exhilaration; nothing in peacetime will ever match it, and those who are affected by it are as traumatized as those who have been wounded, who at least have the visible signs of trauma to show for it. Soldiers are licensed to break the ultimate taboo against killing; some of them get the habit.

Richard has had to fight against many odds; he is the youngest son, coming after two very strong, dominant, assertive brothers— and he is deformed, "unfinished." His eldest brother, Edward, is a profligate, and the spectacle of his brother's success with women is a sharp thorn in his flesh. The age, no less than today, worshipped physical prowess, and Richard is accustomed, though certainly not inured, to pejorative terms like "bunch-backed toad"; he has heard them all his life. We know that he is deformed, but the text repeatedly tells us he is a successful professional soldier. We have to reconcile the two demands of the text. Olivier's interpretation has become central to the mythology of the play, but the deformity that he depicts has never seemed to me plausibly compatible with what Shakespeare wrote. Ian McKellen played Richard with a small hump, he had chronic alopecia, and he was paralyzed down one side of his body. These three handicaps taken together were sufficient to account for all the abuse he attracts and [yet he could] still serve as a professional soldier. Experience shows that even slight deformities are enough to inspire repulsion; modern reactions to disability haven't changed very much in this respect.

It is clear that Richard has been rejected from birth by his mother; she says so unequivocally to Clarence's children, and her words of contempt spoken to her son in front of his troops confirm this. It is impossible to escape the conclusion that Shakespeare is attempting to give some history, some causality, to Richard's evil.

The design of the production emerged empirically. We started with an empty model box, and put minimal elements into it—rows of overhead lamps to create a series of institutionalized public areas, a world of prisons and cabinet rooms and hospital corridors; palaces and areas of ceremonial display, set off against candlelit areas of private pain. We drew some parallels with the rise of Hitler, but these were forced by Hitler himself; his rise shadows that of Richard astonishingly closely, as [Bertolt] Brecht showed in [his play] *The Resistible Rise of Arturo Ui*. Specific elements of Hitler's ascent to power, or [Sir Oswald] Mosley's to notoriety, were echoes that bounced off a timeless sounding board. The play is set in a mythological landscape, even if it draws on an apparently historically precise period; I say "apparently" because Shakespeare treats historical incident with little reference to fact—incidents are conflated, characters meet whose paths never crossed, Tudor myths prevail.

Tyrants always invent their own ritual, synthetic ceremonies borrowed from previous generations in order to dignify the present and suggest an unbroken continuum with old traditions. Hitler played up all the themes of historical restitution. Napoleon, the little man from Corsica, designed the preposterous Byzantine ceremony which is represented in David's painting. Most of the English ritual, our so-called time-honored ritual, is not very old either. The order of the last British Coronation, in 1953, had been almost wholly invented by Queen Victoria. Putting Richard in medieval costume in the Coronation, as we did, was a way of showing how tyrants, the authors of the Thousand Year Reich, would have us believe that medievalism and modern time coexist; the past is consistently made to serve the needs of the present.

Richard III is so much a one-man show in our acting tradition that the miseries visited on woman by the male appetite for power tend to be ignored or obscured. The female characters are as strong as in any of Shakespeare's plays. The legacy of men's cruelty is swept up by women who have been educated by the experience of grief. They have caused pain to Richard and they are taught by him to suffer: Elizabeth—proud, arrogant, and abusive of him—loses her brother and her sons; the Duchess of York—sealed in her own self-importance, openly contemptuous of her son—loses another son and grandchildren at his hands; Lady Anne—blinded by her grief and her hatred and seduced by him—loses her self-respect and, finally, her life. Only Queen Margaret needs no education at his hands; "Teach me how to curse my enemies," says Elizabeth to her. Their models in our times are only too obvious: the women who wait in Chile and in Argentina for news of their sons who have "disappeared," and the mothers I saw in Romania shortly after the Revolution, putting candles and flowers in the streets on the spots where their sons had been killed. The play is called *The Tragedy of Richard III*, and it is the tragedy of the women that is being told.

The crude villain of melodrama has managed to overrule a play of considerable political subtlety. Richard does not appear in an untainted Eden; his England is the world of realpolitik. Clarence and Edward have both committed crimes in the civil wars, Clarence even admitting his guilt to the Keeper; Queen Elizabeth's family are greedy parvenus; Buckingham, Stanley, and Ely are all morally ambiguous. At the beginning of the play Clarence has just been capriciously arrested; such behavior may be exceptional and outrageous, but not unprecedented. What right have any of the characters to call Richard a villain?

Hastings, the prime minister, is a politician's politician, expedient, and amoral—when he is told of the impending execution of his political enemies, he can't fault this transparent abuse of justice; within minutes he is himself under sentence of execution. "The rest that love me, rise and follow me," says Richard, and at this point self-preservation takes over from courage, morality, or political expediency. We all hope that we will never have to face this choice; it takes formidable courage to say "No" when the consequence is imprisonment or worse, and where there is a crying need for reform, it's easy enough to agree that minor infringements of liberty are a small price to pay for the benefit of an able leader. We are comfortably insulated in our unchallenged, liberal, all-too-English assumptions.

The play ends with the triumph of Richmond—a young man, almost a boy, in the hands of mature soldier-politicians who are promoting him. It is essential for their purposes that he succeed, and he is equally determined to show that he can succeed. I set his first entrance against a backdrop of a peaceful country village, in Devon in fact, near where I was born, the England of "summer fields and fruitful vines." If I were asked what I thought Richmond was fighting for, it would be this idealized picture of England. It was more than a metaphor for me; it was a heartland.

When I took my production of *Richard III* to Romania a year after their Revolution, familiar landmarks in Bucharest were obscured entirely by the snow and the people were unrecognizably changed from the years of oppression. Though some claimed that nothing had altered, the mere fact of being able to say this openly contradicted what they were saying. A stagehand said he wasn't at all frightened of being killed in the Revolution; after all, better to be dead than how it was. A small pixielike woman was helping at the theater; she was slightly retarded but had some English. "Are you happy? I am happy" was her refrain. Like many others she was homeless, and lived in the theater, where at least she could get hot water. Outside it was often one hour of hot water a day.

At the end of the last performance I went onstage with the actors and made a speech, starting through an interpreter. She was shouted off: "English! English!" they chanted and I continued in English. I told them the production had come to its spiritual home, that this sort of cultural exchange was the only true diplomacy, and thanked them for their hospitality. They didn't want us to go, clapping rhythmically and incessantly, but we walked offstage slowly, blinking back tears. As we left the stage a man walked up to us and handed a note and a bouquet to one of the actors. The note read: "Nobody can play Sir William Shakespeare's plays better than his English people. I've seen with your remarkable help that somewhere in England Sir William Shakespeare is still alive. Thank you. Signed: a Simple Man."

SHAKESPEARE'S CAREER
IN THE THEATER

BEGINNINGS

William Shakespeare was an extraordinarily intelligent man who was born and died in an ordinary market town in the English Midlands. He lived an uneventful life in an eventful age. Born in April 1564, he was the eldest son of John Shakespeare, a glove-maker who was prominent on the town council until he fell into financial difficulties. Young William was educated at the local grammar in Stratford-upon-Avon, Warwickshire, where he gained a thorough grounding in the Latin language, the art of rhetoric, and classical poetry. He married Ann Hathaway and had three children (Susanna, then the twins Hamnet and Judith) before his twenty-first birthday: an exceptionally young age for the period. We do not know how he supported his family in the mid-1580s.

Like many clever country boys, he moved to the city in order to make his way in the world. Like many creative people, he found a career in the entertainment business. Public playhouses and professional full-time acting companies reliant on the market for their income were born in Shakespeare's childhood. When he arrived in London as a man, sometime in the late 1580s, a new phenomenon was in the making: the actor who is so successful that he becomes a "star." The word did not exist in its modern sense, but the pattern is recognizable: audiences went to the theater not so much to see a particular show as to witness the comedian Richard Tarlton or the dramatic actor Edward Alleyn.

Shakespeare was an actor before he was a writer. It appears not to have been long before he realized that he was never going to grow into a great comedian like Tarlton or a great tragedian like Alleyn. Instead, he found a role within his company as the man who patched up old plays, breathing new life, new dramatic twists, into tired repertory pieces. He paid close attention to the work of the university-educated dramatists who were writing history plays and tragedies for the public stage in a style more ambitious, sweeping, and poetically grand than anything which had been seen before. But he may also have noted that what his friend and rival Ben Jonson would call "Marlowe's mighty line" sometimes faltered in the mode of comedy. Going to university, as Christopher Marlowe did, was all well and good for honing the arts of rhetorical elaboration and classical allusion, but it could lead to a loss of the common touch. To stay close to a large segment of the potential audience for public theater, it was necessary to write for clowns as well as kings and to intersperse the flights of poetry with the humor of the tavern, the privy, and the brothel: Shakespeare was the first to establish himself early in his career as an equal master of tragedy, comedy, and history. He realized that theater could be the medium to make the national past available to a wider audience than the elite who could afford to read large history books: his signature early works include not only the classical tragedy *Titus Andronicus* but also the sequence of English historical plays on the Wars of the Roses.

He also invented a new role for himself, that of in-house company dramatist. Where his peers and predecessors had to sell their plays to the theater managers on a poorly paid piecework basis, Shakespeare took a percentage of the box-office income. The Lord Chamberlain's Men constituted themselves in 1594 as a joint stock company, with the profits being distributed among the core actors who had invested as sharers. Shakespeare acted himself—he appears in the cast lists of some of Ben Jonson's plays as well as the list of actors' names at the beginning of his own collected works—but his principal duty was to write two or three plays a year for the company. By holding shares, he was effectively earning himself a royalty on his work, something no author had ever done before in England. When the Lord Chamberlain's Men collected their fee for performance at court in the Christmas season of 1594, three of them went along to the Treasurer of the Chamber: not just Richard Burbage the tragedian and Will Kempe the clown, but also Shakespeare the scriptwriter. That was something new.

The next four years were the golden period in Shakespeare's career, though overshadowed by the death of his only son, Hamnet, age eleven, in 1596. In his early thirties and in full command of both his poetic and his theatrical medium, he perfected his art of comedy, while also developing his tragic and historical writing in new ways. In 1598, Francis Meres, a Cambridge University graduate with his finger on the pulse of the London literary world, praised Shakespeare for his excellence across the genres:

> As Plautus and Seneca are accounted the best for comedy and tragedy among the Latins, so Shakespeare among the English is the most excellent in both kinds for the stage; for comedy, witness his *Gentlemen of Verona*, his *Errors*, his *Love Labours Lost*, his *Love Labours Won*, his *Midsummer Night Dream* and his *Merchant of Venice*: for tragedy his *Richard the 2*, *Richard the 3*, *Henry the 4*, *King John*, *Titus Andronicus* and his *Romeo and Juliet*.

For Meres, as for the many writers who praised the "honey-flowing vein" of *Venus and Adonis* and *Lucrece*, narrative poems written when the theaters were closed due to plague in 1593–94, Shakespeare was marked above all by his linguistic skill, by the gift of turning elegant poetic phrases.

PLAYHOUSES

Elizabethan playhouses were "thrust" or "one-room" theaters. To understand Shakespeare's original theatrical life, we have to forget about the indoor theater of later times, with its proscenium arch and curtain that would be opened at the beginning and closed at the end of each act. In the proscenium arch theater, stage and auditorium are effectively two separate rooms: the audience looks from one world into another as if through the imaginary "fourth wall" framed by the proscenium. The picture-frame stage, together with the elaborate scenic effects and backdrops beyond it, created the illusion of a self-contained world—especially once nineteenth-century developments in the control of artificial lighting meant that the auditorium could be darkened and the spectators made to focus on the lighted stage. Shakespeare, by contrast, wrote for a bare platform stage with a standing audience gathered around it in a courtyard in full daylight. The audience were always conscious of themselves and their fellow spectators, and they shared the same "room" as the actors. A sense of immediate presence and the creation of rapport with the audience were all-important. The actor could not afford to imagine he was in a closed world, with silent witnesses dutifully observing him from the darkness.

Shakespeare's theatrical career began at the Rose Theatre in Southwark. The stage was wide and shallow, trapezoid in shape, like a lozenge. This design had a great deal of potential for the theatrical equivalent of cinematic split-screen effects, whereby one group of characters would enter at the door at one end of the tiring-house wall at the back of the stage and another group through the door at the other end, thus creating two rival tableaux. Many of the battle-heavy and faction-filled plays that premiered at the Rose have scenes of just this sort.

At the rear of the Rose stage, there were three capacious exits, each over ten feet wide. Unfortunately, the very limited excavation of a fragmentary portion of the original Globe site, in 1989, revealed nothing about the stage. The first Globe was built in 1599 with similar proportions to those of another theater, the Fortune, albeit that the former was polygonal and looked circular, whereas the latter was rectangular. The building contract for the Fortune survives and allows us to infer that the stage of the Globe was probably substantially wider than it was deep (perhaps forty-three feet wide and twenty-seven feet deep). It may well have been tapered at the front, like that of the Rose.

The capacity of the Globe was said to have been enormous, perhaps in excess of three thousand. It has been conjectured that about eight hundred people may have stood in the yard, with two thousand or more in the three layers of covered galleries. The other "public" playhouses were also of large capacity, whereas the indoor Blackfriars Theatre that Shakespeare's company began using in 1608—formerly the refectory of a monastery—had overall internal dimensions of a mere forty-six by sixty feet. It would have made for a much more intimate theatrical experience and held a much smaller capacity, probably of about six hundred people. Since they paid at least sixpence a head, the Blackfriars attracted a more select or "private" audience. The atmosphere would have been closer to that of an indoor performance before the court in the Whitehall Palace or at Richmond. That Shakespeare always wrote for indoor production at court as well as outdoor performance in the public theater should make us cautious about inferring, as some scholars have, that the opportunity provided by the intimacy of the Blackfriars led to a significant change toward a "chamber" style in his last plays—which, besides, were performed at both Globe and Blackfriars. After the occupation of the Blackfriars a five-act structure seems to have become more important to Shakespeare. That was because of artificial lighting: there were musical interludes between the acts, while the candles were trimmed and replaced. Again, though, something similar must have been necessary for indoor court performances throughout his career.

Front of house there were the "gatherers" who collected the money from audience members: a penny to stand in the open-air yard, another penny for a place in the covered galleries, sixpence for the prominent "lord's rooms" to the side of the stage. In the indoor "private" theaters, gallants from the audience who fancied making themselves part of the spectacle sat on stools on the edge of the stage itself. Scholars debate as to how widespread this practice was in the public theaters such as the Globe. Once the audience were in place and the money counted, the gatherers were available to be extras onstage. That is one reason why battles and crowd scenes often come later rather than early in Shakespeare's plays. There was no formal prohibition upon performance by women, and there certainly were women among the gatherers, so it is not beyond the bounds of possibility that female crowd members were played by females.

The play began at two o'clock in the afternoon and the theater had to be cleared by five. After the main show, there would be a jig— which consisted not only of dancing, but also of knockabout comedy (it is the origin of the farcical "afterpiece" in the eighteenth-century theater). So the time available for a Shakespeare play was about two and a half hours, somewhere between the "two hours' traffic" mentioned in the prologue to *Romeo and Juliet* and the "three hours' spectacle" referred to in the preface to the 1647 Folio of Beaumont and

Fletcher's plays. The prologue to a play by Thomas Middleton refers to a thousand lines as "one hour's words," so the likelihood is that about two and a half, or a maximum of three, thousand lines made up the performed text. This is indeed the length of most of Shakespeare's comedies, whereas many of his tragedies and histories are much longer, raising the possibility that he wrote full scripts, possibly with eventual publication in mind, in the full knowledge that the stage version would be heavily cut. The short Quarto texts published in his lifetime—they used to be called "bad" Quartos—provide fascinating evidence as to the kind of cutting that probably took place. So, for instance, the First Quarto of *Hamlet* neatly merges two occasions when Hamlet is overheard, the "fishmonger" and the "nunnery" scenes.

The social composition of the audience was mixed. The poet Sir John Davies wrote of "A thousand townsmen, gentlemen and whores, / Porters and servingmen" who would "together throng" at the public playhouses. Though moralists associated female playgoing with adultery and the sex trade, many perfectly respectable citizens' wives were regular attendees. Some, no doubt, resembled the modern groupie: a story attested in two different sources has one citizen's wife making a post-show assignation with Richard Burbage and ending up in bed with Shakespeare—supposedly eliciting from the latter the quip that William the Conqueror was before Richard III. Defenders of theater liked to say that by witnessing the comeuppance of villains on the stage, audience members would repent of their own wrongdoings, but the reality is that most people went to theater then, as they do now, for entertainment more than moral edification. Besides, it would be foolish to suppose that audiences behaved in a homogeneous way: a pamphlet of the 1630s tells of how two men went to see *Pericles* and one of them laughed while the other wept. Bishop John Hall complained that people went to church for the same reasons that they went to the theater: "for company, for custom, for recreation . . . to feed his eyes or his ears . . . or perhaps for sleep."

Men about town and clever young lawyers went to be seen as much as to see. In the modern popular imagination, shaped not least by *Shakespeare in Love* and the opening sequence of Laurence Olivier's

Henry V film, the penny-paying groundlings stand in the yard hurling abuse or encouragement and hazelnuts or orange peel at the actors, while the sophisticates in the covered galleries appreciate Shakespeare's soaring poetry. The reality was probably the other way round. A "groundling" was a kind of fish, so the nickname suggests the penny audience standing below the level of the stage and gazing in silent open-mouthed wonder at the spectacle unfolding above them. The more difficult audience members, who kept up a running commentary of clever remarks on the performance and who occasionally got into quarrels with players, were the gallants. Like Hollywood movies in modern times, Elizabethan and Jacobean plays exercised a powerful influence on the fashion and behavior of the young. John Marston mocks the lawyers who would open their lips, perhaps to court a girl, and out would "flow / Naught but pure Juliet and Romeo."

THE ENSEMBLE AT WORK

In the absence of typewriters and photocopying machines, reading aloud would have been the means by which the company got to know a new play. The tradition of the playwright reading his complete script to the assembled company endured for generations. A copy would then have been taken to the Master of the Revels for licensing. The theater book-holder or prompter would then have copied the parts for distribution to the actors. A partbook consisted of the character's lines, with each speech preceded by the last three or four words of the speech before, the "cue." These would have been taken away and studied or "conned." During this period of learning the parts, an actor might have had some one-to-one instruction, perhaps from the dramatist, perhaps from a senior actor who had played the same part before, and, in the case of an apprentice, from his master. A high percentage of Desdemona's lines occur in dialogue with Othello, of Lady Macbeth's with Macbeth, Cleopatra's with Antony, and Volumnia's with Coriolanus. The roles would almost certainly have been taken by the apprentice of the lead actor, usually Burbage, who delivers the majority of the cues. Given that apprentices lodged with their masters, there would have been ample opportunity for

7. Hypothetical reconstruction of the interior of an Elizabethan playhouse during a performance.

personal instruction, which may be what made it possible for young men to play such demanding parts.

After the parts were learned, there may have been no more than a single rehearsal before the first performance. With six different plays to be put on every week, there was no time for more. Actors, then, would go into a show with a very limited sense of the whole. The notion of a collective rehearsal process that is itself a process of discovery for the actors is wholly modern and would have been incomprehensible to Shakespeare and his original ensemble. Given the number of parts an actor had to hold in his memory, the forgetting of lines was probably more frequent than in the modern theater. The book-holder was on hand to prompt.

Backstage personnel included the property man, the tire-man who oversaw the costumes, call boys, attendants, and the musicians, who might play at various times from the main stage, the rooms above, and within the tiring-house. Scriptwriters sometimes made a nuisance of themselves backstage. There was often tension between the acting companies and the freelance playwrights from whom they purchased scripts: it was a smart move on the part of Shakespeare and the Lord Chamberlain's Men to bring the writing process in-house.

Scenery was limited, though sometimes set pieces were brought on (a bank of flowers, a bed, the mouth of hell). The trapdoor from below, the gallery stage above, and the curtained discovery-space at the back allowed for an array of special effects: the rising of ghosts and apparitions, the descent of gods, dialogue between a character at a window and another at ground level, the revelation of a statue or a pair of lovers playing at chess. Ingenious use could be made of props, as with the ass's head in *A Midsummer Night's Dream*. In a theater that does not clutter the stage with the material paraphernalia of everyday life, those objects that are deployed may take on powerful symbolic weight, as when Shylock bears his weighing scales in one hand and knife in the other, thus becoming a parody of the figure of Justice who traditionally bears a sword and a balance. Among the more significant items in the property cupboard of Shakespeare's company, there would have been a throne (the "chair of state"), joint stools, books, bottles, coins, purses, letters (which are brought on stage, read or referred to on about eighty occasions in the complete works), maps, gloves, a set of stocks (in which Kent is put in *King Lear*), rings, rapiers, daggers, broadswords, staves, pistols, masks and vizards, heads and skulls, torches and tapers and lanterns, which served to signal night scenes on the daylit stage, a buck's head, an ass's head, animal costumes. Live animals also put in appearances, most notably the dog Crab in *The Two Gentlemen of Verona* and possibly a young polar bear in *The Winter's Tale*.

The costumes were the most important visual dimension of the play. Playwrights were paid between £2 and £6 per script, whereas Alleyn was not averse to paying £20 for "a black velvet cloak with sleeves embroidered all with silver and gold." No matter the period of the play, actors always wore contemporary costume. The excitement for the audience came not from any impression of historical accuracy, but from the richness of the attire and perhaps the transgressive thrill of the knowledge that here were commoners like themselves strutting in the costumes of courtiers in effective defiance of the strict sumptuary laws whereby in real life people had to wear the clothes that befitted their social station.

To an even greater degree than props, costumes could carry symbolic importance. Racial characteristics could be suggested: a breastplate and helmet for a Roman soldier, a turban for a Turk, long robes for exotic characters such as Moors, a gabardine for a Jew. The figure of Time, as in *The Winter's Tale*, would be equipped with hourglass, scythe, and wings; Rumour, who speaks the prologue of *Henry IV Part 2*, wore a costume adorned with a thousand tongues. The wardrobe in the tiring-house of the Globe would have contained much of the same stock as that of rival manager Philip Henslowe at the Rose: green gowns for outlaws and foresters, black for melancholy men such as Jaques and people in mourning such as the Countess in *All's Well That Ends Well* (at the beginning of *Hamlet*, the prince is still in mourning black when everyone else is in festive garb for the wedding of the new king), a gown and hood for a friar (or a feigned friar like the duke in *Measure for Measure*), blue coats and tawny to distinguish the followers of rival factions, a leather apron and ruler for a carpenter (as in the opening scene of *Julius Caesar*—and in *A Midsummer Night's Dream*, where this is the only sign that Peter Quince is a carpenter), a cockle hat with staff and a pair of sandals for a pilgrim or palmer (the disguise assumed by Helen in *All's Well*), bodices and kirtles with farthingales beneath for the boys who are to be dressed as girls. A gender switch such as that of Rosalind or Jessica seems to have taken between fifty and eighty lines of dialogue—Viola does not resume her "maiden weeds," but remains in her boy's costume to the end of *Twelfth Night* because a change would have slowed down the action at just the moment it was speeding to a climax. Henslowe's inventory also included "a robe for to go invisible": Oberon, Puck, and Ariel must have had something similar.

As the costumes appealed to the eyes, so there was music for the ears. Comedies included many songs. Desdemona's willow song, perhaps a late addition to the text, is a rare and thus exceptionally poignant example from tragedy. Trumpets and tuckets sounded for ceremonial entrances, drums denoted an army on the march. Background music could create atmosphere, as at the beginning of *Twelfth Night*, during the lovers' dialogue near the end of *The Mer-*

chant of Venice, when the statue seemingly comes to life in *The Winter's Tale,* and for the revival of Pericles and of Lear (in the Quarto text, but not the Folio). The haunting sound of the hautboy suggested a realm beyond the human, as when the god Hercules is imagined deserting Mark Antony. Dances symbolized the harmony of the end of a comedy—though in Shakespeare's world of mingled joy and sorrow, someone is usually left out of the circle.

The most important resource was, of course, the actors themselves. They needed many skills: in the words of one contemporary commentator, "dancing, activity, music, song, elocution, ability of body, memory, skill of weapon, pregnancy of wit." Their bodies were as significant as their voices. Hamlet tells the player to "suit the action to the word, the word to the action": moments of strong emotion, known as "passions," relied on a repertoire of dramatic gestures as well as a modulation of the voice. When Titus Andronicus has had his hand chopped off, he asks, "How can I grace my talk, / Wanting a hand to give it action?" A pen portrait of "The Character of an Excellent Actor" by the dramatist John Webster is almost certainly based on his impression of Shakespeare's leading man, Richard Burbage: "By a full and significant action of body, he charms our attention: sit in a full theater, and you will think you see so many lines drawn from the circumference of so many ears, whiles the actor is the centre. . . ."

Though Burbage was admired above all others, praise was also heaped upon the apprentice players whose alto voices fitted them for the parts of women. A spectator at Oxford in 1610 records how the audience were reduced to tears by the pathos of Desdemona's death. The puritans who fumed about the biblical prohibition upon cross-dressing and the encouragement to sodomy constituted by the sigh of an adult male kissing a teenage boy onstage were a small minority. Little is known, however, about the characteristics of the leading apprentices in Shakespeare's company. It may perhaps be inferred that one was a lot taller than the other, since Shakespeare often wrote for a pair of female friends, one tall and fair, the other short and dark (Helena and Hermia, Rosalind and Celia, Beatrice and Hero).

We know little about Shakespeare's own acting roles—an early allusion indicates that he often took royal parts and a venerable tradition gives him old Adam in *As You Like It* and the ghost of old King Hamlet. Save for Burbage's lead roles and the generic part of the clown, all such castings are mere speculation. We do not even know for sure whether the original Falstaff was Will Kempe or another actor who specialized in comic roles, Thomas Pope.

Kempe left the company in early 1599. Tradition has it that he fell out with Shakespeare over the matter of excessive improvisation. He was replaced by Robert Armin, who was less of a clown and more of a cerebral wit: this explains the difference between such parts as Lancelet Gobbo and Dogberry, which were written for Kempe, and the more verbally sophisticated Feste and Lear's Fool, which were written for Armin.

One thing that is clear from surviving "plots" or storyboards of plays from the period is that a degree of doubling was necessary. *The Second Part of Henry the Sixth* has over sixty speaking parts, but more than half of the characters only appear in a single scene and most scenes have only six to eight speakers. At a stretch, the play could be performed by thirteen actors. When Thomas Platter saw *Julius Caesar* at the Globe in 1599, he noted that there were about fifteen. Why doesn't Paris go to the Capulet ball in *Romeo and Juliet?* Perhaps because he was doubled with Mercutio, who does. In *The Winter's Tale*, Mamillius might have come back as Perdita and Antigonus been doubled by Camillo, making the partnership with Paulina at the end a very neat touch. Titania and Oberon are often played by the same pair as Hippolyta and Theseus, suggesting a symbolic matching of the rulers of the worlds of night and day, but it is questionable whether there would have been time for the necessary costume changes. As so often, one is left in a realm of tantalizing speculation.

THE KING'S MAN

The new king, James I, who had held the Scottish throne as James VI since he had been an infant, immediately took the Lord Chamberlain's Men under his direct patronage. Henceforth they would be the King's Men, and for the rest of Shakespeare's career they were favored with far more court performances than any of their rivals. There even seem to have been rumors early in the reign that Shakespeare and Burbage were being considered for knighthoods, an unprecedented honor for mere actors—and one that in the event was not accorded to a member of the profession for nearly three hundred years, when the title was bestowed upon Henry Irving, the leading Shakespearean actor of Queen Victoria's reign.

Shakespeare's productivity rate slowed in the Jacobean years, not because of age or some personal trauma, but because there were frequent outbreaks of plague, causing the theaters to be closed for long periods. The King's Men were forced to spend many months on the road. Between November 1603 and 1608, they are to be found at various towns in the south and Midlands, though Shakespeare probably did not tour with them by this time. He had bought a large house back home in Stratford and was accumulating other property. He may indeed have stopped acting soon after the new king took the throne. With the London theaters closed so much of the time and a large repertoire on the stocks, Shakespeare seems to have focused his energies on writing a few long and complex tragedies that could have been played on demand at court: *Othello*, *King Lear*, *Antony and Cleopatra*, *Coriolanus*, and *Cymbeline* are among his longest and poetically grandest plays. *Macbeth* only survives in a shorter text, which shows signs of adaptation after Shakespeare's death. The bitterly satirical *Timon of Athens*, apparently a collaboration with Thomas Middleton that may have failed onstage, also belongs to this period. In comedy, too, he wrote longer and morally darker works than in the Elizabethan period, pushing at the very bounds of the form in *Measure for Measure* and *All's Well That Ends Well*.

From 1608 onward, when the King's Men began occupying the indoor Blackfriars playhouse (as a winter house, meaning that they only used the outdoor Globe in summer?), Shakespeare turned to a more romantic style. His company had a great success with a revived and altered version of an old pastoral play called *Mucedorus*. It even featured a bear. The younger dramatist John Fletcher, meanwhile, sometimes working in collaboration with Francis Beaumont, was pioneering a new style of tragicomedy, a mix of romance and royalism laced with intrigue and pastoral excursions. Shakespeare experimented with this idiom in *Cymbeline* and it was presumably with his blessing that Fletcher eventually took over as the King's Men's company dramatist. The two writers apparently collaborated on three plays in the years 1612–14: a lost romance called *Cardenio* (based on the love-madness of a character in Cervantes' *Don Quixote*), *Henry VIII* (originally staged with the title "All Is True"), and *The Two Noble Kinsmen*, a dramatization of Chaucer's "Knight's Tale." These were written after Shakespeare's two final solo-authored plays, *The Winter's Tale*, a self-consciously old-fashioned work dramatizing the pastoral romance of his old enemy Robert Greene, and *The Tempest*, which at one and the same time drew together multiple theatrical traditions, diverse reading and contemporary interest in the fate of a ship that had been wrecked on the way to the New World.

The collaborations with Fletcher suggest that Shakespeare's career ended with a slow fade rather than the sudden retirement supposed by the nineteenth-century Romantic critics who read Prospero's epilogue to *The Tempest* as Shakespeare's personal farewell to his art. In the last few years of his life Shakespeare certainly spent more of his time in Stratford-upon-Avon, where he became further involved in property dealing and litigation. But his London life also continued. In 1613 he made his first major London property purchase: a freehold house in the Blackfriars district, close to his company's indoor theater. *The Two Noble Kinsmen* may have been written as late as 1614, and Shakespeare was in London on business a little over a year before he died of an unknown cause at home in Stratford-upon-Avon in 1616, probably on his fifty-second birthday.

About half the sum of his works were published in his lifetime, in texts of variable quality. A few years after his death, his fellow actors began putting together an authorized edition of his complete *Comedies, Histories and Tragedies*. It appeared in 1623, in large "Folio" format. This collection of thirty-six plays gave Shakespeare his immortality. In the words of his fellow dramatist Ben Jonson, who contributed two poems of praise at the start of the Folio, the body of his work made him "a monument without a tomb":

And art alive still while thy book doth live
And we have wits to read and praise to give . . .
He was not of an age, but for all time!

SHAKESPEARE'S WORKS: A CHRONOLOGY

1589–91	*? Arden of Faversham* (possible part authorship)
1589–92	*The Taming of the Shrew*
1589–92	*? Edward the Third* (possible part authorship)
1591	*The Second Part of Henry the Sixth*, originally called *The First Part of the Contention betwixt the Two Famous Houses of York and Lancaster* (element of coauthorship possible)
1591	*The Third Part of Henry the Sixth*, originally called *The True Tragedy of Richard Duke of York* (element of coauthorship probable)
1591–92	*The Two Gentlemen of Verona*
1591–92; perhaps revised 1594	*The Lamentable Tragedy of Titus Andronicus* (probably cowritten with, or revising an earlier version by, George Peele)
1592	*The First Part of Henry the Sixth*, probably with Thomas Nashe and others
1592/94	*King Richard the Third*
1593	*Venus and Adonis* (poem)
1593–94	*The Rape of Lucrece* (poem)
1593–1608	*Sonnets* (154 poems, published 1609 with *A Lover's Complaint*, poem of disputed authorship)
1592–94 *or* 1600–03	*Sir Thomas More* (a single scene for a play originally by Anthony Munday, with other revisions by Henry Chettle, Thomas Dekker, and Thomas Heywood)
1594	*The Comedy of Errors*
1595	*Love's Labour's Lost*

1595–97	*Love's Labour's Won* (a lost play, unless the original title for another comedy)
1595–96	*A Midsummer Night's Dream*
1595–96	*The Tragedy of Romeo and Juliet*
1595–96	*King Richard the Second*
1595–97	*The Life and Death of King John* (possibly earlier)
1596–97	*The Merchant of Venice*
1596–97	*The First Part of Henry the Fourth*
1597–98	*The Second Part of Henry the Fourth*
1598	*Much Ado About Nothing*
1598–99	*The Passionate Pilgrim* (20 poems, some not by Shakespeare)
1599	*The Life of Henry the Fifth*
1599	"To the Queen" (epilogue for a court performance)
1599	*As You Like It*
1599	*The Tragedy of Julius Caesar*
1600–01	*The Tragedy of Hamlet, Prince of Denmark* (perhaps revising an earlier version)
1600–01	*The Merry Wives of Windsor* (perhaps revising version of 1597–99)
1601	"Let the Bird of Loudest Lay" (poem, known since 1807 as "The Phoenix and Turtle" [turtledove])
1601	*Twelfth Night, or What You Will*
1601–02	*The Tragedy of Troilus and Cressida*
1604	*The Tragedy of Othello, the Moor of Venice*
1604	*Measure for Measure*
1605	*All's Well That Ends Well*
1605	*The Life of Timon of Athens*, with Thomas Middleton
1605–06	*The Tragedy of King Lear*
1605–08	? contribution to *The Four Plays in One* (lost, except for *A Yorkshire Tragedy*, mostly by Thomas Middleton)

1606	*The Tragedy of Macbeth* (surviving text has additional scenes by Thomas Middleton)
1606–07	*The Tragedy of Antony and Cleopatra*
1608	*The Tragedy of Coriolanus*
1608	*Pericles, Prince of Tyre*, with George Wilkins
1610	*The Tragedy of Cymbeline*
1611	*The Winter's Tale*
1611	*The Tempest*
1612–13	*Cardenio*, with John Fletcher (survives only in later adaptation called *Double Falsehood* by Lewis Theobald)
1613	*Henry VIII (All Is True)*, with John Fletcher
1613–14	*The Two Noble Kinsmen*, with John Fletcher

KINGS AND QUEENS OF ENGLAND: From the History Plays to Shakespeare's Lifetime

	Lifespan	Reign
Angevins:		
Henry II	1133–1189	1154–1189
Richard I	1157–1199	1189–1199
John	1166–1216	1199–1216
Henry III	1207–1272	1216–1272
Edward I	1239–1307	1272–1307
Edward II	1284–1327	1307–1327 deposed
Edward III	1312–1377	1327–1377
Richard II	1367–1400	1377–1399 deposed
Lancastrians:		
Henry IV	1367–1413	1399–1413
Henry V	1387–1422	1413–1422
Henry VI	1421–1471	1422–1461 and 1470–1471
Yorkists:		
Edward IV	1442–1483	1461–1470 and 1471–1483
Edward V	1470–1483	1483 not crowned: deposed and assassinated
Richard III	1452–1485	1483–1485
Tudors:		
Henry VII	1457–1509	1485–1509
Henry VIII	1491–1547	1509–1547
Edward VI	1537–1553	1547–1553
Jane	1537–1554	1553 not crowned: deposed and executed
Mary I	1516–1558	1553–1558

Philip of Spain	1527–1598	1554–1558 co-regent with Mary
Elizabeth I	1533–1603	1558–1603
Stuart:		
James I	1566–1625	1603–1625 James VI of Scotland (1567–1625)

THE HISTORY BEHIND THE HISTORIES: A Chronology

Square brackets indicate events that happen just outside a play's timescale but are mentioned in the play.

Date	Event	Location	Play
22 May 1200	Truce between King John and Philip Augustus	Le Goulet, Normandy	*King John*
Apr 1203	Death of Arthur	Rouen	*King John*
1209	Pope Innocent III excommunicates King John		*King John*
18/19 Oct 1216	Death of King John	Swineshead, Lincolnshire	*King John*
Apr–Sep 1398	Quarrel, duel, and exile of Bullingbrook and Mowbray	Coventry	*Richard II*
3 Feb 1399	Death of John of Gaunt	Leicester	*Richard II*
Jul 1399	Bullingbrook lands in England	Ravenspur, Yorkshire	*Richard II*
Aug 1399	Richard II captured by Bullingbrook	Wales	*Richard II*
30 Sep 1399	Richard II abdicates	London	*Richard II*
13 Oct 1399	Coronation of Henry IV	London	*Richard II*
Jan–Feb 1400	Death of Richard II	Pontefract Castle	*Richard II*
22 Jun 1402	Owen Glendower captures Edmund Mortimer	Bryn Glas, Wales	*1 Henry IV*
14 Sep 1402	Henry Percy defeats Scottish army	Homildon Hill, Yorkshire	*1 Henry IV*

Date	Event	Location	Play
21 Jul 1403	Battle of Shrewsbury; death of Henry Percy (Hotspur)	Battlefield, near Shrewsbury, Shropshire	*1 & 2 Henry IV*
Feb 1405	Tripartite Indenture between Owen Glendower, Edmund Mortimer, and Northumberland (Henry Percy)	Bangor	*Henry IV*
May–Jun 1405	Rebellion of Archbishop of York (Richard Scroop), Earl of Norfolk (Thomas Mowbray), and Lord Bardolph	Yorkshire	*2 Henry IV*
8 Jun 1405	Trial and execution of Archbishop of York and Earl of Norfolk	York	*2 Henry IV*
20 Mar 1413	Death of Henry IV	Westminster Abbey	*2 Henry IV*
9 Apr 1413	Coronation of Henry V	Westminster Abbey	*2 Henry IV*
c.1415–16?	Death of Owen Glendower	Wales?	*2 Henry IV*
Early Aug 1415	Execution of Earl of Cambridge, Lord Scroop, and Sir Thomas Grey	Southampton	*Henry V*
14 Aug–22 Sep 1415	Siege of Harfleur	Harfleur, Normandy	*Henry V*
25 Oct 1415	Battle of Agincourt	Agincourt, Pas de Calais	*Henry V*
31 Aug 1422	Death of Henry V	Bois de Vincennes, near Paris	*1 Henry VI*
18 Jan 1425	Death of Edmund Mortimer	Ireland	*1 Henry VI*

Date	Event	Location	Play
Oct 1428–May 1429	Siege of Orléans	Orléans	*1 Henry VI*
17 Oct 1428	Death of Lord Salisbury	Orléans	*1 Henry VI*
18 Jun 1429	Capture of Lord Talbot at battle of Patay	Patay, near Orléans	*1 Henry VI*
18 Jul 1429	Coronation of Charles VII	Rheims Cathedral	*1 Henry VI*
6 Nov 1429	Coronation of Henry VI as King of England	Westminster Abbey	[*1 Henry VI*]
23 May 1430	Capture of Joan of Arc	Compiègne, near Soissons	*1 Henry VI*
30 May 1431	Execution of Joan of Arc	Saint-Ouen, near Paris	*1 Henry VI*
16 Dec 1431	Coronation of Henry VI as King of France	Notre Dame Cathedral, Paris	*1 Henry VI*
14 Sep 1435	Death of Duke of Bedford	Rouen	*1 Henry VI*
Summer– Autumn 1441	Arrest and trial of Eleanor Cobham and accomplices	London	*2 Henry VI*
20 May 1442	Lord Talbot created Earl of Shrewsbury	Paris	*1 Henry VI*
23 Apr 1445	Marriage of Henry VI and Margaret of Anjou	Titchfield, Hampshire	*2 Henry VI*
23 Feb 1447	Death of Humphrey, Duke of Gloucester	Bury St. Edmunds	*2 Henry VI*
11 Apr 1447	Death of Cardinal Beaufort	Winchester	*2 Henry VI*
2 May 1450	Death of Earl of Suffolk	English Channel	*2 Henry VI*
Jun–Jul 1450	Rebellion of Jack Cade	Kent and London	*2 Henry VI*
Spring 1452	Richard, Duke of York, marches on London	London	*2 Henry VI*

Date	Event	Location	Play
17 Jul 1453	Death of Lord Talbot at battle of Cantillon	Cantillon, Gascony	*1 Henry VI*
22 May 1455	First battle of St. Albans	St. Albans, Hertfordshire	*2 Henry VI*
10 Jul 1460	Battle of Northampton	Northampton	[*3 Henry VI*]
Oct 1460	Richard, Duke of York, holds Parliament	London	*3 Henry VI*
30 Dec 1460	Battle of Wakefield	Wakefield, Yorkshire	*3 Henry VI*
2 Feb 1461	Battle of Mortimer's Cross	Near Wigmore, Herefordshire	*3 Henry VI*
29 Mar 1461	Battle of Towton	Near Tadcaster, Yorkshire	*3 Henry VI*
28 Jun 1461	Coronation of Edward IV	Westminster Abbey	*3 Henry VI*
1 May 1464	Marriage of Edward IV and Elizabeth Woodville	Northampton-shire	*3 Henry VI*
Jul 1465	Henry VI captured	Lancashire	*3 Henry VI*
26 Jul 1469	Battle of Edgecote Moor	Near Banbury, Oxfordshire	*3 Henry VI*
Oct 1470–Apr/ May 1471	Readeption (restoration) of Henry VI	London	*3 Henry VI*
14 Apr 1471	Battle of Barnet; death of Warwick	Barnet, near London	*3 Henry VI*
4 May 1471	Battle of Tewkesbury; death of Edward, Prince of Wales	Tewkesbury, Gloucestershire	*3 Henry VI*
21 May 1471	Death of Henry VI	Tower of London	*3 Henry VI*
12 Jul 1472	Marriage of Richard, Duke of Gloucester, to Anne	Westminster Abbey	*Richard III*
18 Feb 1478	Death of Duke of Clarence	Tower of London	*Richard III*

Date	Event	Location	Play
9 Apr 1483	Death of Edward IV	Westminster	*Richard III*
Jun 1483	Death of Lord Hastings	Tower of London	*Richard III*
6 Jul 1483	Coronation of Richard III	Westminster Abbey	*Richard III*
2 Nov 1483	Death of Duke of Buckingham	Salisbury	*Richard III*
16 Mar 1485	Death of Queen Anne	Westminster	*Richard III*
22 Aug 1485	Battle of Bosworth Field	Leicestershire	*Richard III*
30 Oct 1485	Coronation of Henry VII	Westminster Abbey	[*Richard III*]
18 Jan 1486	Marriage of Henry VII and Elizabeth of York	Westminster Abbey	[*Richard III*]
Jun 1520	Meeting of Henry VIII and Francis I	"Field of the Cloth of Gold," near Calais, France	[*Henry VIII*]
17 May 1521	Death of Duke of Buckingham	Tower Hill, London	*Henry VIII*
29 Nov 1530	Death of Wolsey	Leicester	*Henry VIII*
25 Jan 1533	Marriage of Henry VIII and Anne Bullen (Boleyn)	Whitehall	*Henry VIII*
1 Jun 1533	Coronation of Anne Bullen (Boleyn)	Westminster Abbey	*Henry VIII*
7 Sep 1533	Birth of Princess Elizabeth	Greenwich Palace	*Henry VIII*
10 Sep 1533	Christening of Princess Elizabeth	Greenwich Palace	*Henry VIII*

FURTHER READING AND VIEWING

CRITICAL APPROACHES

Brooke, Nicholas, *Shakespeare's Early Tragedies* (1968). Strong on tragic structure.

Burns, Edward, *Richard III* (2001). Brief but stimulating study in series published for the British Council.

Clemen, Wolfgang, *A Commentary on Shakespeare's Richard III* (1957), trans. Jean Bonheim (1968). Good on language and imagery.

Marienstras, Richard, "Of a Monstrous Body," in *French Essays on Shakespeare and His Contemporaries,* ed. Jean-Marie Maguin and Michèle Willems (1995), pp. 153–74. Cultural-historical analysis of significance of Richard's deformed body.

Moseley, Charles, *Shakespeare: Richard III. A Critical Study* (1989). High-class student guide.

Neill, Michael, "Shakespeare's Halle of Mirrors: Play, Politics, and Psychology in *Richard III*," *Shakespeare Studies* 8 (1975), pp. 99–129. From adaptation of sources to Richard's psychological complexity.

Rackin, Phyllis, *Stages of History: Shakespeare's English Chronicles* (1990). Particularly strong on the women.

Richmond, Hugh, "*Richard III* and the Reformation," *Journal of English and Germanic Philology* 83 (1984), pp. 509–21. Examines religious vocabulary and debates.

Rossiter, A. P., *Angel with Horns and Other Shakespeare Lectures* (1961). Sane, balanced.

Saccio, Peter, *Shakespeare's English Kings: History, Chronicle, and Drama* (1977). Handy comparison with sources and actual history.

THE PLAY IN PERFORMANCE

Brooke, Michael, "*Richard III* on Screen," www.screenonline.org.uk/ tv/id/1022653/index.html. Valuable overview of film and TV versions.

Day, Gillian, *King Richard III*, Shakespeare at Stratford (2002). Survey of productions.

Hankey, Julie, ed., *King Richard III*, Plays in Performance (1981). Innovative edition annotated by means of reference to choices of actors and productions down the ages.

Holland, Peter, *English Shakespeares: Shakespeare on the English Stage in the 1990s* (1997). Discusses key modern productions.

Jackson, Russell, and Robert Smallwood, eds., *Players of Shakespeare 3* (1993). Includes interview with Penny Downie on playing Margaret in the *Henry VI/Richard III* tetralogy.

O'Connor, John, *Shakespearean Afterlives: Ten Characters with a Life of Their Own* (2003). Lively account of some historic Richards.

Richmond, Hugh M., *King Richard III*, Shakespeare in Performance (1989). Useful overview.

Royal Shakespeare Company, "Exploring Shakespeare: *Richard III*," www.rsc.org.uk/explore/plays/richard3.htm. Rehearsal footage, actor and director interviews, commentary on Michael Boyd's 2007 production.

Shakespeare Birthplace Trust Study Materials, *Richard III in Performance* by Rebecca Brown, www.shakespeare.org.uk/content/ view/315/315/.

Sher, Antony, *Year of the King* (1985). Compelling diary of a great actor describing what it is like to play the role of Richard.

Smallwood, Robert, ed., *Players of Shakespeare 4* (1998) and *6* (2004). Each volume contains an interview with an actor talking about playing Richard.

For a more detailed Shakespeare bibliography and selections from a wide range of critical accounts of the play, with linking commentary, visit the edition website, www.therscshakespeare.com.

AVAILABLE ON DVD

Richard III, directed by F. R. Benson (1911), on *Silent Shakespeare* (DVD 2004). Brief tableaux from a very early film version.

Richard III, directed by Laurence Olivier (1955, DVD 2006). Also starring Olivier. Shaped the image of Richard for two generations.

The Wars of the Roses (tx. 22 April 1965), directed by Peter Hall, with text adapted by John Barton. BBC television version of a highly influential project of the RSC in its early years, with Ian Holm as Richard and Peggy Ashcroft as Margaret. Only available in specialist archives such as the British Film Institute in London.

Richard III, directed by Jane Howell (BBC Television Shakespeare, 1983, DVD 2004). Nearly four hours long, due to a very full text, in contrast to the heavy cutting of all other filmed versions. Less successful than the three parts of *Henry VI* by the same director, which were an unexpected highlight of the BBC series.

Richard III in *Shakespeare: The Animated Tales* (joint BBC/Russian television production, 1994, DVD 2007). High-quality cartoon abbreviation, notable in that Richard is voiced by Antony Sher, whose legendary 1984 RSC stage production is not available on screen.

Richard III, directed by Richard Loncraine (1995, DVD 2000). Developed from the McKellen/Eyre National Theatre production. Brilliant transposition to Fascist 1930s setting: a definitive modern revisioning, rendering Olivier into a period piece.

Looking for Richard, directed by Al Pacino (1996, DVD 2005). Quirky but illuminating "metaproduction" in which Pacino explores his fascination with the role and the play, assisted by actors and academics, including Kevin Spacey excellent as Buckingham.

REFERENCES

1. Quoted in E. K. Chambers, *William Shakespeare* (2 vols, 1930), 2.212.
2. Stanley Wells, "Television Shakespeare," *Shakespeare Quarterly*, 33 (1982), pp. 261–73 (p. 266).
3. Thomas Davies, *Dramatic Miscellanies* (3 vols, 1784), 3.440–42.
4. Thomas Davies, *Memoirs of the Life of David Garrick* (2 vols, 1780, repr. 1969), 1.40.
5. Davies, "Mr. Garrick's First Appearance on a London Stage" in his *Life of David Garrick*, 1.37–50
6. Julie Hankey, *Plays in Performance: Richard III* (London: Junction Books, 1981), p. 42.
7. William Hazlitt, review in *A View of the English Stage; or, A Series of Dramatic Criticisms* (1818), pp. 5–9.
8. London Green, "'The Gaiety of Meditated Success': The Richard III of William Charles Macready," *Theater Research International* 10 (1985), pp. 107–28 (p. 125).
9. Review of *Richard III*, *The Athenaeum*, 26 December 1896.
10. Review of *Richard III*, *The Times*, 3 November 1937.
11. Donald Wolfit, *First Interval: The Autobiography of Donald Wolfit* (1954), p. 205.
12. J. C. Trewin, review of *Richard III*, *The Observer*, 17 September 1944.
13. Kenneth Tynan, "Heroic Acting Since 1944," in *He That Plays the King: A View of the Theatre* (1950), pp. 32–113.
14. Sheridan Morley, "A Breath of Fresh Air," *New Statesman*, 30 June 2003.
15. Hugh M. Richmond, *King Richard III*, Shakespeare in Performance (1989), p. 142.
16. Peter Hall, program notes to *Edward IV* [second play of the trilogy, drawn from parts 2 and 3 of *Henry VI*], RSC, 1963.
17. Milton Shulman, *Evening Standard*, 21 August 1963.
18. Ian Richardson on playing Richard III, in Judith Cook, *Shakespeare's Players* (1983).
19. Richardson on playing Richard III.
20. Benedict Nightingale, *New Statesman*, 24 April 1970.
21. S. P. Cerasano, *Shakespeare Quarterly* 36 (1985).

22. John O'Connor, *Shakespearean Afterlives* (2003), p. 113.
23. John Peter, *Sunday Times*, 24 June 1984.
24. Interview with Simon Russell Beale by Peter Lewis, *Sunday Times*, 2 August 1992.
25. Irving Wardle, *Independent on Sunday*, 16 August 1992.
26. Paul Taylor, *Independent*, 13 August 1992.
27. Benedict Nightingale, *Times*, 13 August 1992.
28. Irving Wardle, *Times*, 5 November 1980.
29. Michael Billington, *Guardian*, 5 November 1980.
30. Julie Hankey, *Times Literary Supplement*, 14 November 1980.
31. David Troughton, "Richard III," in *Players of Shakespeare 4*, ed. Robert Smallwood (1998).
32. Anton Lesser, "Richard of Gloucester," in *Players of Shakespeare 3*, ed. Russell Jackson and Robert Smallwood (1993).
33. Henry Goodman, "Richard III," in *Players of Shakespeare 6*, ed. Robert Smallwood (2004).
34. Goodman, "Richard III."
35. Benedict Nightingale, *New Statesman*, 24 April 1970.
36. D. A. N. Jones, *Listener*, 23 April 1970.
37. Irving Wardle, *Independent on Sunday*, 16 August 1992.
38. Henry Goodman on his portrayal of Richard III, *Richard III Online Playguide*, www.rsc.org.uk/richard/current/home.html.
39. Susannah Clapp, *Observer*, 27 July 2003.
40. Benedict Nightingale, *Times*, 25 July 2003.
41. Troughton, "Richard III."
42. Cerasano, *Shakespeare Quarterly 36*.
43. David Starkey, *Times Literary Supplement*, 28 August 1992.
44. Troughton, "Richard III."
45. Goodman, "Richard III."
46. Peter Holland, *English Shakespeares* (1997), p. 231.
47. Lesser, "Richard of Gloucester."
48. Hankey, *Times Literary Supplement*, 14 November 1980.
49. Lesser, "Richard of Gloucester."
50. Lisa Stevenson on playing Lady Anne, *Richard III Online Playguide*, www.rsc.org.uk/richard/current/home.html.
51. Katherine Duncan-Jones, *Times Literary Supplement*, 11 May 2001.
52. Taylor, *Independent*, 13 August 1992.
53. Wardle, *Times*, 5 November 1980.
54. B. A. Young, *Financial Times*, 5 November 1980.
55. Nightingale, *New Statesman*, 24 April 1970.

56. Katherine Duncan-Jones, *Times Literary Supplement*, 11 November 2001.
57. R. Chris Hassel Jr., *Shakespeare Quarterly* 36 (1985).
58. Penny Downie, "Queen Margaret," in *Players of Shakespeare 3*.
59. Andrew St. George, *Financial Times*, 13 August 1992.
60. Taylor, *Independent*, 13 August 1992.
61. Taylor, *Independent*, 13 August 1992.
62. Sean Holmes on directing the RSC's 2003 production, *Richard III Online Playguide*, www.rsc.org.uk/richard/current/home.html.
63. Lesser, "Richard of Gloucester."
64. Troughton, "Richard III."
65. Hassel, Jr., *Shakespeare Quarterly* 36.
66. Charles Spencer, *Daily Telegraph*, 27 April 2001.
67. Barbara Hodgdon, "The RSC's 'Long Sonata of the Dead': Shakespeare-history and Imagined Community," in *Re-visions of Shakespeare*, ed. Evelyn Gajowski (2004), p. 77.
68. Michael Billington, *Guardian*, 5 November 1980.
69. Paul Taylor, *Independent*, 30 October 1998.
70. Jones, *Listener*, 23 April 1970.

ACKNOWLEDGMENTS AND PICTURE CREDITS

Preparation of "*Richard III* in Performance" was assisted by generous grants from the CAPITAL Centre (Creativity and Performance in Teaching and Learning) of the University of Warwick, for research in the RSC archive at the Shakespeare Birthplace Trust. The Arts and Humanities Research Council (AHRC) funded a term's research leave that enabled Jonathan Bate to work on "The Director's Cut."

Picture research by Helen Robson and Jan Sewell. Grateful acknowledgment is made to the Shakespeare Birthplace Trust for assistance with picture research (special thanks to Helen Hargest) and reproduction fees.

Images of RSC productions are supplied by the Shakespeare Centre Library and Archive, Stratford-upon-Avon. This library, maintained by the Shakespeare Birthplace Trust, holds the most important collection of Shakespeare material in the UK, including the Royal Shakespeare Company's official archives. It is open to the public free of charge.

For more information see www.shakespeare.org.uk.

1. Portrait of David Garrick (1745). Reproduced by permission of the Shakespeare Birthplace Trust.
2. Directed by Bill Alexander (1984). Joe Cocks Studio Collection © Shakespeare Birthplace Trust.
3. Directed by Sean Holmes (2003). Malcolm Davies © Shakespeare Birthplace Trust.
4. Photograph of the set design for *Richard III* (2008). Lucy Barriball © Royal Shakespeare Company.
5. Directed by Sam Mendes (1992). © Michael Le Poer Trench.
6. *Richard III* directed by Michael Boyd (2008). Ellie Kurttz © Royal Shakespeare Company.
7. Reconstructed Elizabethan Playhouse © Charcoalblue.